The Digital Gold Rush Secrets

2 BOOKS IN 1

Unleashing the Power of Bitcoin, Blockchain, NFTs, DeFi, Altcoins, and Making Money with Crypto

By **Brian Scott Fitzgerald**

Published By **Fitzgerald Publishing Group**

How to Make Money Online: THE SERIES

I created a series of 12 (twelve) books, of How to Make Money Online

Feel free to read any of my books in the series, which can be found on my Author page on Amazon

You can visit this link or Scan this QR code to get access

https://www.amazon.com/author/brianscottfitzgerald.

Table of Contents

Your Free Gift.

I am offering my readers the FREE PDF version of ChatGPT Prompts.

To get almost instant access, go to this website..
https://go.fitzgeraldpublishing.com/opt-in-page-crypto-bundle

Or use your phone to take a picture of this QR code, and it will take you to the Website for your Gift.

Inside the book, you will discover:

- **3000 Prompts** To help you make even more money online.

- **Save time:** You can search for new topics to create content on ChatGPT.

- **Expand knowledge:** Our Package of ChatGPT Prompts covers various topics, from science and technology to art and culture.

If you want to make even more money online, grab this free PDF.

Wait, that's not all; just for buying this book and getting the free PDF above, you can also earn another free Book. You can use your phone to take a picture of this QR code.

Or type this in your browser to get to the book page on Amazon in the US at https://www.amazon.com/dp/B0C71NQH9K or this if you are not in the US. https://mybook.to/beyondchatgpt.

Use the latest AI techniques to uncover online innovation's future. Take advantage! "Beyond ChatGPT and 50 New AI Tools: The Ultimate Guide to Discovering Cutting-Edge AI Tools Beyond ChatGPT" offers endless possibilities. Explore a variety of cutting-edge AI solutions to transform your work. Discover advanced AI tools beyond ChatGPT on this thrilling voyage. If you want to make even more money online, grab this free book.

Book #1

How to Make Money Online with Crypto

Mastering Cryptocurrency, Bitcoin, Blockchain, NFTs, DeFi, Altcoins, and Other Digital Assets.

Introduction

If you read my book BlockChain Technology for Beginners, you know that Bitcoin is the first scarce resource that can be digitally verified. As I ponder the creation of this book, my latest literary masterpiece, "How to Make Money Online with Crypto," I am struck by the sheer astonishment that such a lucrative opportunity exists in our lifetime. Let's seize the moment and make it count. We don't want to look back regretfully and wonder what could have been. You might wonder who I am to author a book on generating income through Crypto. In 2012, I took the first step towards financial freedom by opening my first account with Coinbase. Although the report was created much earlier, it wasn't funded until later, in 2017. Please take advantage of potential gains more than I did. Invest wisely and avoid my mistake of missing out on purchasing Bitcoin at $100. Although early 2017 was still a great time to invest, I regret not taking advantage of the opportunity sooner. Learn from my experience and make informed investment decisions.

Even in 2017, I made mistakes such as buying more Ethereum than Bitcoin and missing out on the historical BTC bull run of 2017. In 2018 I tried to diversify my portfolio by investing in several ICOs (Initial Coin Offerings), similar to IPOs (Initial Public Offerings) but for the cryptocurrency world instead of stocks. In later years purchasing, selling, and constructing NFTs, I can help you quickly navigate that world of digital assets. With my good and bad experiences in DEFI projects, by participating in hundreds of them, I can help guide these areas as well.

I also invested in pyramid scheme coins, and owning too many Alltcoins can be overwhelming, as I know it well. To make matters worse, having your wallet hacked and losing six figures worth of coins is a hard lesson I had to learn. That's why the most crucial aspect of making money in crypto is knowing how to keep your investments secure. This guide explores the best ways to protect your assets and ensure your peace of mind. In the dynamic world of Crypto finance, a lot has transpired over the last six (6) years. Our book delves into all of it, leaving no stone unturned.

Let's step into the world of online wealth creation with 'How to Make Money Online with Crypto: Mastering Cryptocurrency, Bitcoin, Blockchain, NFTs, DeFi, Altcoins, & Other Digital Assets.' As we embark on a journey into the digital age, generating wealth and managing finances is rapidly transforming like never before. Experience the financial revolution of our time with the emergence of cryptocurrencies, Non-Fungible Tokens (NFTs), Decentralized Finance (DeFi), and other digital assets. These innovative technologies are transforming the financial landscape and providing exciting opportunities for generating income and accumulating wealth. Join the global economic renaissance and participate in a revolution that transcends traditional boundaries. With internet access, anyone can join in this exciting movement. Navigating the world of digital finance can be overwhelming with its complex terminologies, rapidly evolving technologies, and volatile markets. Discover the ultimate solution with this must-have book. Discover the exciting world of digital finance with our comprehensive guide. Whether you're a curious novice or an experienced investor, our book will equip you with the insights and tools to navigate the crypto-economy's dynamic and often turbulent waters. Get ready to embark on a fulfilling journey to unravel the mysteries of digital assets and discover the keys to generating online wealth through cryptocurrencies. Get ready to immerse yourself. The top ways to earn in crypto today;

Investing

Discover the potential for profit by investing in cryptocurrency. Invest in favorite cryptocurrencies like Bitcoin and Ethereum, or diversify your portfolio with a cryptocurrency index fund. Diversify your portfolio and mitigate risk with this excellent method. Before investing in cryptocurrency, conducting thorough research and fully understanding the potential risks is crucial. Invest in cryptocurrency for long-term profit by adopting a buy-and-hold strategy. Investing involves strategically allocating resources, such as capital, with the ultimate goal of generating a profit. Invest your money wisely by using it to fund a business venture or purchase land to sell it for a future payoff. Experience the excitement of the financial markets by investing in financial instruments with the potential to yield a profitable return upon sale.

Investment is all about the expectation of a return, commonly called ROI. Unlike trading, investing is a prudent strategy for accumulating wealth over the long haul. As an investor, your ultimate objective is to amass wealth over an extended period, spanning years or even decades. Discovering promising investment opportunities is multifaceted, but astute investors often rely on fundamental factors to guide their decision-making.

Lending and Earning Interest

Lend your cryptocurrency to maximize its value. Lending cryptocurrency earns interest. Discover your cryptocurrency lending interest rate and investment amount. Explore DLP, centralized, and P2P lending solutions. Like lending money, lend cryptocurrency to make money. Platform selection determines which cryptocurrencies can be lent or collateralized.

Decentralized or centralized cryptocurrency lending platforms. Centralized platforms provide a seamless and safe online environment where a trustworthy central authority efficiently governs and oversees operations and verifies user identities.

Computer-managed decentralized platforms give users some autonomy—to experience blockchain technology's community-verified transactions. The platform makes all transactions visible and secure. Interest rates can be fixed or floating. Choose a fixed or floating interest rate, which changes with market conditions.

Learn how cryptocurrencies can boost your returns by earning interest. You can test yield farming by lending Bitcoin to a platform and receiving welfare. Despite the risks, yield farming can generate passive income. The loan platform and cryptocurrency you choose determine your interest earnings.

Cryptocurrency investments may yield higher returns. In the "yield farming process," you lend your cryptocurrency to a site for interest. Despite the danger, yield-producing crops can generate passive income. Only the platform and type of Bitcoin you lend will affect your interest rate.

Trading

Trading is about exploiting short-term chances, whereas investing is a sensible and patient buy-and-hold strategy. Explore the volatile cryptocurrency market. Enjoy volatile markets where asset prices can rise or fall quickly. Trading success lies in technical and analytical skills.

Cryptocurrency trading offers lucrative opportunities. Trading BTC USDT with market trends and technical analysis might boost your profits. Charts and indicators can effectively predict price changes. Learn about trading—buying and selling assets to optimize earnings. Explore a marketplace where buyers pay merchants. Some trades involve bartering products and services. Financial instruments are exchanged in volatile financial markets. Discover stocks, bonds, Forex currency pairings, futures, options, margin products, cryptocurrencies, and more.

Many traders maximize opportunities by entering and exiting positions quickly. Start trading professionally today. This assumption may be inaccurate. Trading includes day trading, swing trading, trend trading, and others. Rest easy.

Mining

Learn more about mining, which is now the most common way people make money using cryptocurrencies. Feel the power of mining as it verifies transactions on the blockchain and adds new data blocks to the chain without causing any interruptions. Feel the rush that comes with the acquisition of Bitcoin through mining. You will be rewarded with valuable digital assets due to the hard effort you have put in. Discover the full potential of mining with specialist gear or with the use of cloud mining services. Enjoy the benefits of cloud mining without the headache of investing in or maintaining your mining hardware. However, the payouts may be less than those obtained from hardware mining. By utilizing the efficiency of remote cloud mining, you can take the verification of your blockchain transactions to the next level.

Staking

Crypto-staking requires keeping a certain number of coins in your wallet for a specific time. Invest in cryptocurrencies to see their potential. Cryptocurrency investments can generate passive revenue. The interest you get depends on the cryptocurrency you provide as collateral and how much. Make passive money from your idle cryptocurrencies.

Buy crypto assets from a trustworthy exchange to enjoy buying the dip. This tried-and-true investing approach maximizes returns by buying more when prices decline. Sell the asset months or years later for a significant profit. The daily changes in Bitcoin, Ethereum, and

Litecoin are thrilling. Enjoy new coins, likely to debut at a premium because of their popularity. Its value declines, and recuperation takes longer. Long-term investors don't worry about price swings. They're indifferent to tiny setbacks. Discover the power of the holding strategy, a straightforward, low-risk option that can yield spectacular results. Avoid panicking when others do.

Choose a cryptocurrency during a price drop and hold it until it rises. Sell it to profit. Paxful lets you start financial freedom with 10 USD. Strategic investments and timing are essential to enhance earnings. Though difficult, the rewards are worth it. Investment increases risk. This cryptocurrency plan is long-term, like traditional investing.

Affiliates

Discover a variety of cryptocurrency exchanges that offer affiliate programs, allowing you to earn commissions on the customers you refer. Discover an incredible way to make money through cryptocurrencies without trading or investing. Discover the intense competition that characterizes affiliate programs.

Dividends

Maximize the potential of your cryptocurrency investments and boost your earnings by participating in dividends. You're likely familiar with tips if you invest in stocks or bonds. Discover the essence of bonuses - small yet significant monetary payments distributed to shareholders. As a company generates profits for a quarter, the resulting gains are distributed among its esteemed shareholders, who are the proud owners of the organization. When a company generates earnings for an entire year, the organization retains those profits.

Airdrops

Find out why airdrops are quickly becoming the preferred option for crypto aficionados to receive free tokens without paying money. On the other hand, airdrops are unlike typical sales or token launches in that they do not need consumers to make any initial deposits or spend any money. Take baby steps toward achievement by publishing project details on social media, signing up for an online group, or accomplishing minor tasks like watching an instructional video. These are just a few of the many options available to you. Gain Crypto Tokens by Completing Mundane Tasks and Doing So Completely Free of Charge!

CHAPTER 1

The Cryptocurrency Revolution

Understanding The Basics Of Cryptocurrency

Electronic virtual currencies originated way before the inception of the first-ever scalable crypto - Bitcoin. However, these currencies weren't termed cryptos because they do not have the cryptography tech embedded in them. But these are the very first attempts that eventually led to the invention of the currently used cryptocurrencies.

The revolution of digital currencies started in the Netherlands in the 1980s. A group of developers invented an electronic card system to avoid the thefts in Gas Stations that happen at night. Whoever wants to access Gas can use those cards, so the use of real money is eliminated.

The second attempt towards virtual currencies is made by 'David Chaum.' He is an American cryptographer and the inventor of Blinded Cash. The USP of this currency is that it is untraceable. That is, transactions made using this virtual currency cannot be tracked. Chaum used complex encryption techniques to achieve this feat. However, this crypto has failed because of various scalability issues.

We must know that eCash, B-Money, Bit Gold, and Hashcash are notable failed attempts in this space. eCash was the first conceptualized digital token currency to transfer between individuals. B Money was portrayed as an electronic cash system that is anonymous and secured at the same time. Bit Gold is considered the first digital asset with complete decentralized functionality. Bit Gold was pegged to the value of gold while moving away from centralization.

HashCash was one of the most successful digital currencies, getting everything in place except for scalability. It functions almost like Bitcoin and has a similar consensus algorithm too. This digital currency was truly ahead of its time, which could be one reason for its failure. Finally, in 2008, the whitepaper of Bitcoin was released, while in early 2009, the first ever Bitcoin block was mined, and the rest is history.

Cryptocurrency is a kind of digital money that exists only online. There is only an actual coin or bill if you utilize a service that enables you to exchange cryptocurrencies for physical tokens. Typically, you trade cryptocurrencies with another person online, through your phone or computer, without a third party's assistance, like a bank. Cryptocurrencies are unrelated to valuable things – they are irrelevant to anything of actual worth in the real world, which causes their value to fluctuate wildly, as you have probably seen.

In contrast to equities, bonds, artwork, real estate, or precious metals, cryptocurrencies have no intrinsic value or use. For instance, gold is a critical component of electronics and jewelry — and therefore has worth in addition to its scarcity. On the other hand, cryptocurrency costs money solely because someone else owns it and needs money to deliver it to you.

Cryptocurrencies address the following critical issues associated with the use of cash. There is a need for a centralized authority to control these objects' value, manufacturing, and authenticity. Possibility of fraudulent duplicating. To understand this better, one should get a good understanding of some of these basics.

Cryptography

Cryptocurrency uses cryptography — the art of concealing and disclosing information — to guarantee the security of user data and the integrity of transactions. As the name implies, a cryptocurrency is digital or virtual money protected by encryption, making it hard to counterfeit or double-spend.

Blockchain

A blockchain is a subset of Distributed Ledger Technology (DLT), a distributed database distributed among many operators (nodes, computing devices, etc.) Numerous cryptocurrencies are decentralized networks powered by blockchain technology—a distributed ledger maintained by a distributed network of computers.

This is the underlying technology that drives cryptocurrency. It is a digital ledger that validates transactions, accounts, and balances. Blockchain may be used for various applications outside financial transactions, including supply chain management, monitoring art ownership, and even digital collectibles.

A node is a word associated with blockchain technology that will be used throughout this essay. A node is a discrete component of a larger data structure known as a blockchain. Without nodes, the system would implode. Cryptography and blockchain technology assist cryptocurrencies in the creation of new coins, the enforcement of legal transactions, and the establishment of a secure system.

Decentralized

A distinguishing characteristic of cryptocurrencies is that they are not issued by any central authority, which supposedly protects them against government intervention or manipulation. As shown by Bitcoin, decentralization implies that all authoritative source is spread evenly across all peers on a network, and there is no single point of failure. For example, to "hack" Bitcoin, someone must access at least 51% of the vast network of computers that operate Bitcoin, which is considered impossible.

Peer-to-Peer

Without a broker, cryptocurrency may be transferred directly between two individuals. These transactions are made with minimal processing costs that benefit the network, allowing customers to avoid the high transaction fees associated with more conventional money transfer services.

There are many cryptocurrencies in existence. You've almost certainly heard of some of the most prominent cryptocurrencies, like Bitcoin, Litecoin, and Ethereum. Cryptocurrencies are becoming an increasingly popular alternative to traditional online payment methods. Before you convert actual dollars, euros, pounds, or other conventional currencies to cryptocurrencies, it's essential to understand what they are, the dangers associated with their use, and how to safeguard your investment.

A cryptocurrency is a digital money that was developed using encryption techniques. It is a type of alternative payment. Due to the usage of encryption technology, cryptocurrencies serve as both a medium of exchange and a virtual accounting system. A cryptocurrency wallet is required to utilize cryptocurrencies. These wallets may be cloud-based services or software installed on your PC or mobile device. Wallets are the devices that hold the encryption keys that verify your identity and connect you to your Bitcoin.

Cryptocurrencies are still in their initial stages, and their market is very volatile. As banks or any other third party does not regulate these, they are often uninsured and challenging to convert into real money (such as US dollars or euros.) Additionally, since cryptocurrencies are intangible technology assets, they may be hacked like any other. Finally, since you keep your cryptocurrencies in a digital wallet, you will lose your entire cryptocurrency investment if you lose access to your wallet.

Properties Of Cryptos

In the middle of the 2008 Financial Crisis, an unknown person or group of people known as Satoshi Nakamoto published a whitepaper titled "Bitcoin: A Peer-to-Peer Electronic Cash System." At the time, very few individuals were aware of this game-changing breakthrough in money.

Cryptocurrency has become an alternate trade means due to the development of encryption and blockchain technology. Since its inception in 2009, Bitcoin has grown in popularity across the globe. It has garnered so much attention as a result of its unique features.

To properly comprehend the cryptocurrency revolution, it's critical to understand the basic features of cryptocurrencies and blockchain technology that contribute to its revolutionary and game-changing status. While there are many cryptocurrencies in the modern world, each with its distinct features, cryptocurrency, at its core, has three essential traits.

Trustless

Bitcoin is trustless because it was built to require no one to trust anybody else to operate. Before Bitcoin, every form of money needed you to charge a central authority to use it. In each of these instances, the foremost authority becomes the primary weakness that ultimately results in the currency's downfall. With Bitcoin, each ecosystem component verifies what the others are saying without relying on anybody. When a Bitcoin transaction is broadcast, all nodes receive it and verify that the signatures are genuine. If the signatures are invalid, the transaction is discarded.

Because everyone on the network has a copy of the ledger, we no longer need to rely on a single entity, organization, or third party, as there is no need to trust when you can check against this ledger using your copy. The blockchain is the decentralized ledger, and Individual network players being rewarded through a proof-of-work (PoW) consensus mechanism is one of the most revolutionary concepts in contemporary economics.

The incentive may assist nodes in maintaining their integrity. If a greedy attacker can build more CPU proof-of-workers than all the honest nodes, he must choose between defrauding people by reclaiming their money and generating new currencies.

He should consider it more lucrative to follow the rules, which reward him with more new coins than everyone else combined, than to undermine the system and the legitimacy of his riches. While we are still discovering how and why we utilize cryptocurrencies, they are here to stay. Apart from the other advantages of cryptocurrencies and blockchain technology, resolving the centralized trust problem alone is a significant breakthrough that will ensure the long-term viability of crypto.

Unchangeable/Immutable

In the most straightforward meaning, "immutable" implies "unable to be undone." Immutability should be based on three concepts about blockchain and cryptocurrency: Rewriting history should be extremely unlikely or difficult. Anyone other than the owner of a private key should be unable to transfer money. The blockchain records all transactions to ensure the two principles above.

We consult our bank's transaction history to see how our money has been spent from our bank accounts. We entrust our banks with the responsibility of not fabricating transactions or manipulating our money, just as we entrust them with the responsibility of delivering our transactions to receivers. If fraudulent transactions occur, the bank must also be trusted to reverse them and rectify the problem.

As previously shown, a cryptocurrency needs more centralization and trust; there is no longer a third party in whom we can place our confidence to perform these functions. As a result, transaction records are made publicly accessible and irreversible (immutable). Although changing the transaction ledger is not impossible, cryptographic security makes it very difficult. It necessitates the compromising of the whole Bitcoin network.

Distributed

Because "decentralization" is such a hot topic in the crypto world, it's critical to describe it precisely. It may have a variety of connotations "Blockchains are decentralized politically (no one controls them) and architecturally (there is no single point of failure in the infrastructure), but they are centralized conceptually (there is a single generally accepted state, and the system acts like a single computer)." — Vitalik Buterin.

Fault Tolerance: since decentralized systems rely on networks of independent components, they are less likely to fail unintentionally.

Attack Resistance: Because decentralized systems lack susceptible central points that may be attacked at a far lower cost than the surrounding system, they are more costly to attack, destroy, or control.

Collusion Resistance: individuals of decentralized systems find it more difficult to behave in ways that benefit themselves at the cost of others. On the other hand, businesses and governments constantly cooperate in ways that enrich them while harming others.

Besides central banks and governments, banks regulate the supply and production of money via mints and interest rates. Users of fiat currencies are at the whims of central banks regarding money creation.

Scarcity and Limited Supply

Fiat currencies have an infinite supply because central banks can issue and print as many as they wish. Central banks often influence the value of their nations' money as part of their economic strategies. The inflationary nature of fiat currencies implies a gradual decline in the currency's value over time. On the other hand, most cryptocurrencies have a finite and predetermined supply programmed into their underlying algorithm when they are established.

However, with cryptocurrencies, a person or consortia can only control or exercise substantial influence over the money supply with the majority's consent. The most popular cryptocurrencies have limited tokens or an endless pool with pre-defined manufacturing criteria. Like Bitcoin, Litecoin, and Dash, numerous popular other cryptocurrencies have a finite supply, making them naturally deflationary. Any rise in demand or acceptance of the cryptocurrency will result in a price increase.

How Can Cryptos Change The Way We Transact?

To further comprehend this, let us examine the cryptographic transaction process. Assume Julia wants to give Luke $25 in BTC. Luke gives Julia his Bitcoin address ("public key"). This Bitcoin address is associated with any Bitcoin exchange or wallet Luke creates on the Bitcoin Blockchain. It appears as follows:

3GTDmd3JohJ4oDbTnvgw68gEDS3y6CS7Wx.

Julia puts that address and the Bitcoin (BTC) amount — about 0.0009 BTC, equal to a little under $25 — into his cryptocurrency exchange or wallet and clicks send.

Luke gets the BTC less a transaction fee that the BTC miners and the network charge. These costs may vary from $0.05 for an hourly delivery to $0.58 for a ten-minute delivery. It makes no difference whether Julia sends $25 or $25,000,000 - the costs would remain the same. Now, let us dissect what occurs behind the scenes. From the time Julia sends the transaction to the blockchain, every node in the Bitcoin network receives the transaction request. Each node verifies that Julia is really whom they claim to be. The nodes verify Julia's identification using the private key – a private key uniquely identifies the source of the funds being sent. Whoever has access to this small substantial gains access to your funds? This is why it is critical to safeguard your private key. And we always want to use our wallets and not keep the coins on exchanges, more about that later, but remember ***Your Keys, Your Crypto.***

Because the nodes have a copy of the transactions' entire ledger, they can verify that Julia has the funds. If at least 51% of nodes agree on the two components mentioned earlier, the transaction is valid, and the nodes update the ledger with the new marketing.

If we compare this to a typical transaction involving fiat money, we can see how complex crypto transactions are. These additional layers contribute something to the table and may address a weakness in conventional financial systems. Here are a few ways that cryptocurrencies have the potential to revolutionize the way we do business.

Transactions That are Faster, Cheaper, and More Secure Than Banks

Today's banking system needs to be updated. International bank transfers may take up to a week since both require correspondent banks and country-specific clearing institutions. Even cross-border exchange of payment data is fraught with difficulties and frictions. Bank transactions may be done quickly and inexpensively using a digital currency like Bitcoin.

Fraud is a significant issue when it comes to virtually everything involving money. Whether it's a money transfer or just using a credit card on an unsecured website, the potential for fraud is a significant worry for everyone. This is particularly true for individuals who have previously been a victim of fraud.

Because cryptocurrency is not linked to your bank account or cash and is transferred electronically and securely through the blockchain, which records all transactions, cryptocurrency will significantly decrease fraud and provide peace of mind.

Global Remittances Get a Boost.

Each year, migrants from poor nations send over $500 billion in remittances home, surpassing foreign direct investment. With international transfer costs averaging 6-10 percent of the entire amount sent, the impact on some of the world's most disadvantaged individuals is significant. Technology offers the ability to accelerate and reduce the cost of these transfers.

Private users may even transfer money straight to their relatives through cell phones using virtual currency, with the remaining costs coming from currency exchanges. While conventional money transfer businesses must maintain capital to compensate for delays in international money movement, enterprises with digital currencies have considerably lower capital needs. Capital carrying expenses and money transfer charges are just a portion of the cost of doing business for remittance companies. Reduced costs, however, may make it simpler for smaller companies to join and create new remittance corridors or for current players to service smaller cities or new nations.

Money That is Secure for the Impoverished

The inflation and volatility suffered by certain nations' conventional currencies are alarming. While not all nations' currencies are susceptible to exorbitant inflation rates, some may significantly gain from adopting Bitcoin.

For instance, the growth of mobile technology in Africa has already shown that poor nations can be technological leaders. According to estimates, up to 60% or more of trade in Kenya occurs via mobile phone credits as a means of exchange. Anyone who has a mobile phone may use it to store money and transfer credits to another user. The issue is that the costs are high: traditionally, cashing out has cost up to 20%, even though many customers may use credit cards directly without paying significant fees.

Digital currencies have the potential to become another simple and secure method of payment in nations where the majority of people lack bank accounts. While adopting Bitcoin as a secondary currency in a nation exposes people to currency risk, it may be preferable to current alternatives, especially in countries with severe inflation. For instance, it would be more secure physically than keeping cash at home or purchasing gold jewelry. Additionally, a Bitcoin owner may swap it for a more stable currency on one of the worldwide Bitcoin exchanges. This may broaden access to worldwide financial markets, allowing even the unbanked to save and safeguard against inflation.

One possible consequence is that capital restrictions become more challenging to implement.

Unleashing the E-Commerce Potential

Concerns about credit card theft are causing several internet businesses to turn away potential customers today. Such fraud is particularly prevalent in overseas transactions, so many companies refuse to take foreign payments. It cannot be reversed once a transfer is performed using a digital currency like Bitcoin. This reduces merchants' risk of fraud and enables them to sell globally. Additionally, since virtual currencies enable consumers to transfer money as simply as email, online purchasing would become a far more pleasant experience.

Additionally, digital money may enable small companies in underdeveloped nations to participate more fully in global e-commerce. Latin American artisans might sell their wares worldwide, Chinese adolescents could provide Mandarin instruction through Skype, and African businesses promoting their products on online advertising markets would have a payment option that is now absent. Small-value transactions are a compelling use case since minimal transaction costs allow low-value in-app purchases or micropayments to read online news items from media sources worldwide.

Money That Can Be Programmed With Smart Contracts

Once a digital asset is created, it may be transferred automatically. This opens the door for implementing "programmable money" and "smart contracts." Escrow accounts are a realistic example. These accounts are already utilized in significant transactions, like real estate purchases. The buyer deposits funds in escrow, and is released to the seller only when the seller transfers the title to the property. This method may be utilized for even smaller amounts in the digital era when trust can be a significant barrier to people transacting at arm's length.

Another example is multi-sig, which requires several people to authenticate before money can be withdrawn from an account. This may be used to prevent the theft of digital currencies. Still, it could also guarantee that money is not "lost" or stolen when it travels across borders, between business divisions, or between charity groups and contractors in poor nations.

Additionally, programmable money may be used in far more sophisticated contracts, such as financial transactions with many parties and complex derivatives. You might invest some money in a financial agreement that pays out based on the performance of specific stock values. A computer program might be connected to the Bloomberg terminal feed, and then, based on the performance of certain stocks or combinations of equities, various people may get money.

Can Cryptos Replace The Centralized Financial System? Before we address this issue, we must consider how centralized financial systems came to be. This would enable us to assess the function of central financial institutions and determine if cryptos might eventually replace them.

Central Banks: Their History

In 1844, the English developed central banking with the Bank Charter

Act, a legislative initiative that established the foundation for an organization with exclusive authority over currency issuance. The notion was that a bank with so much power might contribute to the financial system's stability during times of crisis. It's a notion that many experts believe played a role in averting catastrophe during the 2007-2008 financial crisis and the subsequent Great Recession.

Over time, central banks have developed. For example, the Federal Reserve utilizes monetary policy to Attain full employment and price stability. Assure the nation's banking and financial systems are secure and sound and allow customers to get credit. In times of crisis, stabilize the financial system. Contribute to the oversight of the nation's payment systems. The Federal Reserve and other central banks may adjust interest rates and create or destroy money to accomplish these goals.

For instance, if the economy seems to be expanding too fast and prices for goods and services become unaffordable, a central bank may raise interest rates to make borrowing more costly. Additionally, a central bank may deplete the economy of money by decreasing the quantity of money it makes accessible to other banks for lending reasons. Because most funds reside on computerized balance sheets, just pressing delete may cause it to vanish. Thus, the quantity of money available to buy products is reduced, presumably resulting in a decrease in pricing.

Naturally, every action has a corresponding response. While demonetization may result in lower costs, it makes it more difficult for companies to borrow money. As a result, these companies may become more cautious, hesitant to spend, and reluctant to recruit new employees.

Central banks may lower interest rates or create money if an economy needs to develop more rapidly. Reduced interest rates make borrowing money less costly and more accessible and attractive to businesses and individuals. Similarly, central banks may expand the funds available to banks for lending.

Additionally, central banks may attempt to influence economies in other ways. These measures may involve the open market purchase of securities (bonds) to create demand. High demand results in reduced interest rates since borrowers no longer need to provide a higher rate because the central bank offers a willing buyer.

Attempts by central banks to guide economies toward prosperity are loaded with danger. Inflation may become a concern if interest rates are kept too low. The economy may stall when prices rise and people need help to afford their desired goods. When interest rates are too high, borrowing is restricted, and the economy is harmed.

Low-interest rates (compared to other countries) encourage investors to withdraw money from one country and transfer it to another, providing a better return rate. Consider the predicament of retirees whose income is dependent on rising interest rates. When interest rates are low, their buying power and capacity to pay their expenses are directly impacted. Sending money to a nation that provides a higher rate of return is a sensible move.

Interest rate and money supply manipulation also directly impacts the value of a nation's currency. A high currency makes exporting products more costly for local businesses. This has the potential to result in domestic unemployment. A depreciating dollar raises imported products' prices, such as oil and other commodities. This may increase the cost of imports for consumers and domestic producers of products that depend on imported components or materials. A weak dollar benefits a slowing economy needing a boost, while a strong dollar benefits consumers.

Because there is a lag between when a central bank initiates a policy adjustment and when that move affects a nation's economy, central banks are always looking forward. They aim to implement policy changes now that will allow them to accomplish future objectives.

Now let's look at the other side of the coin. The inherent complexity of national and global economies provides ammunition for the claim that these economies are too unpredictable to be effectively controlled via the manipulation practiced by central banks. This argument, advanced by adherents of the Austrian School of Economics, may justify the adoption of a peer-to-peer currency like Bitcoin that does away with central banks and their intricate systems.

Since their creation, modern central banks have been a source of contention. And the causes for dissatisfaction are many and diverse. On the one hand, the idea of monopolistic power is very unsettling to many individuals. On the other hand, the presence of an autonomous, opaque organization that can influence an economy is much more alarming.

Numerous individuals (including economists and politicians) think that central banks make errors that significantly affecting citizens' lives. Among these errors are the following: Increases in the quantity of money (creating inflation and hurting consumers by raising prices for the goods and services they purchase).

Interest rate hikes are being implemented (hurting consumers who wish to borrow money). The development of measures that maintain an abnormally low rate of inflation (resulting in unemployment). Abnormally low-interest rates (creating asset bubbles in real estate, stocks, or bonds)

In this vein, no less an authority than former Federal Reserve Chair Ben Bernanke blames the Great Depression of 1929 on central bank manipulation (which increased interest rates).

In an era where technology enables consumers to conduct trade without the intervention of a central authority, central banks are obsolete. This argument is strengthened by a more comprehensive study of the financial sector.

The Great Recession and a slew of scandals were precipitated by banking sector corruption. Bankers have wreaked havoc in Greece and other countries. Several organizations, like the International Monetary Fund, have been accused of prioritizing profits above people. And on a more local level, bankers earn billions of dollars by acting as intermediaries in individual transactions. In this climate, many individuals find abolishing the financial system attractive.

To sum up, at the moment, central banks are the primary mechanism through which countries control their economies and look at every war fought this century. Every battle was in a country with no central bank until the war ended. They have monopolistic power and are unlikely to relinquish it without a struggle. While Bitcoin and other digital currencies have attracted considerable curiosity, their adoption rates are low, and official backing is practically nonexistent. It makes sense when you realize that banks are not just for transactional purposes, as most cryptos are. They have a far broader set of goals than cryptos. All of these make sense on paper, but when the Federal Reserve is no more Federal than Federal Express, and it was created by the Bank of England and the Rothschilds to print money for the financial elite anytime they want, you can imagine they will do everything that can to keep this system in place for their benefit.

Governments and the puppets that run them get out of the control of the financial elite and accept Bitcoin or any other cryptocurrency as a legal currency; it stands little chance of ever completely replacing central banks. Central banks the world over are monitoring and analyzing Bitcoin. Given the high expense of manufacturing metal coins (which often exceed their face value), it is more probable than not that central banks will issue their own Central Bank Digital Currency (CBDC). CBDCs have become the latest trend among central bankers worldwide. The coalition of advanced economies is making strides toward introducing CBDCs globally. At a recent meeting in Washington, Japanese Finance Vice Minister Masato Kanda announced that the G7 has made it a top priority to explore ways to assist developing countries in implementing CBDC by appropriate standards, including the G7 public policy principle for retail CBDC.

CBDCs are the government's response to the rise of cryptocurrencies. They seamlessly blend the innovative technology behind Bitcoin with the tried-and-true monetary policies of fiat currencies such as the dollar, euro, and renminbi. Unlike traditional digital currencies such as bitcoin or even dollar-pegged stablecoins like TetherUSDT or USDC, CBDCs offer governments complete visibility and control over every economic transaction.

Indulge in the deliciousness of a New York City street taco without a worry in the world. Your privacy is paramount as there is no government record of your identity or purchase when you hand over a $5 bill to the street vendor. Experience the revolutionary difference of CBDCs, the complete antithesis of conventional paper currency. Introducing the e-CNY, China's revolutionary CBDC that provides the government real-time insights into consumer behavior. With the ability to track purchases and locations, the e-CNY allows the government to regulate transactions deemed unfit for society. Need medicine, the government will know. Have an addiction that costs money, the government will know everything.

With the ability to replace private-sector checking and savings accounts with government accounts, CBDCs offer a new level of convenience, security, and no civil liberties or privacy. Additionally, they provide the Federal Reserve unlimited ability to print and allocate money, just like today with the paper dollar. CBDCs even allow for the subtraction of money from individuals' bank accounts, making them a powerful tool for governments to manage their economies and control whom they deem wrong. Think about it: with their CBDCs, they can make and enforce their own rules in the digital space. If you want to use your digital currency, let's hope you have an excellent social score and have been a good citizen.

And why wouldn't they? Think about it: with their CBDCs, they can make and enforce their own rules in the digital space. If you want to use your digital currency, let's hope you have an excellent social score and have not been a bad citizen.

The Drawbacks of Central Bank Digital Currencies (CBDCs).

Discover the fascinating possibilities that await you. If you have yet to notice, there are some concerning drawbacks. Experience full traceability with our product - say goodbye to anonymous transactions. Rest assured; physical cash will not be immediately outlawed. You are introducing CBDCs - the ultimate solution to enhance transactional efficiency and streamline cross-border transactions. With this innovative add-on to the existing system, you can experience unparalleled convenience. The inevitability of cash disappearing is undeniable.

This development is noteworthy as it removes our capacity to conduct incognito transactions. Experience the future of digital currency with CBDCs. The government-controlled private ledger technology offers you the perfect balance of anonymity and transparency, all while providing central banks with the traceability they need. Experience a new level of transparency with your financial activity. Just like your debit card transactions are visible to your bank, your central bank will now have visibility into your economic activities. Discover why this could be a more significant issue than initially anticipated, coming up shortly.

Experience the future of banking with negative rates. Say goodbye to physical cash as we introduce a new era of digital transactions. In the world of CBDC, holding your digital tokens under the mattress is not an option for withdrawal. Inevitably, the age of physical cash will come to a close.

Experience greater flexibility in implementing negative interest rates with the help of this solution provided to central banks. Individuals will feel motivated to spend or forfeit their funds by taking this action, ultimately boosting consumer spending. It's undeniable that since the 2008 financial crisis, interest rates have been at an all-time low. With this tool in their arsenal, central banks won't hesitate to drive them even lower.

Discover the concerning turn of events. Experience a new level of financial control with CBDCs. Central banks now have the power to make money "programmable," thanks to the centralization of our relationship with the financial system. Central banks need help regarding monetary stimulus - while they control the price of money (interest rates), they cannot influence the velocity of money. With CBDCs, the game is changing. Now, policymakers have the power to adjust speed as they see fit.

With a direct relationship with your central bank, CBDCs could allow for a currency expiration policy. Maximize the potential of your funds by programming your CBDC account to automatically expire any remaining balance of $5000 by the upcoming Saturday. Are you skeptical about this idea? Discover how China has already done this to its citizens.

Central Bank Digital Currencies (CBDCs) offer a quick and seamless way to deliver currency directly to the pockets of citizens. Experience the convenience of receiving freshly printed fiat currency now in your CBDC account with a button. Unlike traditional quantitative easing (QE), which heavily relies on financial institutions to facilitate the flow of money, this approach is vastly different.

As commercial banks take a backseat in lending, central banks will likely step up to make lending decisions. Are you looking for a mortgage or business loan? Take control of your finances today by completing the application on the user-friendly Freedom App. Rest assured that the central bank will contact you soon after—experience tailor-made monetary policy with our customization feature. Personalize your policy to suit your unique financial needs.

The ethical implications of traceability, the lack of physical currency, and programmability cannot be ignored. In addition, they increase the probability of tailored financial policies. The central bank can now precisely customize its monetary policy by leveraging a vast reservoir of Big Data on personal spending, saving, investment behaviors, and cutting-edge digital identification infrastructure.

Experience the power of CBDCs with their unique ability to control both price and velocity. Our boundaries are expanding into uncharted territory. As a result, stimulus tools can be strategically utilized to maximize rate rather than applied universally. Targeting individuals with lower incomes can effectively deliver the stimulus to those who are more likely to spend. Central banks are often called "independent," but there is a risk that personalized monetary policy could become politicized, which could be detrimental. By segmenting its voters and identifying communities where it may be lagging in polls, a government can strategically deliver targeted stimulus to these groups.

Significant Milestones In The Cryptocurrency Market

Let's look at the timeline of cryptocurrencies from the inception of Bitcoin and a few significant milestones it saw on the way.

2008

The first two cryptocurrency milestones occur. The domain name Bitcoin.org was registered on August 18. Then, on October 31 "Satoshi Nakamoto," the inventor of Bitcoin, released a document that kicks off the process: Bitcoin is a decentralized electronic cash system that operates on a peer-to-peer basis.

2009

On January 12, Nakamoto delivered ten Bitcoin (BTC) to Hal Finney, a computer programmer.

2010

Bitcoin was hacked on August 15, revealing a critical weakness in the system. Jeff Garzik, a Bitcoin developer, notes a very unusual transaction involving 184 billion BTC, stating: "We've got an issue here."

Later that year, the first Bitcoin sale occurred, establishing the first time that cryptocurrency had a monetary value. Ten thousand Bitcoins are exchanged for two pizzas by a Bitcoin user. These would be the world's most expensive pizzas since 10,000 Bitcoin is worth more than $447 million.

2011

Rival cryptocurrencies begin to appear with the introduction of Litecoin, Namecoin, and Swiftcoin. Meanwhile, Bitcoin is under fire after reports that it is being utilized on the so-called "dark web," namely Silk Road. Bitcoin's price skyrockets before plummeting again, demonstrating that no exposure is terrible PR.

2012

Cryptocurrencies became public awareness thanks to a fictionalized trial dubbed Bitcoin for Dummies in the third season of the US drama The Good Wife.

2013

Forbes dubbed 2013 the "Year of the Bitcoin." This was the year Bitcoin captured the attention of many hungry investors, commanding headlines at $1,242 per coin and driving gold prices to a session low of $1,240 per ounce.

Its worth soared as it gained traction at discussion tables, internet forums, and seminars. This rapid growth resulted in widely divergent perspectives on cryptocurrencies, with some seeing them as a hoax while others saw them as lucrative and appealing ventures. The reality is that both positions are very persuasive. Due to the extreme volatility of the cryptocurrency markets, succeeding years saw unpredictable changes in value and opinion.

When Bitcoin holders cannot agree on a new transaction rule, a Bitcoin "fork" occurs, and the blockchain physically divides in half. Two networks operate concurrently for six hours, with two distinct versions of transaction histories, resulting in an inevitable value decline.

Meanwhile, many governments are trying to determine the best approach to cryptocurrency regulation. Thailand prohibits Bitcoin trading, calling it unlawful. Germany's finance ministry would not recognize Bitcoin as an official currency but as a "unit of account," opening the door for a future framework taxing Bitcoin-related activities. The People's Bank of China has prohibited financial institutions from utilizing Bitcoins, resulting in another decline in value. The first Bitcoin ATM is opened in Vancouver, Canada.

2014

Exchange of cryptocurrencies Mt Gox, headquartered in Japan, falls insolvent and leaves investors out of pocket. Microsoft enables customers to purchase games using Bitcoin as an example of the currency's increasing appeal.

2015

The emergence of other cryptocurrencies, including Ethereum and Coinbase (which received $75 million in a financing round, the most significant sum ever raised by a Bitcoin firm). Bitstamp, a Bitcoin exchange headquartered in Europe, suffers a security breach after a hack and restarts trading a few days later, assuring clients that their money has not been lost.

2016

Cryptocurrencies continue to gain popularity. The number of Bitcoin ATMs has increased from about 500 at the start of the year to slightly under 900 by year's end; Uber in Argentina has begun taking Bitcoin payments, while the Swiss national railway and software company Steam are among new users.

The DAO (decentralized autonomous organization) was established in May - a stateless venture capital fund on the Ethereum blockchain and the world's most significant crowdfunded initiative. Users hack it a month after its debut, and a third of its assets are stolen.

Consequently, Ethereum undergoes a "fork," dividing into Ethereum and Ethereum Classic.

2017

This was a watershed year in the history of Bitcoin, and this period permanently altered the way people viewed cryptos. Bitcoin served as an entry point for all newcomers to cryptocurrency in 2017. Individuals were only sometimes considering Bitcoin as a long-term investment. They were trading Bitcoin for altcoins and investing in initial coin offerings (ICOs), throwing away millions expecting to become wealthy.

The general public first became aware of crypto assets in 2017. The regulation was minimal; anybody with money could create and list a token on an exchange. Consumer safeguards were non-existent, and everyone became an expert at assessing early-stage, blockchain-based "investments."

This resulted in the initial coin offering (ICO) frenzy, in which everyone was misled by excitement and burnt by fundamentally poor investments. Bitcoin increased from $900 to $11000 in less than a year. This year was even crazier for cryptocurrencies since coins potentially increased in value from $1 to over $100000 in a single year.

Apart from this excitement, the highly anticipated "Bitcoin cash hard fork" occurred, dividing Bitcoin into two derivative cryptocurrencies: BTC and BCH. Japan enacts legislation allowing for the legal acceptance of Bitcoin as a payment mechanism. At the same time, Skandiabanken in Norway incorporates Bitcoin accounts and recognizes Bitcoin as an investment asset and payment system.

2018

In 2018, we saw one of the most significant price declines in Bitcoin's history (BTC). The altcoins market surged in 2017 during the Bitcoin bull run but collapsed in 2018 because of the downturn. This pattern demonstrated that all cryptocurrencies are inextricably linked to Bitcoin's trends. In other words, what reached an all-time high of $828 billion began to decline gradually. Consequently, interest in cryptocurrencies was waning in the market.

Numerous European countries collaborate on cryptocurrency legislation, and many continue to establish creative collaborations with high-street brands, such as Ripple's 2018 international money transfer app with Santander.

2019

Increased geopolitical tensions, global trade frictions, political instability, and uncertainty were just a few of the main themes that dominated the global market in 2019. As we've seen with the US-China trade talks, investors' expectations have fluctuated between an agreement and a full-fledged trade war. The Brexit issue has cast doubt on the UK's future growth.

Despite a turbulent market environment, Bitcoin outperformed other asset classes significantly in 2019. The performance demonstrates Bitcoin's effectiveness as a hedge against global dangers and stagnation, as well as a risk-on asset with a high rate of return.

Bitcoin may provide investors a 90% annual return in 2019 if they follow a simple buy-and-hold strategy. In 2019, the cryptocurrency sector was a completely different scenario. At the start of 2019, the

Crypto Total Market Cap Ex-BTC was USD 52.66 billion. It surpassed USD 140 billion in mid-June when BTC reached a year high 13330. However, when Bitcoin prices fell, the Ex-BTC Market Cap lost most of its gains in 1H19 and ended the year at USD 55.90 billion.

2020

2020 has been an insane year for everyone, especially for cryptocurrencies. Bitcoin garnered media attention lately after setting fresh all-time highs for the first time since 2017. Global financial markets were shaken by turmoil as concerns of a pandemic-induced economic slump increased. On March 12, Bitcoin dropped below $4,000 for the first time in almost seven years, registering the most significant one-day loss of 27 percent in nearly seven years.

Bitcoin recovered to $7,000 in April, only one month before its third and final historical event - halving. After three months of stabilization, Bitcoin broke over the $10,000 barrier in October. Then, within two months, as investors were still discussing the prospect of Bitcoin falling lower, it surmounted obstacles of $12K, $14K, $16K, and ultimately $19K. In 2020, institutional investors and government sectors will undoubtedly benefit from Bitcoin's growth. JPMorgan Chase was the catalyst for the adoption. And this was the impetus for the 2021 cryptocurrency bull run.

2021

The bull run that began in 2020 lasted far into 2021, with experts and fans issuing lucrative price forecasts for major cryptocurrencies. Elon Musk's support at the start of the year accelerated the pace. All of the optimism surrounding Bitcoin propelled it to new highs and positively influenced virtually all the altcoins.

However, a hurdle occurred in May when Elon Musk changed his stance and said that Tesla would no longer take Bitcoin because it would jeopardize the environment. To make matters worse, a series of crackdown operations against crypto mining was conducted in China in May, the country hosting most of the world's crypto mining. This affected virtually all cryptocurrencies, and it seemed as if the so-called bubble had burst.

On the other side, half the Earth away from China, the year 2021 will be remembered as another South American nation formally accepts the first time Bitcoin. El Salvador has recognized Bitcoin as legal money after Congress received a request from President Nayib Bukele to embrace the cryptocurrency and eliminate all related capital gains taxes. Additionally, the President pledged to harness the country's geothermal energy by instructing a state-owned utility to construct geothermal facilities that harness the power from volcanoes for Bitcoin mining. The height for BTC in 2021 reached $68,000, another record high reached in October 2021, but closed the year below $40,000.

2022.

As we moved from 2021 to 2022, inflation, the energy crisis, and geopolitical upheaval owing to Russia's aggressiveness toward Ukraine lowered BTC and other top cryptocurrencies' values. Prepare for the 2022 Crypto Winter and shifting Bitcoin values. From January to May 2022, Bitcoin's price plummets. BTC dropped below $30,000 for the first time since July 2021 in May. Crypto winters are less defined than bear markets. Like a bear market, this period sees the cryptocurrency markets decrease steadily and sometimes sharply. Cryptocurrencies fell in Q2. Stablecoins like TerraUSD and Terrra Luna contributed to the crypto price drop. Bitcoin traded around $20,700 as cryptocurrency hedge fund Three Arrows Capital defaulted on a bitcoin loan and was ordered into liquidation by a court in the British Virgin Islands. In November 2022, FTX, a major crypto exchange, unexpectedly collapsed, further depressing crypto values. The conversation went bankrupt after its CEO, Sam Blankman Fried, was accused of misappropriating funds. FTX's financial difficulties and possible fraud prevented Binance from bailing it out.

The shocking collapse of FTX sent shockwaves across the financial industry, generating a domino effect in the cryptocurrency market and leaving investors uneasy. Inflation fears and rising interest rates impacted the market. As 2022 ended, Bitcoin's price dropped below $20,000, indicating the cryptocurrency market's health.

2023

The first half of the yeast saw BTC in the $ '20s. We are now experiencing the gradual yet promising rise of Bitcoin's value, reaching approximately $30,000 when writing this chapter and igniting a glimmer of hope that the crypto winter is finally ending. Q1 had seen other cryptocurrencies following suit with similar price trends.

Experience the new heights of Bitcoin mining as we draw closer to the end of May. The recent surge in miner interest has caught traders' attention, who view it as an excellent bullish signal. While inflation remains a concern in the broader markets, there is growing optimism that the measures implemented by the Fed could lead to a gentle landing.

CHAPTER 2

The Bitcoin Phenomenon

The Story Of Bitcoin's Birth

On November 1, 2008, an anonymous entity named Satoshi Nakamoto wrote in an email to a cryptography mailing list with a nine-page white paper containing the first-ever mention of Bitcoin, calling it a "peer-to-peer electronic cash system."

"I've been working on a new electronic cash system that's fully peer-to-peer, with no trusted third party. The paper is available at Bitcoin.org/Bitcoin.pdf." Nakomoto said. The original paper detailing the math and specifics of Bitcoin is still available on the website.

As Nakamoto proposed, the system's main properties would be that the electronic transactions would be peer-to-peer and would not need to involve a financial institution. The plan was to be completely decentralized, meaning that the currency users would not need to rest their trust in a central authority, such as traditional central banks.

Satoshi also expressed dissatisfaction that banks have repeatedly breached the trust of the people who deposit money with them by lending them money in credit bubbles while keeping minimal reserves. "The root problem with conventional currency is all the trust required to make it work. The central bank must be trusted not to debase the currency, but the history of fiat currencies is full of breaches of that trust," Satoshi wrote.

After publishing his revolutionary paper, Nakamoto released Bitcoin's first software and partnered with developers and coders online to improve it.

The first lines of code were posted to the Bitcoin blockchain on January 3, 2009, a few months after the original whitepaper surfaced. These lines of code, known as the "genesis block," are credited to the person or persons known as Satoshi Nakamoto.

On January 12, Nakamoto sent ten Bitcoins to Hal Finney, giving birth to a new finance counterculture, taking impetus away from banks and back to the people. At this point, Bitcoin's monetary value was negligible. Initially, users rewarded each other with Bitcoins for good comments in forums. The first "real" transaction occurred on May 22, 2010, when Laszlo Hanyecz famously bought two pizzas for 10,000 Bitcoin, which was about $30. This transaction would be worth more than $38 million at current prices.

The collaborative environment between Nakomoto and other developers continued until 2011, when, without warning, Nakamoto vanished, or did he?

Many attempts have been made to discover Satoshi Nakamoto's true identity, but with each name suggested, each turned out to be something other than the creator. However, details about the creator, such as Nationality and origins being obscure, made the currency trustworthy and free of any inherent biases. Bitcoin was invented amidst the aftermath of the 2008 financial crisis, and the crisis was an apparent motivating factor that led to its creation.

Many banks and other financial institutions failed worldwide and had to be bailed out by governments at the expense of taxpayers' money. This highlighted the fragility of the modern financial system, where the health of the monetary system was heavily reliant on banks and other financial institutions. We are forced to trust these institutions to make wise and prudent decisions with the money we give them. Too often, they need to carry out this fundamental responsibility adequately.

For most of its history, Bitcoin was associated with three overlapping communities: the small community of original investors, blockchain technology enthusiasts, and speculators just here to make money off this new financial instrument.

Initially, Bitcoin was regarded as money with philosophy. Instead of a central bank backing the currency, it had programming and Nakamoto's whitepaper, both of which suggested skepticism about ordinary financial institutions and proposed significant theoretical advantages against the same. Bitcoin was structured in a way that exposed its ideology. The idea of a peer-to-peer money network was a disruptive one.

You don't have to pay a fee to a third party like a bank or currency exchange to transact money. But the original ideology is even more revolutionary than that: Bitcoin highlights how fundamentally bizarre the concept of money is. In some sense, money isn't "real" in the way a physical asset like a car is. Money is a human invention, a value token that makes exchange easier. But it works and is accurately provided that enough people believe in it, people fight and die for it, and establishments fall for lack of it. You can notice the influences of the banking crisis on Bitcoin's ideology.

It portrays a specific distrust of financial institutions. And in 2009, in an economy reeling in financial distress, many people were keenly looking for alternatives to the mainstream financial system that had failed them. As most people understand it, the banking system's core is money. Of all the previous attempts at internet-based currency, Bitcoin was the one that came out as the best possible alternative to society's common anxieties around the traditional financial system.

Many investors see Bitcoin as a physical commodity, like gold. There's also the finite nature of Bitcoin, as there can only be 21 million Bitcoin in the world under the current protocol. More than 17 million coins have already been mined, and the rest will be released at a predictable mining rate. Central banks or politicians need to be able to make that system run faster or mint new currency to suit their political agenda.

How Does Bitcoin Work?

Digital currencies like Bitcoin are a relatively modern concept, and there are crucial differences between digital currencies and the currently circulating government-issued currencies. Digital currency is similar to real currency, but they are not issued by central banks nor financially backed by the state as digital money. Cryptocurrency issuing is decentralized and is not decided by politicians but by technical aspects that are usually well-defined.

For instance, Bitcoins use a cryptographic algorithm to generate the currency made by the network users and not by a centralized governing body. To open a conventional bank account, one might require several documents, such as a valid ID and proof of residence, whereas to register to a digital currency, a valid IP address will suffice. Individuals can use Bitcoins to pay others or merchants without involving any third party.

When someone talks about Bitcoin or the Bitcoin blockchain, they usually refer to the Bitcoin network. There are two types of participants in the network: wallets and nodes. Bitcoin users typically own wallets with which they can send and receive payments. Nodes are the computers that validate and verify Bitcoin transactions and maintain a history of past transactions. A node can also act as a wallet. Some Bitcoin network nodes are also known as miners.

Anyone can join the network as a wallet or node and then start using Bitcoin on equal terms with everyone else. Although every network participant can send and receive Bitcoin payments, only nodes keep track of the entire history of transactions in real time. This log of transactions maintained by the nodes is called the Bitcoin blockchain. The word blockchain comes from adding new transactions in segments called blocks.

A block is a permanent record of recent transactions. The blocks of recorded data build upon each other to form the blockchain, dating back to the first Bitcoin transaction. The transparency established by the blockchain is essential in securing the validation process as it allows the community to monitor and self-police transaction activity. It also allows for verification of both the spender and the recipient and ensures that double-spending a Bitcoin is impossible. In the case of Bitcoin, new blocks are added roughly once every 10 minutes. Nodes validate every new transaction and ensure that only legitimate transactions get added to the blockchain.

A node can operate autonomously and requires no maintenance; it only requires an internet connection. Thus anyone can set up a node without much effort. Nodes communicate with each other in a peer-to-peer fashion. Peer-to-peer is like a network where each node relays information to a few other nodes, and eventually, the message gets to all the nodes in the network. If a node tries to cheat the network by marking an invalid transaction as valid, it would be rejected by all other nodes on the web. Therefore, nodes collectively guarantee the network's transparency, availability, decentralization, and security. The nodes are spread worldwide, and with over 10,000 Bitcoin nodes powering the network at any given time, cheating on such a network is nearly impossible.

How Do I Get Bitcoins?

Obtaining Bitcoins and learning to use the blockchain network and ecosystem is relatively simple. The three fundamental ways to get Bitcoins include

Transactions: Individuals and businesses can opt to receive Bitcoins for goods and services rendered or for peer-to-peer payments.

Digital Currency Exchanges: A digital currency exchange operates similarly to traditional fiat currency exchanges, allowing individuals to buy and sell Bitcoins at the current market rate. The exchange rate of

Bitcoins varies based on liquidity, demand, and various other market conditions.

Mining: Miners are the backbone of the Bitcoin ecosystem. They receive monetary rewards in Bitcoin for the services they provide for the network. This includes solving the algorithms necessary to process transactions, which helps secure the network and keep it running smoothly.

How Do I Store Bitcoins and Make Transactions?

Individuals must set up a digital wallet to safely store and transact Bitcoins. A wallet is a file that holds all the unique keys (passwords) attributed to an owner's Bitcoins. These keys will be recorded and synchronized when the system sends or receives payments. Wallets usually come in two forms: hot and cold. Hot wallets allow instantaneous transfers online through the Blockchain; they are connected to the internet. Cold wallets are offline wallets on a user's computer or device. Cold wallets offer greater security as they are offline, but the transaction process is longer and more cumbersome than a hot wallet.

To receive Bitcoins, you provide the sender with your wallet address. A wallet address is a long sequence of numbers and letters. It is the unique identifier used to send payments to you. New addresses can be generated for each transaction to maintain greater financial privacy.

Bitcoin technology significantly improves over traditional payment systems when utilizing the currency for both micro and large-scale payments. Micropayments can be made in increments as small as a fraction of a penny (0.00000001). The lowest possible unit of digital money, known as Bitcoin, is called a satoshi. It takes its name from

Satoshi Nakamoto, credited with creating Bitcoin. The exchange rate for satoshi to bitcoin is currently set at 100 million satoshis to one bitcoin. For example, if you bought a $100 item with one bitcoin, your charge might ring up as .00341583 BTC (if BTC equaled $29,275.50). However, it's easier to understand 341,583 Satoshi. Conversely, the system can make large-scale payments without worrying about daily transaction limits or slow deposit processes standard at many traditional financial institutions.

Lifetime Price Analysis of Bitcoin

In its decade-long rise, Bitcoin has changed how global markets work and made many people super-rich. The world's most popular cryptocurrency started on January 3, 2009, by mining the genesis block (Block 0), which created 50 Bitcoins. On January 9, Version 0.1 of Bitcoin was officially released, including the generation system that limits Bitcoin's total circulation to 21 million by 2040.

We now walk through Bitcoin's eventful journey to the top and analyze some of the significant milestones hit by the coin along the way.

2009 - 2011

After its inception in January 2009, Bitcoin remained more or less confined to the developers' circles and didn't catch much attention outside of it. But as October of 2009 came around, A pro-Crypto website named New Liberty Standard, which an original Bitcoin developer ran, displayed the first BTC-USD exchange rate. At the time, they calculated the exchange rate based on the cost of electricity required to mine one Bitcoin, which was around $0.0007 on October 5, 2009. Less than a month later, Bitcoin 0.2 was released with Linux support and new features that upgraded the blockchain capabilities. In May of 2010, the first Bitcoin purchase occurred when Programmer Laszlo Hanyecz bought two Papa John's pizzas for 10,000 Bitcoins (worth about $30) through an exchange on the Bitcointalk chat forum. By late 2010, Bitcoins popularity was increasing beyond the original media, and it was gaining momentum; this led to Bitcoins total market cap hitting the $1 million mark by November 2010. One Bitcoin was worth about $0.5 at this point.

2011 was a significant year for Bitcoin as it breached the $1 mark for the first time and made global headlines, further boosting its popularity. The infamous Silk Road website was also launched around this time by Mr. Ross Ulbricht, who wanted to create a lawless dark web marketplace where people could buy and sell whatever they wanted without a trace. Bitcoin is an obvious choice of currency as it is anonymous and untraceable. However, with the momentum gained from media attention, Bitcoin continued to rise, going beyond $10 to over $30 by June 2011. As this happened, the original creator, Satoshi Nakamoto, disappeared from the internet.

After rallying from $1 in February to highs of $31 on June 8, the dream run of Bitcoin suddenly reversed, the Bitcoin bubble as it was known - burst -and prices tumbled back down to single digits by June 12.

The sudden climb gave crypto fans massive hope in the new digital currency, with some expecting the price to reach highs beyond $1,000 and enter mainstream usage by the end of the year. But the sudden crash brought as much despair as the climb had given hope, and soon the existence of black market applications like Silk Road had people questioning the future of Bitcoin. Bitcoin version 0.5 was in operation around this time.

2012-2017

Bitcoin, being ever-volatile, had been slowly rising again over the past few months after the price peaked back in June 2011, climbing back above $9 for the first time in almost a year. Following this, multiple events of Bitcoin exchanges getting hacked and Bitcoins stolen were reported. Bitcoin continued its bull run, breaking the all-important $100 barrier for the first time, jumping from $96.15 on March 31, 2012, to close at $104.70 the next day.

However, the price was over 70% in two days as a panic sell-off ensued, falling from $228.94 to $68.09 in just six days, leaving the currency back where it had started for the month. The secret online black market called Silk Road that uses Bitcoin for shady transactions was seized by the FBI in October 2013, and Bitcoin prices plunged by over 18% from $127.30 to $103.85 as a result, but the price rebounded the very next day. By November, Bitcoin surged almost ten times in value reaching $1000. China's foreign minister Wang Yi takes a positive stand and announces that people in China are "free to participate in the Bitcoin market" and promises to "adopt a long-term perspective" on the currency, bringing much optimism to the market participants.

By 2015, Bitcoin was now accepted by over 100,000 retailers worldwide: including Microsoft, Dell, Wikipedia, Twitch, Greenpeace, Expedia, and PayPal. The widespread merchant adoption reassured people that Bitcoin has real value as a currency, not just as a digital investment. By late 2017, Bitcoin was trading around the $1000 mark as stray hacking incidents continued.

In a gigantic jump, Bitcoin went from under $1,000 on January 1, 2017, to $10,840 on December 1, making many people very rich. It went on to top a record-breaking high of $20,089 and closed the day at an all-time high of $19,783.06.

2018-2020

Prices sank 3.60% after Twitter announced a ban on cryptocurrency advertisements joining the likes of tech giants Google and Facebook to protect investors from fraud.

The crackdowns came as global regulators started to notice the potential risks in Initial Coin Offerings (ICOs) and other misuse and frauds related to cryptocurrency use. The price dropped from $8,518.64 to $7,471.18 during the week. The seventeenth generation of Bitcoin's original software client, Bitcoin Core 0.17.0, became available with significant upgrades by 2018 as prices kept diminishing. As 2019 came around, the price climbed above $10k, hitting $13,880 on June 26 before sliding back.

The plague struck in 2020, Covid-19 crashed into our lives, and markets worldwide plunged. Bitcoin doesn't escape either, falling by over 50% in less than a week as the world moves toward a total lockdown. On March 12, Bitcoin dropped from almost $8,000 to below $5,000, losing 39% daily. Market liquidity froze up, and investors fled into cash and commodity segments. Amazingly, however, the price was back up to pre-pandemic levels by May as Bitcoin traders got back into the game quickly.

By November 2020, Bitcoin was up 100% on the year at $15,770; the bullish momentum continued, with prices increasing to a daily high of $19,864 on November 30 before closing the month at $19,700. Soon enough, on December 16, the cryptocurrency blows past the $20,000 barrier before charging on up to reach a record-breaking high of $21,576 – a yearly gain of over 180%. The currency kept climbing, passing $24,000 on December 21 and $26,000 on December 26.

2021-present

The bull run is sustained as Bitcoin bowls into a record-breaking 2021 by smashing through the $30,000 barrier on January 2 and smashing past $40,000 less than a week later before reaching a high of $42,000 on January 8, resulting in a 40% gain in the first week of the year. It's been very volatile since Bitcoin topped $40,000 at the start of January, and the currency has displayed immense volatility.

It's lost a quarter of its value since then, dipping briefly below $30,000 on January 22 and again on January 27. In yet another example of the massive influence Elon Musk can wield online, he adds the #Bitcoin hashtag to his Twitter profile, and the price skyrockets, gaining almost 11% in a single day and continuing with a further 10% rise the following day.

Following this on Monday, January 8, Tesla announced in an SEC filing that it had invested $1.5 billion into Bitcoin as part of a new investment policy, sending prices skyward. It's been an excellent year for Bitcoin, and by February 2021, the price bounced through $50,000 for the first time. In a significant milestone, Bitcoin's price reflected 9% on February 19- taking its total market cap past $1 trillion for the first time, climbing above $53,000. Shortly after, Elon Musk announced over Twitter that after buying $1.5 billion worth of Bitcoin last month, Tesla will now accept Bitcoins as payment for its cars - integrating the cryptocurrency further into the financial system.

Bitcoin prices shot up 6.24% to a new high of over $63,000 in anticipation of Coinbase IPO. But soon, the crypto gets crushed under the weight of a reversal by Tesla to cease accepting payment in Bitcoin because of the environmental impact. Bitcoin inks down 13%. Things got worse as Bitcoin went through another lousy patch as China banned financial institutions from offering any crypto-related services, sending prices down over 14%.

Bitcoin's price, which started at around $60,000 in May, dropped to about $30,000; almost every other cryptocurrency also took a nosedive. Bitcoin was still in freefall after ending the week down 25% due to global regulatory obstacles. By May, Bitcoin was trading at $38,400. News from El Salvador sent prices galloping up as it could make the legal currency tender and embrace the digital token in an unexpected move that could dramatically shift the currents of the international crypto marketplace.

At Bitcoin 2021, El Salvador President Nayib Bukele announced that his country was officially adopting Bitcoin as a legal tender. Once implemented, it would be the first country in the world to do so and mark a significant milestone in the history of international monetary policy. It would also mean no capital gains tax for Bitcoin in El Salvador. Meanwhile, as China intensified its crypto mining crackdown and banned most mining operations, Bitcoin plummeted to its lowest price since January.

After a year of record highs and parabolic gains, crypto markets are going through a turbulent time that doesn't look to be ending any time soon. Bitcoin looks to be making a comeback, with prices popping to nearly $43k in August 2021 as Germany moves towards greater crypto adoption, allowing institutional funds to hold up to 20% in crypto assets for the first time.

Inflation, the energy crisis, and geopolitical upheaval owing to Russia's aggressiveness toward Ukraine lowered BTC and other top cryptocurrencies' values in 2022. BTC dropped below $30,000 for the first time since July 2021 in May 2022. This period sees the cryptocurrency markets decrease steadily and sometimes sharply. Stablecoins like TerraUSD and Terra Luna's failure contributed to the crypto price drop. Bitcoin traded around $20,700 as cryptocurrency hedge fund Three Arrows Capital defaulted on a bitcoin loan and was ordered into liquidation by a court in the British Virgin Islands. The FTX exchange went bankrupt after its CEO, Sam Blankman Fried, was accused of misappropriating funds. FTX's financial difficulties and possible fraud prevented Binance from bailing it out 2022 ended, Bitcoin's price dropped below $20,000, indicating the cryptocurrency market's health.

Bitcoin vs. Banks

Bitcoin was created to decentralize the financial system. In other terms, it was designed to replace the centralized banking system. To date, it has not officially been able to capture the banks, but the efforts are still intact. So, the dominance of Bitcoin over banks would decentralize the banking system. Thus, we need to concentrate on the characteristics and features of decentralized and centralized strategies to understand if Bitcoin can take over the current banking system.

Before the introduction of Bitcoin in the market, we were exposed only to the working of the traditional banking system. Bitcoin and other cryptocurrencies work by storing the transactions on a decentralized public ledger. The ledger uses cryptographic algorithms to ensure their records are on point and the user's identity is encrypted.

Bitcoin owners have digital wallets where they can store their coins. And the work of the ledger is to ensure that a proper spendable balance is maintained in the wallet. Moreover, it tracks the transaction history to ensure the owner spends from their wallets.

Unlike traditional currencies, Bitcoin is not created by printing notes and coins. But are made through a process called 'cryptocurrency mining.' Mining solves complex mathematical puzzles to confirm and add transactions to the ledger (block). Now that you know the basic working, we can understand its implications on banks.

Implications for Banks

In recent years, a drastic change has occurred in how people look at businesses and make transactions. One can exchange currency outside traditional banks with a few clicks on a mobile phone.

The significant point is that people need not physically go to a traditional bank if they require financing. With the development of the peer-to-peer network, as in the case of Bitcoin and other cryptocurrencies, it is getting much more popular and familiar, and people are turning away from banks and looking forward to more decentralized systems like Bitcoin.

Bitcoin - A Threat to Traditional Banks?

In short, yes. Cryptocurrency enthusiasts have long ago identified that Bitcoin and its technology threaten the banking industry. Not just them, but banks too have strong perceptions on the replacement of working of banks with blockchain technology. For instance, BNP Paribas, a French banking giant, released a report regarding their discussion on the technology behind Bitcoin and how it could make traditional banks redundant.

Furthermore, an analyst for the bank compared the software behind Bitcoin with an invention like the steam and combustion engine and stated that it has the potential to transform the world of finance. A UK banking report concluded that Bitcoin and the following cryptocurrencies are a menace to traditional banks, especially if they need to consider people's new preferences and behaviors regarding how they wish to transact with money.

The After Effects!

To understand Bitcoin's power, let us assume a scenario where Bitcoin has taken over the financial system. Here are the effects banks can have with the entry of Bitcoin in the world of finance.

The Demise of the Banking System

Banks cannot create reserves and perform fractional reserve lending with Bitcoin. There is no means through which it can control Bitcoin, as Bitcoin has no representative and is fully decentralized. Banks can no longer inflate or deflate away the purchasing power of users' saving accounts. Banks cannot do bailouts with Bitcoin if cryptocurrencies get adopted worldwide.

Banks cannot generate revenue from remittance businesses, which levy 10-30 percent in cross-border transactions.

Banks act as an intermediary for every transaction that is made. But, with Bitcoin in the market, banks can become inexistent as one of the main features of Bitcoin is the absence of middlemen. These possibilities could emerge if Bitcoin came into the mainstream business. And thus, banks consider Bitcoin as a potential threat to themselves. Moreover, some believe that Bitcoin's impact on banks and the current technology will be beyond one's imagination. And the financial elite who control the politicians and the media will do everything they can to stop that from happening.

Advantages of Bitcoin Over the Traditional Banking System

Bitcoin, a decentralized system, has several benefits over the centralized system like banks, mainly because of the capability to operate without any intermediary and no case of failure at any point.

Processing of Transactions

Local transactions in the banking system are settled quickly. However, when it comes to international fund transfers, banks take several days to process the transaction. On the other hand, Bitcoin, a peer-to-peer payment system, can process over $1 billion worth of transactions on average. Thus, transactions are processed within a few minutes, irrespective of the sender and receiver location. Banks work for five business days; typically, no transactions are settled during the weekend or holidays. Meanwhile, Bitcoin is open daily and has no concept of holidays and weekends.

Offshore Banking

Financial institutions like JP Morgan, which dominates the offshore banking industry, have links with large banks, making it possible to clear billions of money very efficiently and securely. However, a downside is that the transfer of billions of dollars requires considerable manual labor, including transaction verification, Anti-money Laundering checks, and payment clearing. But being completely decentralized, Bitcoin does not require any manual work, as mentioned. Moreover, settlement and offshore banking are provided by Bitcoin with significantly lesser costs and a much more robust infrastructure.

Can Bitcoin take over the Banking system? Yes and no. With the incredible benefits Bitcoin offers, there is a possibility of Bitcoin ruling over the banking system. Since the traditional banking system is mature, people rely upon and believe in this system. At the same time, Bitcoin does have downsides in terms of volatility and regulation. Therefore, it cannot be said with certainty that Bitcoin will replace the existing centralized system, even though it can do so.

Bitcoin's Fundamental & Technical Analysis

Fundamental analysis determines an asset's value by looking at its financial performance, prospects, market value, and use cases before investing. We will now look at the fundamental analysis of Bitcoin by studying essential metrics such as market cap, liquidity, and the Bitcoin whitepaper, among other things.

Market capitalization, commonly called a market cap, is the total market value of an asset. Market capitalization is equal to the current market price of the currency multiplied by the number of coins in circulation. The market cap of Bitcoin tells us about its proliferation in the market and the extent of its adoption. It can also be used to predict future growth potential. A coin with a low market cap is likelier to see high growth than one with a very high market capitalization, whereas a coin with a high market cap tends to be more established and stable.

Bitcoin has the largest market cap of all cryptocurrencies. It is a well-established coin and comparatively a safe investment bet. The prominent market cap reflects the trust market participants have in the currency.

Liquidity measures how easily an asset can be bought or sold. Good liquidity is a sign of consistent supply and demand. Liquidity is also directly linked to trading volumes. High liquidity ensures an asset can be quickly and easily traded and exchanged relatively.

Analyzing Bitcoin's liquidity shows us an average daily trading volume of 2 - 4 billion dollars, meaning Bitcoin is a very liquid asset representing buyers and sellers readily available. The high trading volumes also indicate the market interest in the coin.

The nature of a coin's supply is a fundamental characteristic of a cryptocurrency. Bitcoin has a fixed collection of 21 million coins; the mining rate becomes half every four years. This is done to preserve the coin's value and counter inflation. A limited supply is almost always advantageous to a currency as it ensures rarity and counters inflation. This makes Bitcoin superior to many other assets due to the limited supply that gives it anti-inflationary properties. Meaning a Bitcoin investment can counter inflation.

Information such as the rate and number of transactions happening in the Bitcoin blockchain gives us insights into the activity taking place in the network. Transaction value can be used to understand the movement of money in a network as it shows how much matter was transferred in a time. Bitcoin has a very high transaction count and weight, as it is the top cryptocurrency traded currently.

Blockchains run on different algorithms, and the hash rate can be used to assess the health of a blockchain network. Bitcoin's healthy hash rate indicates a high interest surrounding the currency or increased mining rates. In simple terms, the hash rate can be said as the rate of mining of a coin. In combination with other metrics, the hash rate can be used to predict trends in a currency.

Active addresses are the blockchain addresses that remain active in a given period. Methods of calculating this metric vary, but it is also a good indicator of the dynamic market participants in the Bitcoin ecosystem. Several unique addresses can also be studied to see how the addition of new users is progressing in the network. Bitcoin has more than half a million addresses active at any given time, hinting at its popularity and rate of adoption.

The whitepaper is a technical document that gives us an overview of the cryptocurrency project. Reading a project's whitepaper before investing in it is a good idea. A good whitepaper should define the network's objectives and give us an insight into the technology used, use cases, and the roadmap ahead of the coin. Bitcoin has solid and well-defined documentation backing its blockchain technology; only minimal modifications and additions were made from the original paper published by Satoshi Nakamoto in 2009.

A cryptocurrency project is only valuable as long as it stays relevant. It should always have different or well-established applications or some unique, irreplaceable aspect that keeps it appropriate in the crypto universe. Hence while studying crypto, one must pay close attention to the network's integration into real-world use cases. Bitcoin is the most widespread and proliferative. Cryptocurrency enjoys an almost monopoly over transaction volumes and has become a standard index currency in crypto, signifying its relevance.

Using fundamental analysis, Bitcoin traders can understand the cryptocurrency's value and decide whether it is an excellent time to buy or sell. However, relying too much on fundamental analysis without also using technical analysis can prevent a trader from buying or selling at the wrong time.

To limit this risk, traders usually combine fundamental analysis with technical analysis. For instance, a fundamental analyst might look at several demand indicators, conclude that Bitcoin is underbought, and then implement a technical analysis by reading charts to find the optimal entry point.

Alternatively, a trader might use technical indicators to determine an excellent time to sell and then use fundamental analysis techniques to confirm this view by looking at key demand drivers.

Technical Analysis of Bitcoin

Technical analysis is an entirely different ballgame from fundamental analysis. In technical analysis, we take a statistical approach to study an asset by analyzing key metrics and studying charts using mathematical tools and functions. Here we will briefly discuss some essential methods and concepts that fall under technical analysis.

Support and Resistance

A support level is a price level where the desire to buy is so strong that it can withstand the pressure of sellers. As a result, the fall is suspended, and prices start increasing again. Usually, a support level can be determined in advance, according to the trends established by the previous decline. Likewise, a resistance level is opposite to a support level and represents a level above the market, where sellers' pressure exceeds buyers' influence. The prices tend to increase if the asset takes support at a support level, but it is likely to decline further if it breaks the support level and moves downwards. Similarly, if an asset breaks a resistance level, it is expected to keep moving up but is likely to move down if it does not cross the level.

Candlestick Charts

Unlike the traditional linear chart that shows the current and historical price data, Japanese candlesticks and bars use as many as four data points for a given time instead of one:

1. The opening price when the time began

2. The highest point the price reached during the time

3. The lowest point the price reached in the period

4. The closing price when the period ended

These four points increase the information value of the chart, which means they can immediately indicate what is happening in the market. This is why almost always candlestick charts are preferred over regular line charts.

Indicator-Based Trading

Technical indicators are a great way to predict future movement and make better trading decisions; here, we will discuss a couple of technical indicators that traders can use to predict the future moment of Bitcoins market price.

Simple Moving Average (SMA) is the most common trend indicator. It gives an average price of a traded instrument over a particular time and identifies the primary trend. It looks like a smooth line on the chart. Moving averages are of 3 types generally - SMA, EMA, and WMA. All the moving averages need to catch up because we average the cost. If the price on your chart goes up or down sharply, this indicator will react, but you will receive this signal with a delay.

When the price exceeds the moving average, it's a buy signal. When it crosses below, it's a sell signal. So we buy when the closing price is above MA and sell when the closing price is below MA.

Relative strength index (RSI) is a widely used technical indicator. It was developed by American engineer Welles Wilder in 1978. RSI shows how much the price changes in the direction of its movement. It transforms the cost into a percentage, indicating overbought zones (below 30%) and oversold zones (above 70%).

Thus, RSI values of 30% or below indicate an oversold condition, while RSI values of 70% or above indicate that security is becoming overbought. When the price from the overbought zone enters the neutral zone, it is a sell signal; when the cost from the oversold zone enters the neutral zone, it's a buy signal.

Although technical indicators are developed using robust methods of math and statistics, they are not 100% accurate all of the time. Experienced traders use more than one technical indicator and other crucial inputs such as market sentiment, financial news, and fundamental analysis techniques before trading. In addition to diverse information, seasoned traders have sound risk and money management strategies to ensure optimal outcomes.

Why is Risk Management Crucial?

Trading is a game of probabilities. In other words, a trading market is a place that is never certain. Thus, it comes with default risk. As a trader, the primary should be to reduce and manage risk in the best way possible. Professional traders believe understanding risk management is more crucial than having a good strategy.

Risk refers to the probability of an event happening against the intended outcome. Trading involves making predictions between two choices. And risk in this domain is simply the percentage of the money you are ready to lose. For instance, if a trader's account balance is $1000 and says he is risking 2% on a trade, the trader is betting 2% of his account balance, which is $20. So, if the business goes against the trader, he would be at most $20.

Risk Management Techniques

A trader who can manage their risk effectively can automatically maximize their profits. A professional trader's approach is to control their losses rather than running after profits. Here are some risk management strategies that every trader should know mandatorily.

1. Stop Loss and Take Profit

The first and foremost rule in trading is to have a stop loss and take profit for every trade. Stop-loss is an executable order that cuts the positions at a specified price when the market goes in the intended direction. On the other hand, take profit is also an executable order that liquidates the parts when the market reaches a specified price in the trader's favor. A stop-loss will keep a trader safe from further losses, and taking profit will lock in the money even if the market goes against the desired direction later.

2. Position Sizing

Position sizing is the number of units of security invested by a trader. This is not a random number derived using the account size and risk tolerance.

Firstly, account size is the account balance in a trading account. For example, if a trader deposits $1,000 into his trading account, the account size will be $1,000.

Account risk is the percentage of the account size a trader is ready to lose on a trade. For example, if you set your account risk to 1%, you will risk 1% of your account balance on the work.

Trade risk is simply the stop loss for a trade. It is the difference between the entry price and the stop-loss price. For example, if the entry price for a buy is $210, and the stop loss is $160, the trade risk would be $50 per unit traded.

Position size

Using the above two parameters, the position size for a trade can be determined. Mathematically, the position size is obtained by dividing the account risk by the trade risk. For example, if the account risk on a trade is $100 and the trade risk is $2 per unit, the position size would be $100/$2 = 50 units.

3. Risk/Reward Ratio

Another critical risk management tool is the risk/reward ratio. This ratio compares actual risk to the potential gains in a trade. The risk/reward tells you whether a business is worth taking. For example, there could be situations when your stop loss has to be higher than the take profit. In such trades, you would be risking more than gaining.

Thus, this ratio is used to stay cautious with such scenarios. For instance, if a trader is risking $100 on a trade and the risk: reward is 1:1, he is betting $100 to make $100. Similarly, if the ratio were 1:2, he would risk $100 to make $200. Therefore, you should refrain from trading under 1:1 to safeguard your capital.

CHAPTER 3

The Future of Bitcoin

We have seen the creation of the Bitcoin Blockchain, the Bitcoin token (BTC), other cryptocurrencies, Non-Fungible Tokens (NFTs), Decentralized Finance (DeFi), and now what is next. Let's imagine or even dream of the possibilities. What if Bitcoin has become a widely accepted payment method among businesses of all shapes and sizes, from Amazon to Chevrolet? Indulge in the perfect book or product on Amazon and purchase with the power of Bitcoin. Introducing the latest addition to the world of automobiles - the new electric car from Chevrolet and experience the future of payment with Chevy as they now accept Bitcoin for your convenience.

Sounds great so far, but let's say it gets even better, and we get the green light from governments. Bitcoin is being actively promoted and supported by governments worldwide, marking the dawn of a new era of acceptance and favorable regulations. Imagine a world where Bitcoin is widely accepted as legal tender, just like in El Salvador, where it was adopted years ago. This would be the ultimate ideal outcome.

And now, Bitcoin's technology has evolved to enable faster and cheaper transactions while staying true to its anti-inflationary ideals and fundamental philosophy of adequate value storage. Experience the reliability and efficiency of a payment processor with our blockchain technology. Experience seamless Bitcoin-powered cash register checkouts with this giant step forward.

And now let's go even further and imagine if the newfound credibility and increased demand for Bitcoin as Wall Street's top players, including Goldman Sachs and BlackRock, begin to treat it as a mainstream asset class. This platform is embraced by investors of all types and sizes, seeking to safeguard and expand their wealth for the long haul. With its impressive track record of achievements, Bitcoin undoubtedly has the potential to serve as the foundation for a thriving DeFi landscape.

Experience the fascinating thought experiments of the highly Utopian and dystopian reviews above without any firm forecasts. All sounds amazing, and we should and can be prepared for that to happen, but let's come back to reality just a little. Let's assume what a more realistic future holds for Bitcoin. As we look ahead, it's clear that Bitcoin and other cryptocurrencies will experience a mix of positive and negative developments in the coming years. Get ready for a financial revolution! Digital currencies are poised to reshape the global markets. However, the journey ahead may be filled with unexpected twists and turns.

Experience peace of mind by avoiding regulatory uncertainty. As cryptocurrencies gain popularity, governments worldwide face the challenge of regulating them effectively. As the world of digital currencies continues to evolve, some will eagerly adopt Bitcoin and its counterparts, while others will persist in enforcing limitations.

Experience the thrill of extreme market volatility as regulatory news fuels a tug-of-war between market forces.

Experience a gradual adoption of Bitcoin and other cryptocurrencies as more businesses and consumers embrace them. However, the pace of adoption is expected to be steady and measured. Companies may need help embracing new opportunities in today's dynamic business landscape due to potential volatility risks, transaction costs, and regulatory concerns. The unstoppable trend towards increased acceptance continues to gain momentum.

Bitcoin is expected to encounter tough competition from other cryptocurrencies. Discover various options tailored to your needs - from lightning-fast transaction speeds to reduced fees and heightened privacy. Although Bitcoin is the leading cryptocurrency, many other players are in the market. Its continued dominance in the future is still being determined.

Experience enhanced technical upgrades on the Bitcoin network, although they may not be immediate and could spark some debate. Achieving consensus among miners and node operators can be a challenging feat when it comes to making changes to the Bitcoin protocol.

Discover the potential future of Bitcoin's validation process. Could it transition from energy-intensive Proof-of-Work to a more sustainable alternative? Have you heard about the Proof-of-Stake system, similar to what Ethereum has implemented? Bitcoin should do what Ehterum did and say resources for the mining process. Perhaps Bitcoin needs to maintain its lifetime cap of 21 million potential coins; what would that mean? Without a doubt, it's crucial to keep Bitcoin at the forefront of the cryptocurrency market. Otherwise, competing currencies could seize the opportunity to dethrone it from its throne.

Experience the excitement of Bitcoin's continued volatility, with significant price swings being the norm rather than the exception. While the market matures, the volatility may decrease. However, brace yourself for some roller-coaster rides in the meantime. The future of Bitcoin remains to be determined. However, it may fall between becoming the world's leading currency or vanishing altogether.

In the future, cryptocurrencies will be as widely accepted as traditional investment options such as stocks, bonds, and savings accounts. With consistent legal and regulatory frameworks globally, any controversy surrounding these digital assets will be a thing of the past. The promising future remains uncertain as the fully settled directives are yet to be revealed. It needs to be clarified what Bitcoin's specific role will be in this landscape.

Embarking on a journey to comprehend Bitcoin and the vast crypto market is a continuous process rather than a final destination. Stay ahead of the game by staying informed, continuously learning, and adapting your investment strategy as this exciting new field evolves.

Experience the thrill of high-risk, high-reward investments with Bitcoin and its crypto counterparts. While they may have a place in a well-rounded investment portfolio, it's important to note that their volatility can be quite the ride. Only those with a strong stomach need to apply. With a measured approach, I hold a positive outlook for Bitcoin's potential as a victorious contender in the long run. Navigating the cryptocurrency landscape requires a cautious approach. Beware of potential pitfalls and prioritize safeguarding your assets by diversifying with tried-and-true investment options like stocks, cash, or index funds.

Future of Bitcoin

The value of Bitcoin soared by more than 500% in 2020-21 at its peak. One Bitcoin is worth twenty times as much as an ounce of gold. For example, some governments like the Central African Republic and El Salvador have recently legalized Bitcoin as a payment method, increasing the usage of Bitcoin bought with current currencies such as the dollar. This meteoric rise in the value of this cryptocurrency has generated substantial public interest and an increase in its perceived value. It has also led many speculators and gamblers to rush to invest in this currency to achieve future exponential returns. Again, this has played the role of a significant catalyst in the rise of its perceived value and made the currency extremely volatile. The unique features of keeping the digital footprint of those who transact in Bitcoin anonymous and not being controlled by any centralized organization have made some traders perceive Bitcoins as an attractive investment asset. Bitcoin's finite supply concept has also made some traders compare it to traditional assets such as gold and silver. However, the constantly fluctuating value of Bitcoins also makes its valuation extremely volatile.

The lack of centralized control or regulatory body makes it prone to changing compliance issues and vulnerable to money laundering. These aspects have also made many people wonder whether Bitcoin is a bubble that will eventually burst.

Bitcoin has strength by design to make it a viable currency that has elevated its status over the years, more notably its fixed supply. Bitcoin will be mined with diminishing returns every four years until the maximum number of Bitcoins is reached: 21 million. This aspect of Bitcoin is essential for its value. Due to the limited amount of Bitcoins, there will never be an overabundance of Bitcoin. This makes Bitcoin a good asset for investors to put their wealth into, as it generally does not lose value due to inflation. However, as with most cryptocurrencies, the price can fluctuate wildly based on many other external factors.

Cryptocurrency is uniquely positioned as a forerunner in transforming technology to long-standing financial systems. It can fill gaps in current financial technologies by its very nature. Bitcoin's technology allows individuals to exchange currency without needing a trusted third party, like a bank, to oversee the transaction. All that is required to use Bitcoin is a mobile phone, which many people can access. Due to Bitcoin's peer-to-peer networking capability, users can trade Bitcoin with each other by scanning QR codes displayed on their wallet application. This is a genuinely innovative solution to a problem that has existed for many years. The transactions will invariably increase as the user base grows, so the demand for a better cryptocurrency network and applications will come to the forefront.

There is a large, untapped market for developers to create these applications, as this technology could be adopted by any industry that relies on a third-party clearing system. Bitcoin's progression into becoming a transformative technology lies in its ability to solve long-standing problems in combination with an active and growing community of users and developers. Businesses are also beginning to see the benefits of using cryptocurrencies for international transactions. Using conventional methods, the trade can be hit with any unexplained fees as it crosses borders, making sending the correct amount to another business complex. Cryptocurrency has a significant advantage over traditional currencies thanks to its agility in fast peer-to-peer transactions, especially in international business-to-business scenarios.

Internet marketplaces have been thriving and are genuine contenders to conventional brick-and-mortar stores. Amazon.com has grown to a degree that seems almost unexpected. Online shopping is flourishing, and Bitcoin is poised to extend its reach with efficient and easy payments for vendors and customers. One of Bitcoin's most significant opportunities is that it can act as a commodity, similar to gold. The value of gold can shoot up considerably whenever an event threatens the balance of global markets, as we have seen with the COVID-19 pandemic. The commodity market is a widely accepted and well-established form of trade, and cryptocurrency has seemingly begun to mimic the characteristics of gold. Gold has been a long-standing holder of value based on the universal acceptance and trust of its value. Cryptocurrencies could become a significant player in the commodity market. They have the unique property of being able to be purchased through a direct online mechanism, which creates an easy on-ramp for buyers. If Bitcoin remains a valid refuge for inflating fiat currencies, it will gain investors' confidence and move closer to becoming more mainstream.

It is well known that the "mining" of Bitcoins is a very energy-intensive process. Recent studies have shown that a single transaction in the Bitcoin network consumes 800 kilowatts of energy. By contrast,

500,000 Visa transactions can be carried out using the same point. In comparison to other payment methods, like cash or fiat money, Bitcoin is highly energy-intensive. Bitcoin's energy consumption is not unfavorable at its current price. Still, global warming and climate change have raised concerns over non-renewable energy sources used in Bitcoin mining.

We are now experiencing the rise of Bitcoin, which may be the beginning of the next bull run in full steam in 2024.

Expert Price Predictions

Bitcoin has stagnated over the latter half of 2021, falling by more than half from its peak of around $65,000 set in April.

However, the Bitcoin price is still significantly higher than when the massive rally began in October 2020, a bull run that sent the combined crypto market to a staggering $2.5 trillion before pulling back. Predicting the future of cryptocurrencies like Bitcoin is challenging, and the results could be more accurate to a high degree. Bitcoin being one of the most volatile assets out there, makes future valuations very difficult to get right. That being said, let's overview what cryptocurrency experts and financial analysts say about Bitcoin's future.

Tim Draper

Bitcoin bull Tim Draper had one of the most optimistic calls on Bitcoin, predicting the token would be worth $250,000 by the end of the year.

Shervin Pishevar

Shervin Pishevar, a venture capitalist and angel investor who co-founded Hyperloop One and Sherpa Capital, tweeted that Bitcoin will hit $100k. The prediction came soon after meeting with MicroStrategy CEO Michael Saylor, whose company invested more than $1 billion in Bitcoin.

Thomas Fitzpatrick

Citibank's global head of their market insights product, CitiFX Technicals, Thomas Fitzpatrick, made headlines for his Bitcoin valuation of $318,000, which came up after a report was leaked online. His analysis drew similarities between the gold market of the 1970s and Bitcoin's price action and pointed out the acceleration in money-printing by central banks since the emergence of COVID-19, which may fuel the Bitcoin run.

Winklevoss twins

Winklevoss twins – the famous Bitcoin billionaires, have come out and said Bitcoin has the potential to hit a price of $500,000 by 2030. This would put its market cap on par with gold at around $9 trillion.

Wences Casares

Wences Casares is the CEO and founder of Xapo, a Bitcoin wallet startup, and a board member at PayPal, among other roles. Casares said that Bitcoin will hit $1 million sometime before 2027 at the Consensus 2017 conference in New York.

Chamath Palihapitiya

Chamath Palihapitiya is the Founder of Social Capital and Co-Owner of the Golden State Warriors basketball team. He started his Bitcoin investment journey with an investment back in 2012, and by 2013 he had included Bitcoin in all of his portfolios. At one point, he owned 5% of all Bitcoin in circulation.

Palihapitiya has claimed that Bitcoin price will reach $100,000 in the next 3-4 years, adding that it will reach $1 million by 2037. He said, "This thing has the potential to be comparable to the value of gold...This is a fantastic hedge and store of value against autocratic regimes and banking infrastructure that we know is corrosive to how the world needs to work properly."

Jeremy Liew

Jeremy Liew is a partner at Lightspeed Venture Partners. He was one of the first investors in the social media app Snapchat. In an interview with Business Insider, Liew said that the Bitcoin price could "realistically" reach $500,000 by 2030. Following this, Liew's prediction was backed by Peter Smith, the CEO and co-founder of Blockchain — the world's most popular Bitcoin wallet.

Mark Yusko

Mark Yusko is a billionaire investor and Founder of Morgan Creek Capital. He predicts Bitcoin to be worth over $400,000 in the long term, a statement that made headlines because of its grandiose scale.

"It's just math. It is gold equivalent; there is about 20 million Bitcoin available today. Gold today is about $8 trillion. That gives you $400,000. And that doesn't include use cases related to currency," Yusko said. He further alluded to the fact that cryptocurrencies such as Bitcoin strike fear into the hearts of bankers because Bitcoin altogether eliminates the need for banks.

Kay Van-Petersen

Kay Van-Petersen is an analyst at Saxo Bank, an investment bank specializing exclusively in online trading and investment.

According to a feature by CNBC News, Van-Petersen believes that Bitcoin will rise to $100,000 per unit by 2027. He successfully predicted Bitcoin's flow up to $2,000 by 2017. Although optimistic, his most recent estimate suggests that Bitcoin would account for 10% of the global foreign exchange market volume.

Andy Edstrom

Wealth manager for a California-based investment advisory firm called WESCAP, Andy Edstrom is an investor and an avid Twitter user, constantly tweeting about the topic and even having written a book titled "Why Buy Bitcoin."

In February 2020, Edstrom predicted that Bitcoin would reach an $8 trillion market cap by 2030. This would put the price of a single coin at around $400,000 with a market cap around that of gold. Edstrom believes Bitcoin could become the world's default currency.

Mike Novogratz

Mike Novogratz is a former hedge fund manager investing and veteran investor in Bitcoin and blockchain technology. His several past predictions have been both correct and incorrect. In March 2019, Novogratz indirectly made a prediction, claiming Bitcoin would "easily" surpass gold's market cap of $7.5 trillion within the next ten years. This puts his prediction very close to Edstrom's, both in terms of timeline and magnitude. As evident from these testimonials, most experts in the crypto and financial space are bullish on Bitcoin, especially in the long-term perspective.

CHAPTER 4

The Altcoin Market

What are Altcoins?

Since its inception in 2009, Bitcoin has become the first and most popular cryptocurrency globally. It has paved the way for creating many other alternative cryptocurrencies (or Altcoins) looking to outperform each other in a dynamic and fast-moving financial market. Bitcoin has also been the most popular currency for users of Dark Net markets due to its semi-anonymous qualities, lack of regulation, and effectiveness in laundering the profits from online contraband sales. However, users have criticized Bitcoin as lacking true anonymity and have been accused of providing a trail of evidence for law enforcement to trace payments via its blockchain due to its design limitations. This led to an increase in the development of alternative cryptocurrencies (Altcoins) in which anonymity and security are prioritized to make tracing payments and laundering of proceeds almost impossible. But all Altcoins are not geared towards anonymity; any cryptocurrency, not Bitcoin, is termed an Altcoin.

With enhanced security features, an Altcoin can see its price increasing dramatically due to demand. Still, it may be the currency of choice for the wider majority. Each Altcoin project is unique and has its own target niche, objectives, and blockchain technologies it was built upon.

Bitcoin vs. Altcoins

Altcoins work in different ways than Bitcoin does. For example, while Bitcoin produces only new Bitcoins every 10 minutes, altcoins such as Litecoin create new coins every 2.5 minutes. This means Litecoin can process payments faster. Moreover, Litecoin's total supply is capped at around 84 million Litecoin, whereas Bitcoin's total is about 21 million.

Litecoin also uses a different set of rules for mining than Bitcoin. Bitcoin mining requires costly hardware, whereas Litecoin can be mined with standard computer hardware.

Litecoin is just one of the thousands of altcoins available today. However, some altcoins stand out as popular alternatives to Bitcoin; although they don't reach Bitcoin's $100 billion market cap, most have some advantage over conventional Bitcoin. A few examples of such altcoins include:

- **Ethereum -** ETH
- **Ripple –** XRP
- **Cardano –** ADA
- **Solona –** SOL
- **Polygon –** MATIC
- **Polkadot -** DOT

- **Litecoin –** LTC
- **Avalanche -** AVAX

Generally, these altcoins were built and released to improve on Bitcoins flaws by providing faster transactions, faster mining rates, more security, or lower network fees.

However, these altcoins may need more stability, liquidity, and a large market cap that Bitcoin offers.

Early Examples of Altcoins

One of the earliest notable Altcoins, Litecoin, released in October 2011, was marketed as the "silver to Bitcoin's gold." While fundamentally similar in code and functionality to Bitcoin, Litecoin diverges from Bitcoin in several ways. Litecoin allows transactions to be approved more frequently. It also provides for a total supply of 84 million coins to be created, which is four times Bitcoin's total supply. Litecoin is still among the most popular altcoins; some even think it could be a better investment than Bitcoin.

Types of Altcoins

Depending on their functionalities and blockchain mechanisms, altcoins come in many varieties and categories. Here's a rundown of some of the more important ones:

Mining-Based

As their name indicates, mining-based altcoins are generated through mining. Most altcoins that fall into this category use Proof-of-Work

(PoW). Proof-of-work is how computers generate new coins by solving complex problems to create blocks. Examples of mining-based altcoins are Litecoin, Zcash, and Monero. Most of the top altcoins in early 2020 were mining-based coins. Pre-mined coins are the alternative to mining-based altcoins. Pre-mined coins are not produced through an algorithm but distributed before being listed in a cryptocurrency exchange. An example of a pre-mined coin is XRP, also known as Ripple.

Stablecoins

Cryptocurrencies, since their launch, have been very volatile by nature. Stablecoins aim to reduce this overall volatility by clinching their value to various goods or commodities, such as precious metals, fiat currencies, or other cryptocurrencies. This ensures that investors can redeem their money if the cryptocurrency fails or faces problems. Price fluctuations for stablecoins don't usually go beyond a narrow range.

Social media giant Facebook's Diem is the most famous example of a stablecoin. It is a dollar-backed coin, meaning Diem's value is linked to the US dollar. Other examples of stablecoins include USDC and MakerDAO.

Security Tokens

Security tokens are comparable to securities traded in stock markets, except they have a digital origin. Security tokens are similar to traditional stocks, and they typically promise equity in the form of ownership or a dividend payout to holders. The possibility of price appreciation for such tokens is a major draw for investors to buy and hold these coins. Security tokens are generally offered to investors through ICOs or initial coin offerings from major crypto exchanges.

Utility Tokens

Utility tokens are used to provide and avail services within a network. For example, they might be used to redeem rewards or purchase services. Utility tokens, unlike security tokens, do not pay dividends. Filecoin, used to buy cloud storage space on a network, is an example of a utility token.

Crypto Adoption Token (CAT)

The CAT Token was released in 2023 and introduced as a cutting-edge Pro-Crypto Public Education, Adoption, and Awareness Token, Including advertising campaigns to promote Crypto. Join them and others to spread the word about cryptocurrency's benefits and help revolutionize the world of finance. Tokens like this will invest in pro-crypto politicians and support regulatory measures through funding. They will secure a lobbying company and empower the next generation with strategic crypto education and Onboarding. The goal is to provide crypto content to the masses, including schools, libraries, independent seminars, workshops, and beyond.

CAT is revamping the crypto news arena for a seamless experience and introducing the goals to establish a fair and impartial news network and disseminate the news that will revolutionize the industry and surpass what existed before. Discover these high-quality alternatives to other subpar options.

Are Altcoins Good Investments?

The market for altcoins is still very new. And in recent times, the number of altcoins listed in cryptocurrency markets has rapidly multiplied. It has attracted crowds of retail investors, relentlessly betting on their price movements to book quick profits. But retail investors need more capital to generate sufficient market liquidity.

Shallow markets and an absence of regulation produce immense volatility in altcoin markets and valuations.

There is money to be made buying and selling altcoins, but there's also money to be lost. Even though this is true with almost any investment, altcoins come with unique risks.

Altcoin prices are incredibly volatile, and most individual investors cannot manage this volatility. Plus, there needs to be more regulation in place around altcoins. Widespread fraud also happens in the cryptocurrency market when scammers lure investors into buying fake cryptocurrencies.

That doesn't mean you should refrain from buying altcoins altogether. Altcoins be a source of diversification for an investor's portfolio as each altcoin project is usually independent of the others.

Cryptocurrency markets have yet to mature, and there are no defined investment criteria or metrics to evaluate cryptocurrencies. The altcoin market is driven mainly by speculation. Several cases of death and failed cryptocurrencies exist.

Therefore, the altcoin market is for investors prepared to endure the risks of operating in an unregulated and emerging market prone to high volatility and wild price swings.

Looking Ahead

Altcoins improve on the original Bitcoin, aiming to fix the cryptocurrency's shortcomings. Altcoins, such as Ripple's XRP and Ethereum's ether, have already become popular in the mainstream financial world, resulting in high valuations for these coins. The SEC has sued some of these coins, claiming they are securities, making it hard to trade with USD. There is a reason the corrupt financial system does not want these to succeed.

Looking at the current state of the altcoin market, it is likely that all the altcoins will stay. But it is also expected that most of the more than 2000 altcoins listed in crypto markets will not survive. The altcoin market will coalesce around many altcoins with solid utility and use cases, dominating the markets.

Altcoins are an inexpensive way for investors in the crypto space to expand their horizons beyond Bitcoin. Rallies in Altcoin markets have produced returns multiples of those produced by Bitcoin. But there is significant risk involved in Altcoin investing, like the absence of regulation and immense price volatility. Before buying any altcoins, research and have sound risk management strategies. If trades are timed correctly, one can expect multi-bagger returns in the Altcoin markets.

The Market Capitalization of Altcoins

The altcoin market has been booming in recent years; from 2017 to the present day, the total market cap of the altcoin space has increased by more than 100-fold. The altcoin market cap currently stands at 884 billion dollars, higher than Bitcoin's $665 billion. Let's look at some of the front runners in the altcoin space that account for a significant portion of this impressive market cap.

Ethereum ($221 billion)

Ethereum is a cryptocurrency that draws inspiration from the original Bitcoin. While Bitcoin is used primarily as a store of value as a digital form of currency, the idea behind Ethereum is to decentralize applications and services from simple apps to more complex financial agreements. Ethereum uses the same technology as Bitcoin, wherein a blockchain uses a distributed, decentralized public ledger to decentralize the network, so it's not under the control of any single entity.

Ethereum lets you send cryptocurrency to anyone for a small fee and powers applications everyone can use. Ethereum boasts itself as 'the world's programmable blockchain. It builds on Bitcoin's innovation, with some significant differences.

While both Ethereum and Bitcoin let you use digital money without payment providers or banks, Ethereum has the added advantage of being programmable, so you can also use it for many different use cases and business models. This also means Ethereum's application can go beyond fulfilling payments on a network. It can be a marketplace of financial services, games, and apps that can't censor or steal your data. Ethereum was conceived by Vitalik Butarin, Martin Wood, and other members in 2013 and released after a couple of years in 2015. Through the Ethereum project, they wanted to address different limitations present in Bitcoin and allow the execution of short programs in the Blockchain. Vitalik and the rest of the team sought better ways to build decentralized finance systems with apps running on the Blockchain.

At the heart of the programmable aspect of Ethereum lies intelligent contracts and dApps (Decentralized apps). A Smart Contract is a short program that can be deployed and run on a Blockchain. It processes transactions sent to it by executing code and can also hold funds(Ether) on the blockchain ledger. These transactions can pass both funds and data.

Smart contracts can be built to perform all sorts of functions without a trusted third party or central authority. If you consider Smart Contracts as back-end code running in the Blockchain, Decentralized Applications are the front-end or UI. They represent the visible layer connecting users or other applications with the Smart Contracts running in the Blockchain. Eventually, entire decentralized autonomous organizations may exist in an ether economy.

Ethereum was trading at $2,913 as of Aug 2021 and $1,913 as of June 2023. Exactly years ago, it was trading at $390; that's more than a five times increase in market price.

As Ethereum's rally accelerates, many in the crypto industry predict that Ethereum could overtake Bitcoin as the world's biggest cryptocurrency by value. With the latest update to its Blockchain, Ethereum is returning to a cryptocurrency bull market with fresh all-time highs on the horizon. The price boost, pushing ether tokens toward $3,000, has caused the combined crypto market cap to climb to almost $1.7 trillion.

Tether ($83 billion)

Tether or USDT is a cryptocurrency pegged 1 to 1 with the US dollar. Tether is currently the most popular USD-pegged cryptocurrency in the world. According to its developers, the design of USDT is to be worth 1 USD, and the dollar will back each tether unit it issues into circulation in a one-to-one ratio. However, the price of USDT can be volatile, and it was seen trading at a>10% discount to USD in 2018.

Many consider Tether an optimal way for users to move money effectively without a centralized authority. Users can trade the currency actively and use it for international transactions in countries with capital regulations. The massive global payments market is a driving force for Tether's supply and demand movements.

Though the white paper states that one USDT should receive the backing of one USD, there are many questions about its legitimacy. The reserve level has been a mystery as rumors suggest that Tether's reserve is insufficient to back the amount of USDT. The last audit was in mid-2018 by a Washington law firm. The mistrust and speculations brought in a significant price movement in Oct 2018.

The credibility of the Tether has always raised some concerns, especially regarding whether Tether's reserve has sufficient reserves. Despite such speculation, Tether remains at the top, holding ten times more market share than other USD stablecoins. Given the uncertainty surrounding its backing with USD, it will be interesting to see if Tether can maintain such dominance in the future.

Binance Coin ($40 billion)

Binance Coin is the cryptocurrency issued by the Binance exchange, the largest cryptocurrency exchange in the world—binance coin trades with the BNB symbol.

It was initially based on the Ethereum network but is now the native currency of Binance's Blockchain, the Binance chain.

Binance uses one-fifth of its profits to repurchase BNB. They then permanently destroy this purchased currency every quarter in a process known as burning. This keeps inflation at bay and induces scarcity to drive up prices. The updated whitepaper states that BNB burns will now be based on its exchanges' trading volume.

Since Binance began burning BNB in Oct 2017, 10 token burns have occurred, with about 16.7 million BNB worth approximately $208 million burned as of January 2020.

Binance was initially intended as a utility token for discounted trading fees during its release in 2017. But now, its uses have expanded to various other applications, including payments for transaction fees, travel bookings, entertainment, online services, and financial services.

Binance has a market cap of more than $56 billion and ranks among the top cryptos in terms of market cap. Binance's story started with an Initial Coin Offering (ICO) and has grown into one of the largest global cryptocurrency exchanges in terms of volume traded and market share by web traffic.

Cardano ($12 billion)

Charles Hoskinson founded Cardano in 2017, two years after he helped develop the Ethereum blockchain technology. He also co-founded Internet Online Hong Kong (IOHK), the company that built the Cardano blockchain.

Cardano uses a timestamping methodology called Proof of Stake (PoS). PoS is the system by which the miners in the Cardano ecosystem validate and may block transactions. A stake is simply the number of coins (ADA coins) one holds, which also determines one's participation in creating new blocks.

Using knowledge gained from developing the Ethereum project, Hoskinson injected the idea of smart contracts into the Cardano project. Cardano sets itself apart in the crypto-verse in that it was conceived through peer-reviewed research. The research yielded unique features like unparalleled platform security, system sustainability, and a robust professional development community.

According to the project's website, IOHK created the Cardano blockchain to "restore trust to global systems" by availing a new standard in inclusive and open-source technology. Therefore, "changemakers, innovators, and visionaries" can leverage the technology to create a society that is "more secure, transparent, and fair."

ADA is the digital currency facilitating transactions among Cardano network participants. ADA ranks among the top ten tokens in terms of market cap. It enables peer-to-peer transactions in a decentralized, secure environment free from intermediaries. For this reason, transactions over the Cardano blockchain are fast and inexpensive.

Cardano's cryptocurrency claims to have legitimate advantages over fiat currency. The Cardano Foundation adopted a limit of ADA's total supply at 45 billion coins. The idea is to avoid inflation and keep the coin's value in check. ADA is far better than a fiat currency in terms of transaction speed by peer-to-peer transactions. Fiat currencies require intermediaries like banks to enforce trust, leading to bottlenecks along the transaction chain.

XRP ($30 billion)

Ripple is a cryptocurrency token equivalent to digital cash, purpose-built for payment networks and banks. XRP or Ripple is a native token on its Blockchain known as RippleNet. RippleNet is a payments system run by Ripple Labs and built on the XRP Ledger, decentralized and open-source blockchain technology. It boasts breakneck transaction speeds with an average transaction settlement speed of four seconds. Comparably, the transaction settlement time on the Bitcoin network is 3,600 seconds.

One of the areas where Ripple had an immediate impact was cross-border payments. The developers created RippleNet to streamline transactions. Consumers and businesses often suffer the inconveniences of converting between currencies and losses arising from exchange rate differences when transacting in fiat currency. RippleNet uses the XRP token as an intermediary to streamline fiat currency exchange without suffering slippage.

Moreover, digital currency facilitates faster settlement of transactions at speeds unseen in the traditional payments sectors. Due to the utilization of the peer-to-peer transaction system, users enjoy micro-fees where the average fee is less than $0.0003403. RippleNet's competitors in the conventional payments sector, such as VISA, charge thousands of times higher for an equivalent transaction.

Ripple draws its strength from blockchain technology. Most blockchain platforms obtain consensus through Proof of Work (PoW) or Proof of Stake (PoS) mechanisms. The PoW system is slower and consumes more power, unlike the PoS system, which supports faster validation and approval of transactions while consuming less power.

However, blockchain platforms like XRP Ledger utilize another form of consensus, in this case, called the Ripple Protocol Consensus Algorithm (RPCA). Peace is how nodes in a blockchain network maintain agreement and correctness with each other. RPCA runs through the more than 150 nodes that make up the global XRP Community.

The robust consensus system is a significant reason behind Ripple's seven years of stability, enabling its developers to expand the product range of the ecosystem. For example, the developers have expanded RippleNet's capacity to offer on-demand liquidity to its enterprise clients. This makes global payments faster and cheaper.

Promising Altcoins

Some altcoins have immense potential to dominate future markets. We will now look at such altcoins whose market cap has been gradually increasing over the years.

Basic Attention Token (BAT) is a utility token built on the Ethereum blockchain, which is the foundation for the Brave web browser platform. The Brave browser allows users to browse the internet anonymously and completely ad-free and then enables users to opt-in to watch ads in exchange for BAT tokens.

Publishers also get BAT when users watch or click on ads on their sites. Advertisers benefit from lower overhead costs for advertising and higher engagement from users. And users get increased privacy without sacrificing the benefits of tailored advertisements and can get BAT tokens. The BAT token is designed to be exchanged between users, advertisers, and publishers. It is based on the concept of user attention, which is critical to advertising companies operating in the digital age. BAT is an ERC-20 token secured by a rigorously tested proof-of-work consensus algorithm supported by an extensive Ethereum miner network. This algorithm ensures that only valid transactions are confirmed, while the combined work of the Ethereum mining network ensures BAT transactions are irreversible once approved.

The developers of BAT seek to improve how advertising is done in the digital space. They see the current system as disadvantageous for users, publishers, and advertisers. Users are relentlessly targeted with ads and trackers, and they are subjected to malware that is becoming increasingly aggressive and powerful.

Conventional publishers have seen their ad revenues decline dramatically as monopoly platforms like Google and Facebook drive down the price of information while taking a hefty cut from the advertising revenue. In addition, bots and malware can inflict increasing damage each year, and platforms have suffered credibility issues. Moreover, advertisers need more accurate targeting methods and information to deliver their content sufficiently because platforms monopolize these functions.

The creators of BAT believe that tracking how users interact with digital advertising content and storing that information in a distributed blockchain ledger will enhance and improve the digital advertising experience for advertisers, publishers, and users. Users will experience fewer ads and content that is better tailored to them, while Publishers will find new sources of revenue. And advertisers will be able to target particular users better based on documented user content preferences and interests. They will also be able to avoid fraud more efficiently.

Basic Attention Token has a maximum total supply capped at 1.5 billion tokens. Almost all of this supply is currently in circulation. Hence, the Basic Attention Token can be considered almost entirely liquidated.

In its 2017 ICO, 1 billion BAT tokens were sold to investors, the remaining 200 million coins were locked in a development pool, and 300 million BAT was reserved for the user growth pool (UGP). As of November 2020, the development pool and UGP pool addresses are almost empty. Basic Attention Token can be bought and sold on every central cryptocurrency exchange platform and has excellent liquidity.

Chainlink (LINK) is a cryptocurrency blockchain network that provides a link between real-world data and smart contracts. The platform helps execute smart contracts, which are blockchain agreements that automatically complete upon filling in necessary preconditions. It offers a tradable cryptocurrency token called LINK, used to pay for innovative contract transactions on the Chainlink network. LINK tokens also hold their value in comparison to fiat currencies.

Chainlink was created in 2014 and launched in 2017 by its founder Sergey Nazarov, a 32-year-old entrepreneur with a significant presence in the crypto market. Initially, the Chainlink network was designed to be a centralized oracle system that could verify incoming information. However, it has since transformed into a decentralized oracle network that pairs with smart contracts to secure transactions using external data sources and APIs.

Chainlink helps bridge the gap between oracles that send real-world data and smart contracts on the Blockchain. Chainlink can generate multiple subcontracts while taking data from only the most trustworthy nodes and oracles to maximize accuracy. Although there is no limit on the number of smart contracts the platform can handle, the number of LINK tokens that will ever exist is capped at one Billion. The Chainlink network is a reasonably open system. Anyone can join it, provide data to the network, or help operate its corresponding nodes and oracles. These operators are paid in LINK tokens, which are the native currency of the Chainlink network.

As the proliferation of blockchain technology is increasing daily, networks such as Chainlink can supplement innovative contract implementations, acting as alternatives to mainstream blockchains such as Ethereum.

Polkadot (DOT) is a network designed to 'join the dots with all other networks. Unlike networks like Bitcoin, which operate independently, Polkadot can link multiple networks.

Its ultimate aim is to act as a standard integrated framework for all blockchains that opt-in to use its technology. The idea is to take care of complex and costly cryptocurrency mining processes that include validation of transactions and security protocols and enable developers to focus solely on creating efficient dApps and smart contract functionality. Gavin Wood, a co-founder of Ethereum, built Polkadot.

Developers building innovative, decentralized systems must engineer these systems from the ground up, including the Blockchain. This means that time, talent, and resources are diverted into building competing networks rather than creating a standard everyone builds off. That's Polkadot's aim, to make way for developers to build value on top of all blockchains rather than just one.

Blockchains can connect with Polkadot and work in parallel as "Para chains" to access the network's proof-of-stake validation system for transactions and security. In the network's "relay chain," transaction addresses are checked, and data is standardized so that every participating system can understand it.

While functionality is covered, blockchains connected to Polkadot can use their PoS mechanism to decide when and how to update their code and run the dApps or tokens they prefer. Polkadot is a pick-and-choose layer that allows networks to keep their security intact and incorporate new protocols simultaneously. The two fundamental issues blockchain-based systems must address are scalability—the number of transactions per second the network can handle—and governance: how the system manages protocol upgrades and changes. Polkadot aims to solve both of these problems efficiently.

DOT, the native token of the Polkadot network, allows holders to vote on potential code changes, which automatically upgrade across the network if a consensus is reached. Polkadot launched its main net in early 2020 and quickly gained traction among investors, developers, and cryptocurrency traders.

In less than a year, it has already racked up several impressive accolades and developments, including Climbing to become the fourth-largest cryptocurrency and achieving a peak market capitalization of almost $18 billion.

Undergoing redenomination, a process through which old DOT tokens are split 100 times to produce new DOT tokens—increasing the supply from 10 million to 1 billion and Seeing a dramatic surge in developer activity, with over 350 projects now being actively developed on the platform.

With blockchain technology penetrating conventional business models and use cases, we can expect more developers to get on board the smart contract and dApps universe; a framework model that Polkadot proposes will be of paramount importance in such a situation where developers are required to be more focused on creating robust smart contracts and dApps rather than devoting time to build a blockchain from the ground up.

Future of the Altcoin Market

With the astronomical price of Bitcoin, Altcoins have become a viable investment option for new investors because these cryptocurrencies are reasonably priced; they are bought much more.

Most traders in the present-day cryptocurrency market are small retail investors who cannot buy and sell Bitcoin as they need to possess adequate capital, so they naturally trade.

Altcoins are generally cheaper than Bitcoins and are available to users at a better price. Moreover, these coins have better future growth potential when compared to Bitcoin. If proper research about a blockchain project and the potential for scalable growth can be identified, such altcoins can be a great investment opportunity that can produce multifold returns quickly. Ethereum is an example of such an altcoin that rewarded early investors that identified its potential.

Cryptocurrency represents the beginning of a new period of technology-driven markets that will eventually disrupt conventional market strategies, longstanding business methods, and traditional regulatory policies. Cryptocurrencies carry the ground-breaking potential to allow their consumers access to a global payment system in which participation is only a matter of internet availability or ownership of a crypto wallet rather than by factors such as having a bank account.

CHAPTER 5

Decentralised Finance

What is DeFi?

Decentralized finance (abbreviated as DeFi) has taken the world by a whirlwind since its inception in 2017. The basic constitution of this term indicates the involvement of finances and Decentralization. While "finances" is self-explanatory, Decentralization is a descriptive term requiring extra elaboration for comprehension. "Decentralization" here highlights that this system is free from the control of any chief body like banks; in other words, it is not centralized. It stands at the crossroads of financial services and technology.

DeFi has amalgamated the two sectors with such efficiency that the need for intermediaries like brokers or banks has been eliminated. Compared to the financial handling by mediators, DeFi does not require an account, government-issued ID, address proof, etc. In other words, DeFi allows vendors, lenders, borrowers, etc., to engage in monetary transactions much like a bank but without the actual involvement of a centralized authority like that of a bank. It is a much less cumbersome finance system that does not require the service seeker to go through extensive processes like generating bank statements, producing many documents, etc.

The operation of these services is facilitated by blockchain technology. Blockchain is an immutable ledger that successfully stores, tracks, and records transactions in the simplest form. Such a system makes the exchange process of financial services between the seeker and receiver smoother using intelligent contracts embedded in the blockchain. A smart contract is a digital agreement between two or more parties with terms agreed upon by both and subsequently signed. A well-formulated smart contract promises security in terms of its information. Since the contract would be present in blockchain, the accessibility to the signed contract for malign purposes can be reduced, thus bolstering the security of the insurance.

How Does DeFi Work?

DeFi uses cryptocurrencies and smart contracts, driving out the need for interventions by brokers or other intermediaries. The functioning of DeFi can be understood by first understanding the essential components of DeFi.

Components of DeFi

Before understanding the features and characteristics of DeFi, it is crucial to understand the components that constitute DeFi. Due to the premise that DeFi is a financial ecosystem, it is only pertinent that it works akin to other economic ecosystems. Due to this, The broad categorization of components of DeFi includes:

Stable Currencies (Stablecoins)

Additionally, for every financial service exchange on DeFi, smart contracts are used. Intelligent contracts are central to DeFi's functioning because they secure the terms and record the transaction activities to ensure the agreed-upon terms are met. Now, let's move on to understanding the components of the DeFi system in the context of a software stack.

The consolidation of multiple layers characterizes a software stack. These various layers, in turn, have components that have a definitive specific function to cater to in developing a DeFi system. The four layers comprise the

Defi Software System Stack is:

The Settlement Layer is the first of the four layers constituting the DeFi software system. It can be comprehended as a base layer providing the platform for DeFi transactions. A settlement layer is paramount because it is the anchor of the financial ecosystem of DeFi. A public blockchain and cryptocurrency are their essential constituents for functioning. For example, Bitcoin and Ethereum are the quintessential representatives of the settlement layer.

Blockchain Protocol: These protocols are pertinent rules and regulations necessary to secure the reliable functioning of the system. Compliance with these rules allows operators in this industry to work unhindered. This layer ensures the conversion of the assets into cash in the DeFi ecosystem providing liquidity.

Application Layer: This layer simplifies the protocol mentioned above to ensure interface services, making the system and its services available to consumers. For example, this layer can allow borrowing services to be disseminated here. While there are different categorizations of the various layers, these layers mentioned above have been compressed to ensure the readers' understanding and avoid ambiguity.

Having understood the essential components of the DeFi ecosystem, let's understand the actual working process of these systems. Since the DeFi works on blockchain networks only thus, its working process is quite similar to that of blockchains. The DeFi blockchain ensures the security of financial services and transactions by issuing users encrypted keys. These keys enable the users to receive a unique identifier they can only access. This system has two essential keys- private and public keys.

These dual keys cater to different functions. For example, a Public key is used by interested service seekers or peers to find the system's owner. The owner can use a private key to access and authorize any financial activity or transactions involving their funds. The private key is crucial as it acts as the owner's digital wallet through which the user can exchange cryptocurrencies. Only the owner can put the transaction into motion by authorizing the transaction with the private key. The transaction is set into action once the transaction request is verified by all the relevant parties involved. It is pertinent to mention that a unique ID accompanies every transaction to maintain high-security standards and prevent any malpractices on the platform. With an understanding of the working of DeFi, let's move on to see the features of this system.

Key Features of DeFi

The central characterizing features of DeFi also fall in tandem with the benefits offered by this decentralized method of disseminating financial services across the globe. Most of these features are reinforced by DeFi services' Blockchain network. From defining features like decentralization and permission nature of the systems to implicated qualities like increased transparency, immutability, etc., DeFi constitutes numerous characteristics. Some of the major ones have been outlined below:

The Premise of Decentralization

The first and foremost feature of DeFi, as its constituent term indicates, is Decentralization. As explained in the previous sections, Decentralization means no centralized authority or intermediary to add to the tediousness and intricacies of the basic financial services process. In the absence of any such intermediaries, the seekers of such financial services can access these services without any constraints placed upon them. This feature is elaborated upon in the next part, which is permissionless and closely related to Decentralization.

Permissionless Nature DeFi Systems

'Decentralized finance' defines this feature, and including the word decentralized indicates the flagship feature being permissionless. Decentralization of financial services has allowed the seekers and receivers to interact on a platform that requires no oversight by an external centralized authority like a bank. It also reduces the dependency on banks and other intermediaries while seeking financial services easily accessible by DeFi platforms. This feature confers the advantage of being independent and user-friendly to the DeFi systems. So any individual can access these services with the minimal requisites of a crypto wallet and, of course, an internet connection. For example, Ethereum has its basis in a permissionless blockchain which has assisted the proliferation of this platform. Today, Ethereum is leading the DeFi industry.

The permissionless nature of DeFi's operation might even instigate doubts about security. The security of the operational activities on DeFi's systems is supplemented by intelligent contracts, which ensure that the terms and conditions of financial services are met, thus ensuring the security of the finances. Also, all the transactional activities are stored on the blockchain itself.

The Premium Level of Transparency

Against the general notion that Decentralization might decrease transparency, Decentralization offers openness to a great extent. Since the distributed ledger encompasses all the transactional activities on the blockchain network, it provides scope for solidified clarity. Transparency extends to financial data and activities and applies to smart contracts. Transparency in the case of intelligent contracts expands the content of the review of its code by anyone. It ensures the presence of information for each individual.

Therefore, any individual might make an informed decision for availing of the financial services offered by the smart contract in focus based on its review. Furthermore, the context of transparency in the case of DeFi systems is also supported by the basic cryptographic regulations applying to the blockchain, which promise that the information is added only after proper verification and authentication procedures. The DeFi protocols existing on the Ethereum platform necessitate the openness of the source code for users to review. In the case of a public Ethereum chain, the information is broadcasted to all the users, bolstering the premise of transparency.

Immutability

One of the significant advantages DeFi offers is the immutability of financial data by reducing the possibility of any malicious data tampering. Data storage on Blockchain networks makes the records extremely secure, reducing the case of any unauthorized change in the papers. This, in turn, decreases the prospect of fraudulent practices reigning in this financial system. Also, smart contracts on the blockchain make the terms and conditions unchangeable by a single party due to the availability of activity regarding the intelligent agreements to all the concerned parties. This distinguishing feature of DeFi ensures a highly secure space and dialogue for exchanging financial services.

Accessibility

As mentioned in the previous section, anyone can use DeFi financial systems with minimum prerequisites of a crypto wallet and an internet connection. This allows users across the world to relish the advantages offered by DeFi. Although such ledgers are permissionless in their essence, they might create many problems, like the proliferation of fraudulent activities or perpetrators disrupting the financial ecosystem set up by DeFi. Due to the same, it is pertinent for service seekers and givers on DeFi platforms to authenticate the other party by checking the Know-Your-Customer (KYC) requisites and, sometimes, Anti-money laundering (AML). Due to relevant strategies to prevent malpractices, accessibility still weighs more towards the side of benefits conferred.

Flexibility and Autonomy

The permissionless feature of DeFi systems offers untamed flexibility and autonomy to the users. Again, this is because there is no regulating body to hinder the progression and evolution of services and their scope of DeFi systems. The users are not required to display compliance with a defined set of rules and regulations forced on them by external authorities. The flexibility offered to the software, for example, in the case of smart contracts, leads to autonomy. Once the interested parties have entered into intelligent agreements with mutual alignment, smart contracts are self-functional, requiring nothing from the involved parties except complying with the terms stated. Thus they can easily carry out their business without needing external authority, augmenting autonomy.

Now that we know the characterizing features of the DeFi systems let's compare this system with the traditional financial methods and assess which system has more significant advantages.

Comparison Between DeFi And Traditional Financial Systems

The traditional financial systems include conventional banks and other financial institutions governed by a centralized authority, thus often used interchangeably with Centralized finance (CeFi). Centralized exchanges, part of the CeFi, jeopardize user funds, data security, and privacy as these centralized authorities manage both. However, these centralized exchanges allow various financial services like margin trading, borrowing, lending, etc. Also, CeFi effectively provides cross-chain services standing in strong contrast to DeFi. CeFi considers a multitude of chains for taking complete control of the funds, and only after that, it allows the trading of coins. Also, they have the feature of transfer of ownership that reinforces its simplicity in the case of cross-chain services. Additionally, CeFi systems also offer flexibility in working with fiat currency. Despite the advantages of CeFi or traditional financial methods, DeFi systems are gaining mainstream traction in the financial world due to their many benefits.

Agents of Regulation of Service

The essence of traditional financial systems is the presence of a central authority. Conventional economic systems or CeFi (Centralized finance) operate under the aegis of an umbrella authority that lists the rules and regulations of different components constituting it. In the case of DeFi, as reiterated in the previous sections, intelligent contracts are responsible for the absolute management and regulation of financial services. These smart contracts are publicly available for audit by any user. Such a facility of contract audit is not available in the case of CeFi, as the operation of financial services needs to be made public for review by a more significant number of individuals. Critics might reason against this by implicating that the presence of intelligent contracts publicly can undermine the privacy of the parties involved. In this context, DeFi ensures that the public projection of the smart contracts is pseudonymous, which means that the identities and preliminaries of the parties involved are not involved.

Also, in the case of a financial institution acting as a platform for disseminating financial services, the culmination of financial services is delayed by the engagement of many people with different allocated responsibilities. Such a tedious and cumbersome process often drives the seekers of financial services away. Smart contracts, in the case of DeFi, ensure robustness in services with little to no human interventions in the process.

Permissionless

CeFi and DeFi are also different regarding permissions required to process financial services. As outlined under the features of DeFi, the permissionless nature of DeFi helps economic activities to be carried out without much effort. The users can connect their existing wallets to their platform of DeFi service and engage in the requisite financial services. However, in the case of CeFi, with the requirements of KYC to avail services, the process becomes relatively longer.

Operational Space

Another basic premise of the difference between traditional financial systems and DeFi is the operational platform. Most conventional economic systems need a physical space for their proper operation. It also requires human labor and services to keep disseminating their services in the physical area, thus necessitating a good amount spent on incentivizing human work. While DeFi is based on Distributed ledger technology (DLT) and runs effectively on blockchain networks. DeFi's entire operation employing technology and advanced software stacks eliminates the need for a formal setting in a physical space, on the one hand. It reduces the need for human labor, on the other.

Currency

DeFi and CeFi also stand in contrast in terms of the characteristic flagship assets and their nature. For instance, DeFi, as we know, uses cryptocurrencies as all the transactions, in this case, occur on a blockchain network in a digital space. However, CeFi necessarily uses fiat currency. Thus the transactions occur with coins, paper notes, etc.

Contract

In the case of DeFi, the interaction occurs directly between the interested parties, and the transactions subsequently take from peer to peer. Intelligent contracts support these transactions. In the context of traditional financial services, multiple points of contact or intermediaries often impede the smoothness of financial services.

Custodianship of Funds and Assets

DeFi users have absolute custodianship of their funds and can choose when to make the transaction, with whom to make the transactions, and by how much. However, traditional financial systems do not offer such control over the funds and assets. The individual must cede their funds to the central authority in these systems. For example, banks substantiate this premise. Instead of being in control of the owners of the funds, the funds are actually under the power of the top central bank, and then the second bank follows.

Innovativeness and Interoperability

The innovativeness also characterizes deFi that it offers in adapting to the evolving standards of expectations of the users. The streak of innovation of these systems is also substantiated by the use cases, as outlined in the next section. With innovation at its core, these systems are getting into many industries. However, due to the centralized approach, the traditional finance ecosystem only offers rapid innovation and adaptation. Due to the centralization of the authority, any proposal for creation goes through a multitude of executives at different levels in the hierarchical structure of these authorities. Such a thorough hierarchical structure ensures that the central authority makes well-deliberated decisions. While such a rigorous approach for multiple checks makes the proposal relatively risk-proof, it often leads to delay or rejection of the proposal altogether. Due to evolving trends, such a time gap might make the proposals redundant.

Accessibility and Reach

DeFi, being a digital finance system, is available and accessible to all individuals around the globe with the basic requirements of a stable internet connection and crypto wallet. Transactions between people sitting far apart on different continents can also successfully occur. These platforms work 24/7. At the same time, traditional financing systems are bound by time and space constraints. Due to the physical space requirements for the operation of maximum financial activities, these economical systems need to catch up to the evolved systems offered by DeFi. Additionally, due to the condition of human labor to put most financial services, activities, and transactions in motion, these systems need to be more useful in digitization.

The DeFi systems stand in strong contrast to the conventional financial systems. DeFi has more advantages in the financial world than traditional economic systems. The utility of DeFi systems is on an exponential rise, with more and more industries attempting to find the crossroads between DeFi and its application to complement their functionality. While the DeFi systems are visibly booming with the current digitization trends, they still have a long way to go. Despite the unprecedented proliferation of technology and increased accessibility of Internet services, only 65% of the world's population has Internet access, making it impossible for them to avail the benefits these systems offer. Thus, they continue to seek financial services from intermediaries under the umbrella of traditional economic methods.

Lack of reliable information provides concreteness to an individual's misconceptions about the working of DeFi platforms. They are falsely implicated in digital financial services as a hoax by magnifying and overdoing the risks. While it is imperative to warn the users of the dangers that might befall their digital journey in the finance world, it is essential to make them aware of the mitigation and manageableness related strategies corresponding to the risks. Additionally, many downsides of the DeFi systems have been discussed in the later sections, which contribute to tantalizing these platforms' reputation and trust quotient. Thus, even individuals accessing DeFi services refrain from venturing into these platforms. They instead turn to traditional financial service systems to receive economic benefits.

Use Cases of DeFi

DeFi has taken the world by a whirlwind with its efficacy, resilience, immutability, and transparency in financial operations. It has set into motion many economic opportunities for its global user base. Due to the plethora of advantages DeFi offers, the scope of its application is already widening. It is expected to widen even further with the refinement of the system and the advancement of technology. DeFi is enabling the integration of digital finance services with multiple industries which initially didn't witness crossroads with these systems. It applies to conventional financial services like borrowing, lending, trading, marketplaces, etc. These economic systems have found application across varied sectors, from increasing the efficiency of traditional financial activities to introducing DeFi in unhackneyed industries. The use cases of this system are already growing at an unprecedented rate and are expected to follow an ascending graph line. A few prominent use cases have been delineated below.

Borrowing and Lending

With DeFi's influence on systems of finance and transactions increasing, the loopholes in the traditional finance system are becoming all the more evident to the users. Traditional financial markets have proliferation in revenue generation by the interest they pay the lenders and the interest they charge from the borrowers. Such a system often discouraged the borrowers from approaching these markets due to rigid protocols for qualifying for a loan, including viable collateral and a hefty amount of interest charged. The digital ledger technology bolstered by DeFi opens opportunities for borrowers who need a loan and fail to procure it due to rigid requirements. With smart contracts in place, lending/borrowing loans and maintaining the terms of conditions outlined in the smart contracts smoothens the dual lending and borrowing processes. The dynamics structuring DeFi support peer-to-peer lending and borrowing. This use case is finding widespread application in the form of an increase in DeFi projects about this.

For instance, Compound is a DeFi protocol that stands out because it has an autonomous interest basis. Compound welcomes lenders to earn interest on various cryptocurrencies. It provides the lenders with tokens, which are then siphoned off to the borrowers at algorithmically decided autonomous interest rates. The compound is highly efficient because the intelligent contract identifies the lenders and borrowers with concurring interests and lays out interest rates following the borrowed and lent assets ratio in the discussion. Another prominent example of such a project is 'Pool Together,' which uses akin mechanisms in lending and borrowing money.

Tokenization

One of the significant use cases of the DeFi system is in the context of tokenization. Tokenization refers to curating, issuing, regulating, and transferring digital assets on a blockchain network. Tokenization is highly pertinent because any form of investment can be converted into tokens for their storage on the blockchain. Ethereum blockchain successfully utilizes tokenization and has granted the world a secure and easy means of trading in the form of Ethereum-based tokens. Out of the many advantages conferred by the usage of tickets, the main benefits emerge as fractional aspects of these tokens and available options for their customization. Thus tokenization is one of the central features of the booming DeFi ecosystem due to its digital alternatives and efficacy in complementing trade.

Efficacy of Stablecoins

One of the significant downsides of cryptocurrency is the profound volatility that is widespread in the crypto ecosystem. Such fluctuations of prices that experience frequent ascent and descent in their value result in the reduction of the reliability of cryptocurrency. Stablecoins pose as a savior in this context. Stablecoin can be understood as a type of unique cryptocurrency because it is tied with an or bulk of them. These assets can be anything ranging from fiat to gold or even any other kind of cryptocurrency. Their consolidation with acquisitions offers stability in contrast to the volatility in the crypto market. They also provide the blockchain greater credibility as a reliable payment method. Stablecoins are now used for borrowing, lending, etc., in the DeFi ecosystem.

Process of Asset Management

DeFi allows users to exercise greater control over their assets. With no central authority for regulation, Decentralization helps the users gain absolute control of their assets. It will enable the users to manage their assets according to their volition. It can involve buying, selling, lending, or transferring digital assets. By removing an intermediary, only the users can access and manage their assets in any way they deem perfect. For example, in many DeFi projects, including Gnosis Safe, Argent facilitates the users' complete control of their information and ensures safe data storage with the user only.

Application in the Insurance Industry

Another major use case of DeFi is in the insurance industry. DeFi is revolutionizing the insurance industry by eliminating the significant limitations posed by the traditional handling of insurance systems. Such rules include unfathomable amounts of paperwork, the flawed claim handling process, time-consuming, etc. The insurance industry also experiences setbacks due to the fraudulent practices of false claims. Blockchain's decentralized technology can verify the presented documents, ownership, policy registration-related details, and claim authenticity. With smart contracts in place, the process of financial exchange as a result of insurance becomes easier for both the seeker and the insurance company.

Compliance Supported by the KYT mechanism

Know-your-customers (KYC) protocols majorly guided compliance in countering-the-financing-of-terrorism and anti-money laundering (AML). However, KYC protocols often interfered with DeFi's premise of privacy. It also did involve the external authority at one step or another contradicting the decentralization aspect of DeFi. Therefore, Defi has introduced a relatively evolved and better Know-Your-Transaction (KYT) mechanism. This mechanism lays the ground for the focus to shift from the identity of the user to digital addresses and the transaction behavior of the users. Such a mechanism assesses the live behavior of transactions and maintains the users' privacy. This mechanism helps assess risk or crisis proliferating in the system, early detection of which can combat eventual large-scale frauds and siphoning of hefty amounts.

Decentralized Exchanges

Decentralized exchanges (abbreviated as DEXs) refer to the transactions of cryptocurrency that occur P2P (peer-to-peer) without the involvement of any central authority, thus supporting the basic premise of DeFi. The assets in such exchanges are non-custodial to any external exchange platform. It allows users to interact, transact and maintain control of their assets. The significant advantage conferred is in terms of mitigation of risks. Since the assets are not under the direct supervision of any external authority or platform, it reduces the chances of hacking, fraud, and price manipulation. Currently, many DEXs are used in the user-friendly and easily accessible DeFi space. The most popular ones are Liquality, AirSwap, Mesa, etc.

Bolstered Digital Identity

Digital identity systems based on blockchain are coming to focus as viable and efficient identity systems. Mainly when amalgamated with the DeFi protocols, these identity systems can experience a boost in their efficiency in terms of immediate processing when required to avail of financial services. These systems are also changing the indicators of creditworthiness. According to the traditional finance systems, the hands to authenticate the credibility of financial service seekers used to be their possession of assets (owned houses) and income level. However, the digital identity reinforced by DeFi and blockchain protocols authenticates the seekers by their transactional behavior, financial activities, online reputation, or any other attributes that deem practical and necessary. This helps financial service seekers overcome the hindrances from collateralization and receive requisite services based on indicators they are mindful of.

Risk Mitigation and Management

The flagship features of DeFi highlight transparency and Decentralization, which have, in turn, become highly crucial for mitigating risks arising on the respective platform. This is done by thorough data analysis that the users can engage in with the data repository provided to them. Following their data analysis and being well informed about the risks associated with and predicted, the users can make decisions of their volition. Such comprehensive frameworks help users know the risks and ways to mitigate them. It also keeps the users updated about the financial opportunities arising in the market. The proliferation of DeFi has brought tools like DeFi Pulse and CoDeFi Data to light, which are involved in the processes mentioned above.

DeFi and Prediction Markets

Despite the critical views regarding the ethics of predicting and betting, these attract many people. The prediction markets allow the users to place bets or vote in favor or against the outcome of an event that hasn't occurred. Events under the umbrella of predictive use cases include predictions regarding sports events and election outcomes, to name a few. The prediction markets' functionality resonates with the traditional predictive needs regarding function only.

The amalgamation of blockchain with these markets eliminates the need for an intermediary. There are many contenders for the top spots in the list of DeFi prediction markets—for instance, Augur, Gnosis, Polymarket, Predictit, FTX, etc. Augur has emerged as the strongest contender on the list. This platform specializes in prediction and allows users to bet on political or economic events. DeFi-backed prediction markets were spotlighted in 2020 during the U.S. presidential elections due to the number of users involved in predicting results and the magnitude of bets in terms of values. Augur was reported to record the amount of about $8 million during these elections.

Gaming and DeFi: The Wonder of no-loss games

An essential feature of DeFi is the composability that the system offers. This composability has motivated the product developers to design protocols of DeFi into the platform itself. The latest video games have options for in-app purchasing, which provokes the users to use the live currency to purchase characters, elements, or other aspects of the game. The developers in the field of gaming are integrating their area with the DeFi systems by incentivizing the playing users.

Curating reward models often do this to target the relish points of the users utilizing DeFi coins. For example, PoolTogether is a game that is based on the premise of no loss. The users are indicated to submit the DAI stablecoin, purchasing digital tickets. These stablecoins are pooled together and stashed away till the end of the month. At the end of every month, this stash again resurfaces to award one player who earned the interest, and the deposited amounts are returned to all the players.

Exchange of synthetic assets

Synthetic assets can be understood as tokenized derivative that works much like another asset in value and functionality without having any actual physical relationship with the asset. These crypto-assets indicate assets of other kinds like fiat, gold, etc. These synthetic assets can be easily used as collateral by tokens in intelligent contracts with predetermined rules, regulations, and agreements. The understanding of synthetic assets can be supplemented by the example of a platform that allows users to curate and trade tailor-made synthetic asset versions. The Synthetix platform enables the exchange of synthetic versions of various assets like gold, fiat, commodities, etc.

Efficient trading practices

The DeFi ecosystem includes many transactional activities, from exchanging synthetic assets to exchanging tokens and margin trading. The advantage conferred by DeFi to the trading industry is the reduced reliance on brokers for trading to be initiated. Crypto traders also relish the benefits of DEXs due to reduced exchange charges, quick transactions, and absolute custody of the assets to the owner.

Blockchain-Based Online Marketplaces

DeFi has enabled digital spaces for the proliferation of marketplaces that link interested buyers and sellers. These markets are widening in their scope and magnitude as well. These digital markets drive out the need for an intermediary and brokers. This allows the sellers of many commodities to access the global user base of DeFi platforms without listing on retail brokerage platforms like Amazon. A significant part of online markets is supported by DeFi protocols enabling the exchange of products and services via peer-to-peer transactions. As mentioned above, the scope of these marketplaces is widening due to the advances in the technology corresponding to DeFi. It can also be attributed to the increasing applications and advantages of DeFi. These cater from established retail products like apparel to new business models like freelance gig platforms. For example, freelance gig hubs like Freelancer and Upwork are witnessing competition from platforms like Anytask built on the blockchain. The advantage that this blockchain platform of Anytask brings is that, unlike Freelancer and Upwork, it does not charge the service sellers any fee for accessing the gigs on their forum.

As outlined above, DeFi finds applications in various cases like borrowing and lending, asset management, insurance cases, stablecoins, compliance supported by KYT mechanisms, trading, no-loss gaming systems, etc. Despite our attempts to include the majority of use cases of DeFi, many use cases still need to be found mentioned in the section above. DeFi, a relatively new system, constantly evolves in its dynamics and application to different sectors. With such an evolving nature, the scopes of applications keep changing with new additions with its proliferation. Nonetheless, the objective of encompassing use cases in the narrative was to highlight the applications of DeFi and to give the readers an idea of how widespread DeFi is becoming, including industry after industry under its umbrella.

Significant Considerations of DeFi

Even though the DeFi systems offer a vast array of advantageous facets due to the culmination of finance and blockchain networks on DLT, it is still fraught with many risks and limitations, which the users should be aware of before venturing into the DeFi ecosystem. With the increasing applications industries, DeFi has also become home to cyber perpetrators on these platforms. Reports published by CipherTrace (a firm involved in crypto analytics) brought to light threatening figures of crypto crimes. According to this report, DeFi thefts in 2020 alone were about $100 million. In the latter half of 2020, about half of the cryptocurrency thefts were due to DeFi protocols. These staggering figures indicate the risks associated with DeFi. In addition to these risks, this system has many downsides, which will be explained in the sections below.

Before delineating the cons of this system, it is pertinent to note a few things. To begin with, the more significant part of the downsides of DeFi is because of the technology upon which they are built. The challenges of the base technology, in turn, propels the minor downsides of DeFi to become profound in their impact. If the blockchain network or technology that DeFi apps are built on suffers from issues of instability. If the base technology they are built upon is stable, the subsequently developed protocols will also be safe.

Additionally, some of the risks associated with DeFi can be mitigated and managed if the users know them.

Risks Arising Due to Smart Contracts

The first and foremost disadvantage branches from the essential components of this system: smart contracts. Although intelligent contracts have eased the process of exchanging financial services, ensuring high reliability, even then, it is fraught with a few technical limitations. Smart contracts, at their outset, are at the disposal of humans, as the lines of the code are written by an individual only before its public upload on the blockchain. This introduces the first instance of the possibility of human error. No matter how strict a smart contract is, it can still have many loopholes. The availability of these smart contracts on the public blockchain offers the content multiple sets of eyes to skim through the contract for the slightest loopholes. While just a few individuals form an intelligent agreement, it is available for audit to the global database accessing it. Such math opens up opportunities for exploitation of the loopholes present in the smart contract. Even a single loophole can be misused to drain millions from the smart contract.

Since smart contracts are available on the public blockchain, prospective investors can review them themselves or often outsource the review to security firms for auditing. This brings to light the second possibility of losses due to human error. Humans can miss out on loopholes in the contract, which then leads to exploitation in the future and financial losses eventually.

For example, Decentralization Autonomous Organization (DAO) was built on an open-source code allowing absolute autonomy and supplementing Decentralization. Launched in April 2016, it was a venture capital fund directed by investors. It saw exponential growth, which soon made this platform one of the most significant crowdfunding ventures, collecting around $120 million. By June 2016, however, an array of hackers emerged who identified a few flaws and vulnerabilities in the smart contract. These vulnerabilities helped the hackers in siphoning off about $50 million. The siphoned amount made it impossible for investors to access their funds for weeks. This became the biggest hack in the history of crowdfunding.

Efforts are being made to prevent the exploitation of smart contracts. For instance, Nexus Mutual is a team focused on structuring aspects of decentralized insurance that will help ensure the interests and security of the users in case they are faced with scams and frauds by cyber perpetrators on these systems.

Hacking and Frauds

The proliferation of fraud occurs in a way that often goes unnoticed at the outset and comes to the spotlight in retrospect. There have been reports of funds laundering on DeFi platforms like Kyber Network, Uniswap, etc. As explained in the previous sections, another source for fraud to occur is hacking by identifying the loopholes in the smart contract that are available on the blockchain network. Such activities put shade on the security of the funds on the DeFi platforms, raising concerns in the context of the trust quotient. While this may lead to users losing their money, on the one hand, it discourages non-existing users from switching from traditional financial systems to DeFi.

Problems with the Scalability of the Host Platforms

The DeFi protocols are well-suited for ensuring the inclusion of more people to cater to their financial services irrespective of geographic impediments. However, blockchain-based projects need to improve the scalability of these host platforms. DeFi suffers as the transactions take longer to process after confirmation. This can be attributed to the fact that these DeFi systems can process a definite set number of transactions at a single moment. For instance, the DeFi-based platform - Ethereum, even at its total capacity, can only process about 13 transactions per second. At the same time, traditional centralized financial systems can allow many transactions in the same period without any error. Therefore, despite the ease offered by DeFi in initiating a transaction, it needs substantial waiting periods for the confirmation of the transaction. Additionally, transaction costs increase at times of such congestion.

The basic premise of DeFi systems is bringing Decentralization to the table and replacing the conventional financial plans with the central authority as an impediment. This Decentralization provides transparency, flexibility, and accessibility, increasing the trustworthiness of DeFi projects and reducing the possibilities of fraud and scandals. However, despite the claims, not all services of DeFi systems are decentralized. For example, a critical use case of these systems in the form of stablecoins introduces the role of central authority either directly in the case of fiat currency-based stablecoins or indirectly in the case of commodity-backed stablecoins.

Apart from the abovementioned issues, many other problems inflect the DeFi systems. To begin with, the anonymity DeFi systems provide can often accelerate the chances of scams and fraud. With the public space open to all users around the globe, the risk factor becomes prominent. Since the DeFi platform does not require KYC from its users, it often includes the bad actors on the forum who indulge in malpractices. Although the verification systems used by DeFi are efficient, robust, and less time-consuming, they can often be misleading. Since authentication is facilitated by tracking online behavior, transactional activities, and other such practical attributes, these attributes can be manipulated, thus tricking the authentication system.

Secondly, insurance is given requisite attention in the case of centralized finance due to its necessity in ensuring the customers' trust and protecting them from events of hacking or fraud which might lead the customers to incur substantial financial losses. However, the aspect of insurance in the case of DeFi is rarely given due importance, if ever. Also, such insurances demand a place, especially when the users have to take responsibility solely.

Even if DeFi has no associated risks or issues, the responsibility for everything will be on the user's shoulders. With the complexity of the operation, room for mistakes is always there, especially for users with less experience with operating technology or those who have just joined DeFi platforms. Their likelihood of losing their funds due to a tiny mistake causes them significant financial problems. Thus, more work is required in the DeFi space to make the platform user-friendly and create tools that minimize the risks of potential human errors.

Despite the risks and limitations of DeFi, it is still booming as it continues to offer advantages to various industries in the form of its successful and efficient applications. Especially after 2020, these systems must focus due to the increasing number of locked assets.

There has also been an increase in the use cases of DeFi, which has yielded more recognition of the system. Even though the technology used by DeFi requires refinement in terms of the necessary tools to reduce the associated risks, nonetheless, it is expected to reign in the financial world due to its interoperability and innovativeness, amongst other factors.

CHAPTER 6

Non-Fungible Tokens

What are NFTs?

Non-Fungible Tokens or NFTs, as the name suggests, are tokens, much like other crypto tokens such as Bitcoin or ether; however, the critical difference is that they are non-fungible, meaning they cannot be copied or replicated. Each of the tokens is unique by itself. E.g., when you buy a cryptocurrency, such as a Bitcoin, and then you exchange it for another Bitcoin, in the end, you have the same thing; there is no way to differentiate between the Bitcoin that you were holding earlier and the Bitcoin that you are holding now, this means that they are fungible.

Non-Fungible tokens are unique because if you exchange one NFT of similar value with another NFT, then what you have in your hand is something different. The fungibility of currencies and cryptocurrencies usually helps us use them as a medium of exchange since everyone has an agreed value common to all the units of the said currency. NFTs, on the other hand, can be compared to collectibles such as unique sports cards or art pieces.

NFTs use blockchain technology to register the transaction, typically, it is the Ethereum blockchain, but other blockchains are also used, which keeps track of the ownership of the NFT. NFTs are created on these blockchains using the ERC-721 and ERC-1155 frameworks. More often than not, NFTs are artwork such as images, GIFs, videos, and music. What happens is that the person purchasing that original piece of art has proof of their ownership, the transaction, stored on the blockchain. Since we know that blockchain has immutable and permanent data, the transaction cannot be altered and is thus a set proof of the fact that the person owns that particular asset.

The value of most things is directly proportional to the scarcity of the said thing. When we say that gold and diamonds are expensive, they are only available in a limited amount, and we cannot create any more natural gold or diamonds. Similarly, art pieces such as those by Picasso, Monet, Banksy, or Basquiat carry astronomical values during auctions and other sales because they are only a limited number of such pieces. Further, each piece is unique from the other. Before the advent of blockchain technology and NFTs, there was no such scarcity of digital art forms, one could search for a song or a photograph and they would get thousands of copies of the same. With NFTs, however, there is a newfound scarcity in the ownership of digital assets, which increases the value of these digital assets.

NFTs work as financial assets; they can be compared to physical art, except they are digital art forms. Just like physical art has no intrinsic value, and most people purchase it either for the bragging rights of having the ownership of the said piece of art or for using it as an investment which will give them returns when they sell it off at a higher value in the future, NFTs are similarly either owned to be flipped for profit in the future or for the fact that one holds the original version of a digital asset.

What one needs to understand, however, is the fact that just because they have ownership of an NFT doesn't mean that the same digital art can't be reproduced by anyone else. Think of it as a painting, such as The Starry Night by Vincent Van Gogh; At the same time, various painters made multiple copies of The Starry Night, and it is even available as posters or drawing aids; the ownership of the original Starry Night lies in the hands of a single person, or this case, the Rijks museum. Similarly, the same gif or image will be available online on various web pages or search engines. Still, the original art lies in the hands of the owner of the non-fungible token.

When a person purchases art using an NFT, the artist or the original owner encrypts digital information and metadata onto the blockchain. This data is used to prove the ownership of the NFT. Further, since blockchains have timestamps, one could even trace back the right of the digital asset to see when and how many times it has changed hands over time.

NFTs can be traded like any other digital assets; there are markets for NFTs where one can go and purchase the token they like. Any fixed market force does not set the price for NFTs; much like art, their price is determined by what the buyer is willing to pay for the asset. NFTs can even be programmed so that the owner is paid a certain amount every time the NFT changes hands, so in case the price of the NFT skyrockets, the original owner is still compensated. NFTs use distributed ledger technology such as blockchain, which means there is no need for an intermediary or an exchange for the transfer of NFTs, bringing down the transaction costs.

NFTs have little to no regulations in the global markets, and their future is very much connected with cryptocurrencies and blockchain technology. For example, if cryptocurrency trade is banned in a particular country, then the sale and purchase of NFTs will also be restricted there.

While NFTs have become increasingly popular, their criticisms have also increased. One of the significant criticism associated with NFTs is their carbon footprint. The world is currently dealing with a climatic disaster partly fuelled by using non-renewable and polluting energy sources. We know that blockchain is a very energy-intensive industry. It takes electricity to run the servers responsible for mining on the blockchains. NFTs, to be created also need similar mining requirements, causing pollution and climate change. Some artists have pulled out of making their NFTs after getting to know about the environmental impact of NFTs.

Properties of Non-fungible Tokens

Non-fungible tokens have certain features which help it function the way it does. Some of these features are:

Unique: Every NFT is unique, i.e., an NFT cannot be copied. Unlike other cryptocurrencies, one NFT does not equate to another NFT, even if they are of the same value. If one trades NFTs, they have something different in their hand and not just a separate copy of the same thing.

Indivisible: NFTs are also indivisible, which means that NFTs cannot be broken down into smaller parts of lesser value and then sold, collected again, and reassembled. An NFT is always traded as a whole.

Indestructible: The data for an NFT is stored on blockchains. Most of the NFTs are stored on the Ethereum blockchain. Since we know that the data on blockchains are tough to destroy or alter, especially on public blockchains, the NFTs cannot be destroyed.

Absolute ownership: When a person owns an NFT, they carry total ownership over the digital asset; it is not like purchasing the license to use a particular image, song, or gif. This means that the owner has unrestricted access to these NFTs.

Verifiable: Since the data regarding the ownership of an NFT is stored on blockchains and such data is always timestamped and, at the same time, assured of authenticity, it is easy to verify and trace the ownership of an NFT.

Limited: NFTs are limited in number; they are scarce. Most NFTs are only produced singularly; however, an artist may have a limited number of similar products, such as 10 or 50, much like little edition clothes or cars by real-life manufacturers.

Transferable: NFTs are digital assets or certificates that pronounce the ownership of digital assets; hence like any other digital asset, NFTs can be transferred from one person to another for a price.

Permanent: The data stored on blockchains are endless; once entered, it is always there. Unlike real-life paintings or art forms that might get spoilt over time, the NFTs will be permanent.

History of Non-fungible Tokens

The idea behind non-fungible tokens started with something called "colored coins" in 2012, which were being offered on the Bitcoin blockchain. These colored coins denote the real-life ownership of cars, metals, real estate, etc.

Non-fungible Tokens were first minted in the year 2014 by Kevin Mckoy. He coined the first non-fungible token called "quantum" before using NFTs extensively in crypto art. Quantum is a pixelated image of an octagonal object that changes shapes and colors.

The NFTs started catching public attention after the introduction of CryptoKitties on the Ethereum blockchain and that of crypto punks. Crypto kitties are non-fungible tokens depicting cats, each with unique age, size, and color features. It means that none of the cats are the same; they are thus traded as collectibles among people, much like sports cards or Pokémon cards in real life. Cryptopunks, conversely, are avatars or profile pictures that have been converted into NFTs, which people can use for various social media platforms. Again, each cyberpunk avatar differs from the others and has its value. The NFTs were growing in the crypto community, but they entered a mainstream boom in 2021.

The NFT Revolution in 2021

In the year 2021, the interest in NFTs ballooned to unprecedented heights. While this was in line with the bull market that saw the prices of cryptocurrencies such as Bitcoin, Ethereum, and even dogecoin during the first quarter of the year, it was observed that despite the fall in the prices of these cryptocurrencies from their peaks in the second quarter of the year there was continued growth in the sale and purchase of non-fungible tokens during the same period.

The NFT market has grown by leaps and bounds in 2021. In the first half of 2021, compared to the 13.7 million dollars in sales in the first half of 2020, the NFT sales had surged to an almost unbelievable 2.5 billion dollars. Within this, we saw an increase in Quarter 1 to Quarter 2 of about 114.6%. In this same period, there was a substantial increase in the number of wallets that store NFTs, at about 151.89%. NFT trading platforms such as Open Sea have also increased, with Open Sea currently worth around 1.5 billion dollars. Sales of NFTs have moved on from being only on trading platforms to being made by traditional auction houses such as Sotheby's and Christie's.

It is not just the quantum of NFT sales that has increased in 2021. The value of the NFTs also increased substantially, with a majority of the most expensive NFT sales ever made being in 2021. In February, we saw digital art by the musician Grimes being sold for an amount nearing 6 million dollars, while the GIF for Nyan cat fetched a price of almost half a million dollars or 300 ethers. In March, the artwork by Beeple, pseudonym of the digital artist Michael Winkelmann, called "Every Day: The first 5000 Days" was listed by the auction house Christie's and sold for a record price of 69.3 million dollars. The same month, Jack Dorsey, Twitter's founder, and CEO, sold his first-ever tweet after converting it into an NFT. This tweet was sold for a price of 2.9 million dollars. Similarly, the cost of various avatars by Cyberpunks has continuously been sold for prices ranging from a few hundred thousand dollars to 7.6 million dollars or 4200 Ether for CryptoPunks #7804.

Some of the most popular NFTs that one should know about are:

CryptoKitties: Crypto kitties were one of the first NFTs readily traded by the public. CryptoKitties were developed by the Canadian development studio called Dapper Labs in 2017. Since then, the popularity and the price of the various cats in the game have increased manifolds, with some rarer cats, such as "dragon," costing more than a million US dollars. Crypto Kitties is a game based on the Ethereum blockchain. Users can purchase, breed, and sell cats in this game.

The cats in the game are all unique. Each cat has its color, size, name, and other characteristics which cannot be copied. The users own the cats and thus cannot be taken away by anyone, including the game's developers. The cats can also be used as collectibles, wherein people collect a specific type of cat and then display these collections. Depending on their attributes and rarity, a few different types of cats are in the game, such as Exclusive Cats, Fancy Cats, and Special Edition Cats.

CryptoPunks: Cryptopunks are the other path setters in Non-fungible Tokens, along with CryptoKitties. Much like CryptoKitties, crypto punks were also introduced in 2017. Cryptopunks were created by the American development studio called Larva Labs. The cyberpunk movement inspired the creation of crypto punks. The crypto punks, in turn, inspired the ER-721 standard of Ethereum that is now used in most digital art NFTs.

Crypto punks are avatars that people can use to display pictures on various platforms. In total, 10,000 crypto punks were created by Larva Labs. Of these 10,000 crypto punks, 6039 are male, 3840 are female, 88 are zombies, 24 are apes, and 9 are aliens. Each of these crypto punks is unique and thus carries its value. The price of the crypto punk depends on the rarity; with the nine alien crypto punks being the rarest, they have been purchased at the highest prices till now.

Crypto punks regularly feature on the list of most expensive NFTs sold, with CryptoPunks #7804 selling for 7.6 million dollars, CryptoPunks #6965 selling for 1.6 million dollars, and CryptoPunks #4156 selling for 1.3 million dollars. Even mainstream companies have started purchasing punks, with Visa shelling out almost 176,000 dollars on a crypto punk in July 2021.

Rare Pepes: Rare pipes were the first NFTs that were offered on the platform known as counterparty. Pepes are images of green-colored frogs that are edited in various ways. The Pepe images of different kinds have been converted to NFTs and then sold to the highest bidder. The 'rarest' of pipes, a picture of Homer Pepe, i.e., the famous TV character of Homer Simpson, edited to look like a Pepe, was brought for a price of 320,000 dollars in March 2021

Everyday: The first 5000 days and other Beeple arts: The first 5000 days are the most expensive NFT to have been sold till now. It was sold for 69.3 million dollars or 42329 Ether during an auction by the auction house Christie's. It is a collage of five thousand images created by Beeple. It was purchased by Vignesh Sundaresan, who is now displaying it in a digital museum.

It is not only the most expensive digital art piece till now but also one of the most expensive pieces sold by a living artist. Beeple is the pseudonym of the American digital artist Mike Winkelmann, who has converted many of his digital pieces into NFTs and sold them. His artworks are some of the most in-demand NFTs in the crypto world, with most selling in minutes and charging exorbitant prices. Another one of his pieces, called Crossroads, a 10-second video, sold for approximately 6.6 million dollars in February 2021.

Decentraland: Decentraland is a 3-D virtual reality world. In this world, the products, lands, and other amenities are sold as NFTs, connecting the virtual and real worlds. It was initially started by Argentinian developers in 2015. It slowly moved from a pixelated sphere to a 3-d world. Recently, the prices of virtual real estate have increased manifolds, with some of the prime real estate in decentral costing as much as 100,000 dollars. Real-world companies such as Sotheby's and Republic Realm are purchasing digital real estate in this world to use as digital offices and shopping places.

Alchemy Toys: Alchemy Toys is a game based on the Binance Smart chain, developed by a German software company called Backupdev UG. It is being promoted as an amalgamation of non-fungible tokens, massively multiplayer online role-playing games, and decentralized finance. In this game, players can own unique and rare alchemy toys, which can then be combined to form newer toys or sold to the other players for the actual value. It is also possible to sacrifice or burn these toys. If a person offers all the different toys, they are rewarded with Binance coins.

Pancake Swap: Pancake swap is also based on the Binance bright chain. On the platform, the users are provided with bunnies that are NFTs. The bunnies have no purpose other than being decorative, except that the users can also trade them for Cake coins, the cryptocurrency of the said platform.

Gods Unchained: Gods Unchained is much like real-life card trading games. In the game, the players are given actual ownership of their cards which are tradeable NFTs. These cards, when sold, provide the players with cryptocurrencies and real value. The value of the cards depends on the rarity of these cards, with some costing upwards of ten thousand dollars. The game was created by Immutable, a development studio based in Australia specializing in blockchain games.

Differences Between NFTs and Typical Cryptocurrencies

Before we look at how non-fungible tokens differ from the otherwise mainstream or typical cryptocurrencies such as Bitcoin, Ether, or Cardano, we must first understand their similarities and what connects them. NFTs and cryptocurrencies are, in essence, digital assets that can be sold or purchased on online platforms with little to no inherent or intrinsic value. Both NFTs and cryptocurrencies are based on blockchain or distributed ledger technologies. The transaction history in both cases is stored on blockchains and is permanent and immutable. NFTs, much like cryptocurrencies, are also in a grey area when it comes to regulation in most countries.

Nature: The first point of difference that we see between NFTs and cryptocurrencies is their essential nature. When we talk about cryptocurrencies, we consider them, as the name suggests, as currencies, i.e., they are to be used as tools or money-like instruments that will be used for purchasing other things or assets. However, in some places and by some people, they are treated as investments that might grow in value and then be sold off. On the other hand, when we talk about NFTs, as earlier discussed, they are not currencies despite being tokens. NFTs are like assets in nature. They are not to be used for purchasing other stuff but rather as collectibles. While cryptocurrencies can be compared to money in real life, NFTs can be compared to works of Art and Luxury.

Fungibility: The most crucial characteristic of NFTs that differentiates them from typical cryptocurrencies is the one that is in their name, i.e., fungibility. Fungibility is the ability of similar goods or assets to be interchangeable or replaced by an identical item. Fungibility is an essential feature of currency. It ensures that people can freely use cash anywhere, and there is no difference between one unit of money with another. Cryptocurrencies like fiat currencies are fungible. If you trade one ether for another, there is no difference between the two; you essentially have the same thing in hand. On the other hand, NFTs are not fungible; each one is unique and thus cannot be copied. If you exchange one NFT for another, you have something different now than you had earlier.

Value determinant: The way NFTs are determined is also different from how the value of cryptocurrencies is determined. Since cryptocurrencies have a very high volume of sales and exchange hands very frequently, thus the price of the cryptocurrencies is determined by the prevailing market forces, i.e., demand and supply. NFTs are unique, and each carries a different value; further, the price of the NFT is determined by what the buyer is willing to pay for the said product. In the case of NFTs, the market's supply side is constant.

Cost: The cost or price of NFTs and cryptocurrencies also differ to a great extent. When we talk about cryptocurrencies, the most popular and expensive cryptocurrency is Bitcoin. Bitcoin, during the bull market of 2021, reached a peak price of just above 64,000 dollars. This, however, completes pales in comparison to the kind of prices that people have paid for some NFTs. People regularly pay upwards of a million dollars for NFTs, with the most expensive NFT netting around 69 million dollars during an auction in March 2021.

Divisibility: Another difference between NFTs and cryptocurrencies is their ability to be divided into smaller pieces. Cryptocurrencies can be broken down into pieces, which can further be broken down into parts. This is essential for expensive cryptocurrencies like Bitcoin so people can purchase them in smaller quantities. NFTs always exist as a whole, and they are like art pieces. They can't be broken down, traded, collected, and reassembled.

Blockchain used: The blockchains that are used for the two also differ. While for cryptocurrencies, almost every cryptocurrency runs on its blockchain, which stores the transactions of the said currency. For example, the trades of Ether are recorded on Ethereum. Whereas NFTs are more often than not running on the ether blockchain, some of them are also on the Binance bright chain. These are the two most commonly used blockchains for NFTs.

Purchase platforms: The platforms at which the two are traded are also different. At the same time, Cryptocurrencies are traded on crypto exchanges, such as Binance and Coinbase. These crypto exchanges can be both centralized or decentralized in nature. NFTs are bought and sold on NFT platforms like Open Sea and Nifty Gateway. At the same time, NFTs are also being sold by auction houses such as Sotheby's and Christie's.

Currencies Accepted: The money that can be paid for the purchase of the two is also different. When we talk about cryptocurrencies, one can pay for them in fiat currencies or other cryptocurrencies, depending on their crypto exchange. Thus we see that cryptocurrencies are readily convertible to real-world money. On the other hand, to purchase NFTs, one has to pay only in cryptocurrencies. If the NFT is based on the Ethereum blockchain, it is paid for in Ethers (ETH), and if it is on the Binance Smart Chain, then it is paid for in Binance coins (BNB)

Timeline: The timeline of the emergence of the two is also very different. Cryptocurrencies were first created in 2008, the first being Bitcoin. Cryptocurrencies came into the mainstream in the middle to late 2010s, with the first bull market in 2017 and the second in early 2021. On the other hand, the first NFT was introduced in 2016, it became slightly famous in 2017 due to crypto kitties and punks, but it only entered the mainstream in 2021 when the NFT market ultimately ballooned.

Workings of NFTs

Creating an NFT is relatively easy; various platforms allow people to make an NFT. To make a non-fungible token, one needs two things, the digital art or asset that will be converted into a non-fungible permit and the payment for doing the minting. Recently, much stuff has been converted into non-fungible tokens, including digital art, songs, videos, and even tweets; anything with a digital form or signature can be converted into an NFT. Once created, the NFTs can be viewed by the owner on wallets, just like cryptocurrencies. These NFTs similarly exist on addresses on the blockchain, which can be accessed by the person holding the key.

During the minting process of an NFT, the owner or creator of the NFT executes code that conforms to different NFT standards. NFTs use standards and protocols such as the following:

ERC - 721: ERC - 721 was the original standard developed to create NFTs in 2017. It was written in Solidity on the Ethereum blockchain. This standard allows minting new NFTs easier, faster, and non-repetitive. ERC-721 is the most commonly used standard; anyone can create their own NFT.

ERC - 1155: ERC - 1155 is another standard on the Ethereum blockchain. It was developed after ERC-721 and is considered an upgrade over the previous one. The bar has smart contracts executed in a way that makes new non-fungible tokens. One of the significant advantages that ERC - 1155 has over ERC - 721 is that one can create multiple NFTs on a single, smart contract. On an ERC-721, one had to run the intelligent contract for a new NFT every time. The ERC-1155 is more efficient and takes less storage space, but it is also more diverse since it can make fungible tokens and non-fungible receipts.

Hedera Token Service - This is a non-Ethereum-based standard that Hedera offers. This is much cheaper than the Ethereum standards and also faster. Infinite by SUKU is one company that has shifted to Hedera from Ethereum.

Currently, we see that NFTs are proprietary and have single owners. There are plans to introduce fractional NFT standards shortly, allowing multiple users to own a fraction of a single NFT. This would align with the decentralizing and multiple-node nature of blockchains in general.

NFT Use Cases

NFTs can be used in various sectors. Some of these use cases are:

Gaming: Non-fungible tokens, primarily online gaming, are extensively used in the gaming sector. Some of the first NFTs, such as CryptoKitties, were just games set up on blockchains. NFTs can be used in gaming in two broad ways, either the collections and storing of the NFTs is in itself a game, and people are trying to get NFTs, convert them into something else within the game, and then try to win a reward, as is the case in crypto kitties or alchemy toys. Conversely, it is also possible that the NFTs are being used as appendages to other games. These can be cosmetic (skins, avatars, helmets, etc.) and utile (weapons, pets, etc.).

In Massively Multiplayer Online Role-Playing games, people can use NFTs to own certain in-game items, giving them the exclusive right to use these. The gaming industry is one of the fastest-growing industries in the world. With the increase in mobile-based games and internet penetration in previously untapped regions, it is set to expand even further in the next few years. The gaming industry will be worth over 300 billion dollars by 2023. This provides NFTs with a large market base and potential growth in this sector.

Digital Assets: The digital asset marketplace is also one of these tokens' most critical use cases. It is possible to purchase assets that only exist in the digital world. Decentraland is among the most common names when buying digital assets as NFTs. Decentraland is a virtual world with a certain amount of finite and scarce land. A prospective buyer can purchase this land from others or even the developers. The price of the land is dependent, much like in the real world, on the location of this 'plot.' Some of the game's prime location digital real estate is being sold for thousands of dollars. Companies are planning to set up their digital stores in these spaces. 'Cryptovoxel' is another project where people can purchase and sell digital assets.

Art: Currently, Art is the sector where NFTs are used most. Digital art for years was plagued with the problem of being easily copied, and thus with no scarcity for the said product, the price of digital art could have been higher. This completely changed after people started converting their digital art to NFTs. When Art was combined with NFT, it became a lot easier for the owners of the said pieces to authenticate their ownership. This created a limited supply of digital art, which caused it to shoot in value. Over the last couple of years, we have seen some digital paintings being sold for astronomical prices, such as every day: The First 500 Days, which was sold at 69 million dollars.

However, it is not just famous artists like Beeple profiting from NFTs. Even smaller artists can convert their art into NFTs and thus monetize their work. Further, using smart contracts, it is also possible for the artist to attach a clause to the NFT that gives them a cut of the price every time an NFT is sold to protect their economic interest if their work gets popular and increases in price in the future. NFTs would also remove the need for mediators and other intermediaries between the artists and the art collectors. NFTs could finally bring the digital art world on par with the physical art world.

Identification: Non-fungible tokens are also being used for providing proof of identity. NFTs can be programmed to contain unique information within them, and at the same time, we know that NFTs can only have a single owner at a time, and the data within an NFT cannot be mutated; thus, NFTs can be configured in such a way to issue identities, licenses, qualifications, etc. For example, suppose a person is to be given an identity card for club membership. In that case, the digital version of the card can be configured with an NFT to ensure that it is the original card shown upon entry. In case of identity theft, even if the culprit can copy the identification cards, they will not be able to copy the NFT that is attached to these cards.

Collectibles: Another of the most common and popular uses of NFTs is currently in the collectibles sector. We know that NFTs are non-fungible and unique tokens, meaning that every NFT differs. Collectibles had been absent in digital form as they could easily be copied and duplicated, but this problem has been solved with NFTs. It is now possible to create an item in a finite amount. Thus even if a product is copied, its authenticity cannot be proven. This creates a form of exclusivity in the ownership of the said items. Some of the collectibles that are being produced with NFTs are:

Trading Cards: For years, trading cards have been one of the most sorts after collectibles in the real world. Trading cards can be of many types, such as for sports like baseball or basketball trading cards or in the form of games such as Pokémon or yu-gi-ho. The rarer cards have sometimes been sold for millions of dollars. Now we are seeing the start of digital trading card games like Gods Unchained.

Avatars: Crypto punks were one of the first NFTs and have become some of the most popular ones. The purchase of the limited edition alien crypto punks has regularly exceeded the value of a million dollars. These punks have no intrinsic value but are just being as collectible because of their rarity. One can use them as avatars or display pictures on various platforms.

Original Copies: Just like the original documents of various products in the real world, such as comic books, novels, and album covers, are kept by collectors and worth thousands of dollars, the digital version of the audiobooks, comics, etc., are also collected by collectors. Not just books, but recently even the original copy of the first tweet by the founder and CEO of Twitter was sold for 2.9 million dollars to the highest bidder by using NFTs.

Sports: Sports have also started venturing into the world of NFTs. NBA sold the first sport-based NFT. Using NBA top shots, collectors can purchase the original highlight of an image or a sequence of play by their favorite players during an NBA game. Formula 1 and boxing are both launching their own NFT collections.

Domain Names: It is also possible to purchase and collect domain names. The ownership of the domain name is stored in the NFT. One of the common ways of buying and storing names is through the Ethereum names service.

Finance: NFTs, though popularly used for their superficial purposes, can be helpful too. This provides the NFT holders with value for holding the NFT in itself. For example, if an NFT allows the holder to enter an exclusive pool of investors, the said NFT can be traded or sold for that right. Their holders can also stake NFTs to earn passive income. Some NFTs also double as discount coupons or combos, such as in the case of BAKE coupons. These financial NFTs can also have artwork attached to them, but their value comes from their use, not their art.

Music and v]Video: Just as it is possible to attach an NFT to an image file or a GIF, it is also possible to link NFTs to audio and video files. By connecting the NFT to an audio file or album, musicians and video makers can start selling the original versions of their products. Just because a person holds the NFT to a song or video does not mean they have the copyright to it. It continues to be with the artist. Currently, the recording studios and other intermediaries earn from songs and music videos; using NFTs would diminish the need for these third parties, thereby increasing the income for the musicians. Kings of Leon was the first central rock band to release a digital version of their album; each album copy was uniquely numbered with NFTs.

Real-World Asset: Real-world assets, such as shares, deeds, contracts, etc., could also use NFTs. Forgery and fraud are commonplace in the physical form. However, blockchain technology could prove its authenticity if these assets were given proper NFTs. In 2021, an NFT was created, which included the ownership of a property in California. Whoever owns the NFTS also holds ownership of the said property. It could also help prove the ownership of valuable items such as jewelry.

High fashion is another probable use case for NFTs. Most luxury fashion has no purpose other than the identity and exclusivity its ownership offers. This makes it a very logical use for NFTs. People can buy digital fashion products, such as digital sneakers or sunglasses, which are authenticated using NFTs. Big fashion houses have already started producing NFT-based digital products. A luxury virtual hoodie by Overpriced was sold for 19,000 pounds.

Licensing: NFTs could be of great use in the software licensing sector. Firstly they would bring down piracy in the industry as it is tough to forge your ownership details when stored on NFTs. Secondly, NFTs allow people to sell their licenses directly to others who need them. So people won't be stuck with licenses or year-long memberships. They could go to an NFT marketplace and sell it to someone who needs it.

How To Safely Buy NFTs And Where?

Non-fungible tokens, like other crypto tokens, are unavailable for sale and purchase on regular stock exchanges. Some specific platforms and businesses deal with NFTs. Some of them have been created specifically for this purpose. The process of purchasing an NFT is straightforward and can be done by following a few steps.

Purchase Cryptocurrency: The first step in purchasing an NFT is cryptocurrency. NFTs are based on blockchains, each of which has its cryptocurrency. NFTs must be bought by paying for the value in the blockchain cryptocurrency. It is not possible to purchase NFTs directly using fiat currencies. They must be first converted to cryptocurrencies. If one wants to get an Ethereum blockchain-based NFT, one purchase ether, and if it is a Binance smart chain-based NFT, one must purchase Binance coins. Cryptocurrency can be bought on various crypto exchanges like Binance, Coinbase, etc.

Transfer Crypto to a Wallet: The next step is to transfer your ether or other cryptocurrencies to a wallet like MetaMask. These wallets store access to cryptocurrencies and provide security from hacking. It is also possible to directly use the crypto to pay for the NFT if it is bought on the identical blockchain, for example, if purchased on Binance.

Choose an NFT Marketplace: The next step is to choose the marketplace. There are many marketplaces that one can choose from. Each of these marketplaces has its features, transaction costs, and other characteristics. One must consider these all before selecting the marketplace they want to purchase their NFTs.

Attach Your Wallet to the Marketplace: The next step is for the buyer to attach the wallet in which they have their cryptocurrency to the market. This allows the cryptocurrency to be transferred from your wallet to the seller's wallet via the market.

Choose the NFT: One of the most critical steps in this process is choosing the NFT that one wants to purchase on the platform. Thousands of different NFTs are available on these platforms, and the market is growing daily. Choosing an NFT is a crucial decision and must be made in an informed manner as it is a long-term investment decision.

Purchase for the NFT: The final step is to purchase the NFT you selected. Purchase on platforms can happen in two ways either they can be done in an auction format, and the highest bidder gets the NFT, or the seller can quote a price, and the buyer pays the amount to purchase the product. Once the cryptocurrency is transferred, the transaction is stored in the blockchain, and the ownership changes to the new person.

This is the usual manner in which NFT purchase takes place. However, we have also seen recently that some real-life auction houses have started selling digital art pieces through auctions.

How to Choose an NFT?

Choosing an NFT should be an informed decision that depends on the following factors:

Price: The first and most important factor before choosing an NFT is the price at which it is sold. One must look at their budget and then decide which NFTs are in their budget that they can buy.

Blockchain: Another factor that must be considered is the blockchain on which the NFT is minted. Most NFTs are on Ethereum; however, other blockchains also offer the minting process. One should choose a trustworthy and well-established blockchain.

Rarity: The rarity of an NFT is the factor that impacts the future price of the NFT. For example, the alien punks in crypto punks are worth more now than the human punks because there are only nine strange punks.

Creator: Like when purchasing an actual art piece, digital art NFTs should also be bought according to who the piece's creator is. One could invest in an artist's NFTs, who they believe will become popular and famous.

Type: The type and kind of NFT are also necessary. Some people use NFTs as digital assets, some as collectibles or game purchases, while others treat them as financial instruments.

How to Choose an NFT Marketplace?

Choosing the correct NFT marketplace is also very important. When selecting the NFT marketplace, it is essential to consider the following:

Token standard: Multiple different token standards are used for making NFTs. Depending on the NFT you want to purchase, you should check whether the marketplace offers NFTs of that token standard.

Transaction cost: Every time one purchase or sells an NFT, a transaction takes place, and it is recorded on the blockchain. For every transaction, the marketplace charges a fee or a commission. This rate of the price differs from one marketplace to another and should be considered when deciding on a

Type: There are different types of marketplaces. Some are universal and allow all kinds of tokens to be traded, while others only offer a specific ticket.

Verification process: Marketplaces have verification processes for the creators who want to sell their NFT on the marketplace. This must be a stringent process to restrict the presence of fakes and fraudulent NFTs.

Pricing method: The Pierce discovery process also depends on one marketplace to another. In some, it is done through an auctioning process, while in others, it is quoted by the seller or creator.

Popular NFT Platforms

Some of the most popular Marketplaces for non-fungible tokens are:

OpenSea

- Nifty Gateway
- Bakeryswap
- Viv3

- Axie Marketplace
- NFT showroom
- Enjin Marketplace
- Binance NFT marketplace
- Myth Market
- Atomic Market
- Rarible
- Foundation

CHAPTER 7

The Blockchain Technology

What is a Blockchain?

Blockchain is often confused with the first-ever cryptocurrency - Bitcoin. This is because the term blockchain became popular only after the inception of Bitcoin. In reality, blockchain is the primary technology that enables the working of cryptos. If not for blockchain, we won't be seeing any of the cryptocurrencies that are in circulation today. It is essential to know that cryptocurrency is just one of the various potential applications of blockchain technology.

In simple terms, a blockchain is a distributed electronic ledger built around a Peer 2 Peer system. This ledger can be shared among infinite users for their reference. The transactions entered into the blockchain are tamper-proof and time-stamped individually. A set of valid transactions makes a block complete. Each verified block is linked to the previous block to form a chain of blocks. Hence the name - Blockchain!

The working of the Blockchain is different from that of centralized systems. It is a distributed ledger and works as a consensus-based network, thus, making it decentralized. Following is the step-by-step working of a transaction on the Blockchain.

1. A node, a computer in the blockchain network, receives a transaction from the sender. It initiates that transaction on the web by creating it. Later, the cryptography technique gets the transaction digitally signed with a private key.

2. The transaction information is passed from that node to all the other nodes on the network to validate the transaction based on some criteria preset by the Blockchain. This process is called the Gossip protocol. In technical terms, it is called the Proof of Work, the standard consensus algorithm of Blockchain. According to the algorithm, the nodes must solve a complex mathematical puzzle to authenticate a transaction. Usually, two or more nodes are required to validate the transaction.

3. Once the nodes validate the transaction entirely, it is included inside a block and is propagated toward the leading blockchain network. This is when the trade gets its first confirmation.

4. Later, when a new block is created for the same transaction, it goes through the same process above and gets linked to the first block, referred to as the "genesis block." The league gets its first confirmation, and the transaction reaches its second confirmation.

5. The same process is repeatedly reconfirmed for every new block created. Typically, about five-six confirmations are required for the transaction to be officially complete. And finally, the ownership of the cryptocurrency/digital asset is moved to the receiver.

Smart Contracts

One of the most fundamental purposes of using a blockchain is that no intermediary is involved. Because blockchain is decentralized and all the functions that the intermediaries do are replaced with complex computer algorithms. A revolutionary application of blockchain that can potentially eliminate many intermediaries is known as Smart Contracts.

Smart Contracts can be defined as computerized agreements stored in a blockchain network. In smart contracts, all contract terms can be pre-coded, and the execution of these contracts can automatically be done once the contract conditions are met. Since these Smart Contracts are stored in a blockchain network, the security, transparency, and accessibility of the contract are increased exponentially.

Also, these smart contracts are immutable. They are tamper-proof, and no one can change the terms once the contract is activated. If any parties attempt to alter the contract terms, the agreement will get rejected while intimating all the parties involved. More importantly, these contracts are cost-effective as we can eliminate fees to typical intermediaries such as authorizers, document creators, etc.

Blockchain technology has become very popular over the last decade, primarily thanks to significant cryptocurrency investments. Blockchain is the technology on the basis on which cryptocurrency is based. Many people hear about it and need clarification or think it is a complex technology well beyond their understanding; however, that is untrue.

In simple terms, a blockchain is a database or ledger used to store information. It is also called distributed ledger technology (DLT). A database is data stored on a computer or electronic device that is organized to allow it to be used and viewed easily. Data up until recently was held in the form of databases, but that has changed with the advent of blockchain technology.

In a blockchain, data or information is stored in groups known as blocks. Whenever an alliance with a finite storage capacity becomes full, it gets chained to the previous block. Then, a new partnership is created, creating a long chain of blocks of information stored in that chronological order, known as a blockchain. Each new block is added after its storage fills up, and the chain continues to grow longer and longer.

Blockchains are different from the other traditional forms of databases in that, while other databases store their data as a whole, the data in a blockchain is kept together in smaller units. Another key difference is that blockchains store their information with timestamps, which means we always know when that data was entered into the system. It ensures that the time entry related to data is valid. In effect, a blockchain also acts as a timeline of data.

Another critical component that makes blockchain different is that it is decentralized, which is apparent from its "decentralized ledger technology." While other databases need servers stored in a single place owned and operated by a single party, In contrast, blockchain holds its data over multiple servers known as nodes. This way, any single party does not control the data, and every time a new data entry is made, it is duplicated over all nodes using predetermined algorithms. blockchain

Due to its features that make it an authentic, transparent, and non-editable database, blockchain is slowly being adopted by many companies and governmental organizations.

Blockchain is one of the biggest game-changers the technology sector has seen in the past few years. According to the World Economic

Forum's Future of Jobs report, blockchain will be one of the largest employment generators over the next five years till 2025. Blockchain is predicted to bring a significant change in the way many industries work, such as the Finance Industry, Banking Industry, Retail industry, Supply Chain industry, and even Governmental Administration.

History of Blockchain

The idea of having a decentralized ledger with data stored in blocks has existed for a few decades. However, a developer (or developers) created the first real blockchain with the pseudonym of Satoshi Nakamoto in 2008. The following year, in 2009, Satoshi, for the first time, used Blockchain practically to maintain a public ledger for keeping track of the transactions of Bitcoin. It was then that Bitcoin was invented.

The first use of Bitcoin for a purchase happened in 2010 when a Florida-based man paid 10,000 Bitcoins for two pizzas from Papa John's.

The use of blockchain exclusively as a ledger for storing cryptocurrency transaction details continued until 2014. This is called the first stage of blockchain. After 2014, the second stage of blockchain technology started. During this stage, the uses of blockchain moved past being just for cryptocurrencies. In 2014, Ethereum started creating computer codes that acted as financial instruments called smart contracts. The same year, R3, a group of blockchain companies, was formed to explore the different areas where blockchain can be used.

In 2015, NASDAQ and Chain, a blockchain company, came together to test blockchain to trade shares of a private company. After 2016, companies like Facebook and IBM started working with blockchain technology.

Types of Blockchains

Public Blockchains: These are the most common type of blockchains. As the name suggests, Public blockchains are open to everyone, and anyone can access the data on these kinds of blockchains. Public blockchains are the most transparent form of blockchains. Public blockchains are used to track the transactions of the cryptocurrencies such as Bitcoin and Litecoin. These blockchains are slightly slower than private blockchains since there are more nodes in a public blockchain, and the transaction must be recorded in every node.

Private Blockchains: Private blockchains are the other primary type used blockchains. In a private blockchain, the number of users is restricted. Only the people authorized to have access to the blockchain can see the data on the blockchain and record transactions on the same. Organizations and firms can have private blockchains to store data, with only people from within the organization having access. Private blockchains are much faster than their public counterparts; however, since the entire point of blockchain technology is to have multiple nodes through which verification is confirmed, private blockchains are not considered as secure as public ones.

Hybrid Blockchains: Hybrid blockchains are a mix between a public blockchain and a private blockchain, so they try to have the advantages of both public and private blockchains. In a hybrid Blockchain, some of the data is open to the public, and the rest of the data that may be more delicate can be kept only to be accessed by a select few. This makes the blockchain faster and more secure at the same time.

Federated Blockchains: Federated blockchains are also called Consortium blockchains. They are similar to private blockchains, but instead of one organization, in a federated blockchain, access is given to multiple organizations that are part of a larger body, such as the government.

Critical Components of a Blockchain

To understand how a blockchain works, one must first know what a blockchain is made of. The components of a blockchain are:

Blocks: The blocks are the most basic units of storing information on a blockchain. After each block is full of data, it is connected to the previous block, thereby creating a chain of data that we call a blockchain. Blocks themselves consist of multiple parts. These parts are:

Data: This data has been stored on the block for safekeeping.

Nonce: A 32-bit whole number is generated for every block when creating a new partnership. This nonce then creates the hash.

Hash: The hash is a 256-bit number unique to every block. This hash encrypts the data on a block and connects one block to another in a given blockchain.

Block header: The block header provides us with the metadata related to the block, such as the hash of the previous block, the time stamp, and the nonce.

Transactions: The block contains all of the transactions that have been stored on the block.

Nodes: Nodes refer to the people or servers with whom the blockchain has been shared. A blockchain has no central authority, and data is stored on distributed ledgers. Each of these ledgers has its node. The more the number of nodes in a blockchain, the more secure it is. Since the same data is secured on every node, the hacker will have to access each node and then change their data to hack into it or make a change.

Miners: Miners are the people who are responsible for adding new blocks to a blockchain. To add a new block to a blockchain, one needs to solve a complex mathematical problem; this problem can only be solved by trial and error and hence requires significant computing power. A nonce is a 32-bit number, and the hash is a 256-bit number, so about 4 billion nonce-bit combinations are possible. The process of finding the correct combination is called mining. For undergoing this process, the miners are rewarded in cryptocurrencies.

Principles of Blockchain

Blockchain technology works based on certain principles; these principles are:

Distributed Database: The most basic principle behind blockchains is that the database in a blockchain is not stored in a single location and is spread across various nodes and servers. It means that for a transaction to be entered into a blockchain, it must be entered in every node, making it a very secure form of data storage, albeit a bit slower.

Peer-to-peer Transactions: The transactions and communication in a blockchain happen directly between the peers and nodes and not via a moderator. This ensures a certain amount of trust and transparency between blockchain network users.

Transparency: The transactions stored in a public blockchain are transparent. Anyone can access these transactions, making it harder for people to cheat or defraud others by creating false entries.

Irreversibility: The transaction, once stored on the blockchain, is marked with a timestamp, and it is stored as such. The data, once entered, cannot be changed after that. The entire chain must be mined again to make even a small change on one of the blockchain blocks. This would require massive computing power and would be nearly impossible.

Computational Logic: The data is stored on the blocks in a logical format, so the users don't have to add it manually. They can create algorithms to enter the transactions by themselves.

Cryptography in a Blockchain

A blockchain uses two basic kinds of cryptography: the asymmetric key and the hash function. These two are used at the same time and have different processes.

The asymmetric key means two types of keys are needed to access the blockchain. For every blockchain, there is a public key and a private key. The public key is available to everyone on the network, and it is the same for everyone. However, the private key is unique to every node and is only available to the node owner. In this kind of cryptography, the public encrypts the plain data into cipher text. The node owner then uses the private key to decipher the reader to plain text. Combining the private and public keys creates a signature unique to the node owner.

The hash function is the cryptography used for chaining the blocks to each other. Every block has its hash; at the same time, it also carries the previous block's hash. E.g., block number 21 in a blockchain will have the hash of block number 20, which will chain it to the last block. Meanwhile, block number 22 will have the hash of block number 21; this is how they connect and create a chain. It ensures no new person can create and attach random data to a blockchain. The block's hash is made via the Merkel tree, where every transaction has its hash, which keeps combining until we get a hash for the whole block.

How do the Transactions go Through?

- The process of transactions being recorded on the blockchain goes through the following procedure:

- The transaction is requested by the people who want to purchase a cryptocurrency.

- The transaction is broadcasted via the peer-to-peer network to all the nodes.

- The node owners then validate the transaction on their records
- The node owners are compensated in the form of cryptocurrency.
- The transaction is then recorded on the block that is open at the time being.
- Once they are filled with transactions, the blocks are attached to the blockchain.
- The transaction is completed and timestamped.

Fundamental Properties of Blockchain

Some of the fundamental properties of a blockchain are:

Distributed: One of the most essential features of blockchains is that they have a distributed ledger. They are also called distributed ledger systems for the same reason. It means a blockchain has multiple nodal centers instead of having a single central authority or a central node from where the data is disseminated. The data is hence stored on all these servers at the same time. These various nodes ensure the security of the data since it is nearly impossible to mutate the data on all nodes simultaneously. This also reduces the cost of the database since there is no need to have large servers on which the data is stored, thereby saving the cost of purchasing these servers and the rent of physically holding all these servers in a place.

Immutable: The data in a blockchain is immutable, i.e., the data is permanent in nature, and it can't be mutated. This is so because once the various nodes verify the transaction on a blockchain, it is stored on a block, which is then attached to the chain. To change the data on a block, one needs to have the correct nonce and hash combination, which is one out of four billion and can only be found through the hit and trial method. Further, each block has its hash in the next block, so to change one block, one needs to change the data in every one of the blocks in the chain.

Timestamped: One of the defining features of blockchain technology is that all of the transactions stored on the platform are time-stamped. This means the time and date are also simultaneously attached as soon as the transaction is entered on the block. This ensures that no one can backdate and change the values. It provides us with a record in chronological order. This feature allows us to keep track of all cryptocurrency transactions and ensure that the cryptocurrency is not doubly sold or bought.

Unanimous: The data stored on the blockchain platform is unanimous because everyone on the forum is verified and accepted through all nodes. One of the nodes may carry a different value or transaction, and the other takes an additional weight or a trade. Due to this feature, everyone has access to the same data, reducing the risks of discrepancies and errors in communication.

Anonymous: The transactions recorded on the blockchains do not carry the name or identity of the people involved. Most of these transactions are either anonymous or pseudonymous. This allows people to carry on transactions without associating themselves with it and, to a certain extent, pass various laws and regulations. The transactions cannot be traced back to the people.

Secure: The data history on a blockchain is considered incredibly fast. Since the data is not stored on a single server and the same data is stored on multiple nodes across the network, it is tough for someone to hack into the blockchain network and change the data at every node. In a traditional database, central servers are easy to break into; however, this is not so in a blockchain. Hence, blockchains are much more secure than the usual servers.

Programmable: Blockchain is a programmable data-storing service. This means the data must be manually put into the servers only sometimes. One can set up mathematical and logical algorithms that verify the transactions themselves. It also allows for setting up intelligent contracts over blockchain technology, a feature now increasingly used by blockchain companies such as Ethereum.

What Industries Can Blockchain Revolutionise?

Banking Industry

Banking is one of the biggest industries that blockchain technology will completely transform. Banks, as of right now, keep all of their data on central servers, which are susceptible to data hacks and largescale monetary hacks, which result in losses worth billions of dollars every year. Once the banks start storing their transaction histories on a blockchain, they will be provided additional security. Further, another added advantage for the users or customers of these banks would be that the data would be transparent and accessible to all.

When such data is available to the public, it reduces financial irregularities, and the kind of banking failures that have happened over the years, such as the Lloyd brothers, will not happen again.

Some of the uses of blockchains in banking would be:

- Payments across borders will be much faster.
- Easier loans will be provided through peer-to-peer loans instead of using central banks.
- The clearance systems being used by the banks would be more rapid as well.
- The use of cryptocurrencies as a form of parallel payment system along with fiat currencies.

Government Record-Keeping Sector

The record-keeping industry, especially in the government sector, would benefit heavily from the advent of blockchain technology. Since the data recorded in blockchains are immutable and permanent, along with timestamps, it would ensure that false certificates and records regarding identification, ownership, death, birth, and property transfer are not furnished. This would also make it easier to access these certificates and information.

The transparency of data afforded through blockchain technology would mean that everyone would have the option of looking at this data, and it would not be secretive, meaning that people can easily verify if the government records being provided to them are authentic. This would decrease benefit fraud, and government facilities could be better targeted toward those who need them.

Health Care Sector

Data storage is one of the most significant issues faced by the healthcare sector. There are multiple forms, documents, and records that patients must fill out repeatedly in different hospitals every single time. This issue can be quickly resolved with the use of blockchain technology. Further, this way, all the hospitals can access the older records of their patient's illnesses and injuries from a transparent and authentic open source.

Worldwide, more and more doctors and medical professionals are advocating for universal health care that includes all kinds of information required by doctors from their patients in a digital form. This universal health care can be achieved via the use of blockchain.

Media and Entertainment Sector

The media industry has changed significantly over the past decade with the advent of online media platforms such as Netflix, Amazon Prime, and YouTube. Using blockchain technology in the field, we could better track the payments made to purchase these accounts and further prevent instances where multiple people use it through a single charge.

It will also help the companies in the media field to keep track of their records as to how and when a product, such as a song, film, etc., was released and how the actual reception was, without the tampering that is done by the promoters. Unique views or impressions will be counted via blockchains, not duplicated ones.

Supply Chain Sector

The supply chain is a sector that will be different once blockchain is ultimately adopted and integrated into it. Concerns about the sourcing of products from across the globe have made it necessary for global companies to trace where each product comes from and who its producers are. Consumers have become increasingly conscious about not using products sourced from places employing child labor or violating labor laws. For this purpose, blockchain technology can keep track of such data. Through it, everyone will also have access to it to ensure that the corporation provides the data correctly or not. Blockchain will also enhance the streamlining of the supply chain. Since if a producer can trace the supply chain to the manufacturer of the products, then he may reduce wastage.

Transportation Sector

The transportation sector in itself will be a great benefactor of the adoption of blockchain technology. In the airline sector itself, we see that there are multiple checkpoints at which payments are made, such as the agents, the insurers, the passengers, and the airlines. With blockchain, the costs will be settled much faster, thereby increasing the ease of making bookings. Further, it could increase the efficacy affected by the overbooking process since everyone can see the number of bookings from a single central space.

A blockchain system can be set up that provides a single factor of identification that goes through all the different steps at the time of boarding, reducing the time for the passenger and the travel company. Blockchain will also help lower the redundancies and discrepancies in data collection in the shipping and cargo sectors.

Agricultural Sector

With the addition of blockchain technology to the agriculture sector, we could see a significant change in how logistics is handled. Firstly it would help us ensure that only the best quality crops are being provided to the consumers and that they are healthy. It will also help keep track of where the produce came from in case their quality could be better. One of the most significant issues that farmers face is that their payments at times are delayed, and they need these payments to secure seeds to sow for the next season; without these payments, their season could be affected heavily, with blockchain the prices will become almost instantaneous which would immensely help the farmers.

Retail Sector

The retail sector could use blockchain technology in multiple ways, the major one being to keep track of the stock. This easily accessible data option would allow everyone to see how much inventory is being used and at what rate; this way, the restocking process can be scheduled appropriately, thereby saving the retail company costs of stockpiling.

Further, in the retail sector, it would make it easier for the customers to verify the authenticity and safety of the products offered at the retail store and that they are ethically sourced. Having transparent supply chains visible to suppliers also helps resolve disputes between them and the retailers faster and saves legal costs.

Insurance Sector

In the insurance sector, blockchain applications are trying to increase operational efficiency. One of the significant differences with other sectors is that in this sector, the technology is not aimed at creating new products or services but rather at cutting down costs, increasing the speed of service, and providing better customer service. By having a transparent and permanent record, the industry will also reduce instances of insurance fraud or multiple insurances. At the same time, it is also helpful to the insured parties as it will allow the person to get quicker claims and payouts from the insurance companies, which, if delayed, can significantly impact these people's lives. Smart contracts, an application of blockchain technology, would also help reduce the time and costs of the underwriting processes.

Real Estate Sector

The Real estate sector will get a boost after introducing blockchain technology in its record-keeping and payment processes. In real estate, the trust between the buyer and seller is imperative; the buyer must be assured that the seller is the actual owner of the property and does not have any incumbent interest in it, and the seller must be guaranteed that the buyer is a genuine buyer who will pay him wholly for the said property. This trust is enhanced with blockchain technology's decentralized, transparent data-keeping methods. Further, through safer and faster payment methods, the cost of transferring the property will be significantly reduced, benefiting both parties. Companies like Safewire use blockchain technology to minimize wire fraud prevalent in real estate transactions.

Pharmaceutical Sector

The pharmaceutical sector has fake medicines, expired patents, and long testing periods. Blockchain technology can help resolve most of these issues. Firstly, having an open and transparent ledger would make it easier for consumers to check whether the medicines sold are authentic and have not expired. Further, the high cost of most drugs is because of the patents that have been claimed on them by pharmaceutical companies through blockchains; one could easily keep track of which all patents are expiring soon enough and thus provide a generic version of the same medicine to the consumers at lower prices and consequently save many lives. The testing phase can also be bettered with blockchains as if and when there are errors, they can be caught quickly and then be traced back to the same batch of medicine.

Education Sector

In education, people often provide fake degrees, diplomas, and certificates. This can be checked by ensuring all certificates are on a public blockchain platform. The educational institutions can confirm and verify that the proper authority has issued the provided certificates and belong to the right person. Further, credentials can be lost or damaged, and even carrying them from one place to another is an issue; by having them on a secure and authenticated platform, the students and degree holders can only take them physically, sometimes for authentication. Blockchains would also help the working of libraries, as it helps keep better track of the books being lent and who has which book, allowing even the set up of peer-to-peer libraries.

Stock Trading Sector

Much like how transactions regarding cryptocurrencies are stored on blockchain technology, the whole asset trading sector can completely shift to blockchain technology. This sector is the closest to the crypto industry, for which blockchain technology was primarily created in the first place. Using the transactions that are time-stamped, it is straightforward to find who is the owner of a particular share and if he has already sold it to another person or not. Further, if trading starts through blockchains, the trades will be settled much faster, and the seller can be credited with his money instantly. Through the use of algorithms and smart contracts, it would also become more accessible for stock traders to execute trades by themselves.

Energy Sector

The energy sector has in the past been one of the most centralized sectors, where energy collection and distribution is done through power corporations, private or public, depending on the countries and territories. With blockchain, this could completely change with people moving on from these centralized power producers to acquiring power from decentralized sources, that is, peer-to-peer purchase of power, which reduces the intermediaries and, thus, the cost of energy and production. Also, using this technology, one could find the source of the point they are using, i.e., whether the energy they consume is clean or made with non-renewable sources. Some blockchain companies use energy certificates, which may be sold from one person to another and then redeemed for power. Another way that blockchains can impact the energy sector is the introduction of cryptocurrencies to pay energy bills.

Food And Beverage Sector

Food and beverages typically have a concise shelf life and, if spoilt, can cause many diseases, such as salmonella or diarrhea. Via blockchain, one can track how old a specific food product is, and the consumer can then make an informed decision. The food supply chain can easily be monitored via blockchains. By using smart contracts, companies can also automate the orders for more products, thereby increasing efficiency and decreasing the workload. Also, if an issue arises, it is easier to trace where the raw material came from and where the problem might have occurred.

Election Sector

Elections all over the world, and especially in developing countries, are marred by allegations of voter fraud. Elections would become much more secure once blockchains store the votes. This would happen in various ways. Firstly, when the voters' data is stored on a blockchain, it is transparent so everyone can see who are the voters in a particular area, how many of them have cast their votes. Further, verifying and tracing the vote means one can prove that the voices are not being hacked and changed to help a particular party or person. Also, blockchain companies are working on ways to start casting votes via blockchains themselves. Do we need to remind anyone of the chaos of the 2020 US presidential election?

Auditing Sector

The auditing process will become a lot easier once the data and information of the companies and firms are uploaded on the blockchains. This would make it difficult for the companies to falsify their accounts, and it would show an accurate picture of the monetary state of the companies. Further, it makes it easier to keep track of the purchases and sales made over the year by a firm, and with the time-stamped transactions, it becomes even harder to hide such expenses.

Mining Sector

The mining industry has started adopting blockchains as well. In the mining sector, there are multiple intermediaries. All of them can be brought on the same page quite quickly using this technology, which makes getting the mined product from the mines to the end consumers much more accessible. Further, the consumers can trace their products back to the mines from where they are claimed to be. This ensures that a certain amount of value is attached to the origin of the stone or metal. De Beers, the diamond company, has developed a blockchain solution called Tracr, which traces the source of the diamonds from the mine to the buyer.

Public Assistance

Public assistance, with the application of blockchain, could reduce wastage significantly. This way, the Non-Governmental Organisations and other inter-government bodies can keep track of their assistance funds and verify that the aid's end receiver is the person for whom the support was intended or not. The World Food Programme of the united nations has already adopted blockchain technology for directly sending assistance to needy people by using blockchain authentication. In some countries such as Jordan, World Food Programme has attached the people's biometrics to their blockchain-based accounts; once the person's identity is confirmed, the money received via aid in the said account is automatically detected, thus allowing instant settlement at the grocery stores.

Gambling Industry

The online gambling sector has grown by leaps and bounds; however, the biggest issue is the lack of transparency. This is something that the introduction of blockchain platforms can easily handle, as this would ensure transparency and inculcate trust between the business and the consumers. It removes the adage of "the house always wins" as the ledger stores all the data and is open. Decentralizing betting through blockchain also allows for anonymity which is necessary for numerous gamblers who do not want to disclose their gambling habits.

Ride-Hailing

Ride-hailing companies like Uber and Lyft rule this sector now; however, these companies represent a central authority or a mediator through which the driver is connected to the passenger. With the introduction of companies that use blockchain technologies, companies will offer a direct peer-to-peer network for ride-hailing. This would mean any central authority is not controlling that driver and is free to create his own market space and provide services as he sees fit at their rates. It is also beneficial to the passenger as the cost of the rides will be lower since the intermediaries' commission is removed from the equation. Some blockchain ride-sharing apps, such as arcade city and Drive, are already available. The users can also make payments through cryptocurrencies on these apps.

Charity

How charitable institutions handle donations will also change if they adopt blockchain to track the money in the institution. This way, the donor can follow exactly where the donated money has been utilized and that the institution has not used it for other purposes. This provides transparency in charity which could encourage more people to donate since many do not do it because they think that charitable institutions are corrupt. Various companies are working in this sector, such as Bitgive Foundation, a Bitcoin-based charity, and Givetrack, a blockchain-based donation platform with a permanent record of global charitable transactions. '

Popular Blockchain Companies That Are Already Making An Impact

Since we know that cryptocurrencies are the most crucial blockchain applications, let's discuss the top two cryptos in the world.

Bitcoin - Bitcoin is the original cryptocurrency and the first instrument to use blockchain technology commercially. It was started in 2008. Bitcoin is a peer-to-peer payment network through which you can pay another person without any central bank or authority. Bitcoin uses the blockchain technology underneath it to manage and keep track of the transactions. Bitcoin has popularized the concept of cryptocurrencies among the masses and currently has a market capitalization of around 950 billion dollars.

Ethereum - Ethereum is one of the most famous blockchain companies and is credited with introducing the concept of smart contracts. Ethereum works in the financial services sector, allowing individuals to lend, borrow and save products via the Internet. It also runs ether, the second-largest cryptocurrency by market capitalization. Ethereum lets people conduct operations through its smart contracts.

Other Popular Blockchain Companies

Chorus One: Chorus One is a community of ambitious, self-reflective people building high-reliability infrastructure for decentralized networks. They believe that crypto economics and decentralized networks will enable collaboration on a global scale and propel the next stage in human evolution. Chorus One is building validator nodes and inter-chain communication for decentralized networks, allowing our users to earn more tokens and shape the emerging open financial system. Their work lies at the intersection of financial services and cryptocurrency. Experience the power of proof-of-stake blockchain networks with Chorus One's top-notch validation and staking services.

Chorus One has been awarded a grant by the Celo Foundation and the Interchain Foundation to develop essential building blocks for an Inter-Blockchain Communication (IBC) module. This module will enable seamless communication between the Celo blockchain and other networks built on the Cosmos SDK.

Experience the ultimate blockchain security with our proof-of-stake network, where validators are the key to safeguarding your platform. Blockchain projects seek dependable validators capable of operating validator nodes. Experience the power of staking your funds with our reliable validator nodes. Maximize your rewards as a validator node by increasing your stake and securing the blockchain.

Sciencesoft - Established in 1989, the company serves non-IT enterprises and software product companies and is frequently approached for custom and platform-based development in CRM, Data Analysis, Collaboration & Knowledge Management, and Information Security. The company also offers end-to-end blockchain software and application development. The company serves midsize-large international organizations, including Walmart, IBM, Nestle, eBay, and NASA JPL.

Ripple Labs - Established in 2012, the company works with the existing financial systems of its customers to improve and streamline their infrastructure. The company provides open-source code and developer tools to further the development of blockchain technology and is the only enterprise blockchain company with products for commercial use.

R3: R3 is significant in providing distributed ledger technology to banks worldwide. It recently even partnered with the central bank of Switzerland to settle large cryptocurrency-based transactions between banks.

Pledgecamp: Pledgecamp is a crowdfunding platform. It uses the transaction history and tracing feature of blockchains to allow the backers or investors in crowdfunding projects to see where the money they have put into a project is being spent. On this platform, the money is moved to an escrow account and slowly discharged to the company, and the records are always transparently available to the backers.

Binance: Binance is one of the largest crypto exchanges in the world right now. Cryptocurrencies are not listed on traditional stock exchanges and are only available for purchase and sale through crypto interactions. The crypto exchanges typically charge a small fee for every transaction on their platform.

Zweispace: Zweispace is a Japan-based company that has developed a blockchain-based automatic settlement procedure for wills and inheritance. The deceased's assets are passed on to the beneficiaries automatically on the confirmation of the trustee's death, thus avoiding the lengthy court battles that typically follow a will.

Republic: Republic is an investment platform based on blockchain technology. One can invest in real estate, startups, and even cryptos through this platform. Republic is a secure platform where very particular companies are afforded the option of being listed; hence one can be assured of their investments through Republic.

SALT: SALT is a blockchain platform that works as a bridge between cryptocurrencies and the real world. Users can leverage their crypto assets on SALT to procure loans in fiat currencies. The loanees can take loans for up to a period of 3 years.

Drife: Drife is an Indian ride-hailing app that is currently operational only in the city of Bangalore. It is a blockchain-based app where the drivers and passengers are provided with a peer-to-peer platform on which they can decide the kind of service and price by themselves. This means that the app is not paid a commission for each ride. However, the passenger must pay a yearly fee for the use of the application.

Winding Tree: Winding Tree helps hotels and airlines by providing a decentralized platform for making travel bookings. This reduces the commissions the intermediaries earn and directly connects the customers to the service providers. Winding Tree has already worked with airlines like Lufthansa, Air France, and Air Canada.

Propy: Propy is a blockchain-based company that works in the real estate sector. It uses intelligent contracts created under blockchains to process purchases, sales, and real estate leases. Realtors can use it to streamline their process, making it easier to go through a deal and decreasing the time for each sale. This also helps to give a more customer-friendly experience.

Hashed Health: Hashed Health is one of the most popular blockchain companies working in the health sector. It aims to provide distributed ledgers of records of patients and physicians. One of their projects will allow physicians to produce their licenses showing where they are allowed to practice. They are partnering with healthcare firms to provide distributed ledgers for improved transparency.

Follow My Vote: Follow My Vote is a decentralized application platform that, as the name suggests, has been set up to follow the voice of every voter in a constituency; this provides transparency in the voting process and, at the same time, avoids voter fraud. It can offer services in all kinds of votes, within an organization, in the collegiate system, or even on a larger scale.

Open Bazaar: Open Bazaar is an e-commerce platform based on blockchain technology. Unlike any other e-commerce platform, it acts as a peer-to-peer platform where one can sell anything they wish to sell and pay no fees as there is no central authority. The payments are made through cryptocurrencies, and transactions are recorded on blockchains. These purchases could be for anything ranging from art to everyday products.

Consensys: Consensys is a blockchain software engineering company that provides end-to-end solutions to companies regarding blockchain technology. It has recently teamed up with Microsoft and Moët Hennesy Louis Vuitton to create blockchain software that will help them trace the luxury products produced by the company and its subsidiaries and provide for their authenticity. It also allows the customers to trace their products from design to purchase.

How to choose a Blockchain? (For business owners)

Depending on the needs of a business or an organization, they may choose the blockchain. The decision to select the correct blockchain is dependent on the following factors:

Adaptability: The first factor when adopting blockchain technology to your business is checking whether the blockchain is applicable in your field. Blockchain requires information on servers that are open to everyone, so it might not be suitable for dealing with sensitive data. Further, blockchain is not a cheap technology, at least not yet. Hiring blockchain specialists is expensive and might not be possible for smaller-scale firms.

Scalability refers to the number of transactions handled on a single blockchain platform. If the business requires a large number of transactions, then it may choose a platform accordingly. While some platforms, such as Bitcoin, offer TPS (Transactions per Seconds) of only about 7 TPS, others, like Stellar, can go up to almost 1000 TPS. The scalability of a blockchain is measured on three factors: speed, security, and decentralization.

New vs. Existing: Organisations can decide that their needs require the use of blockchain technologies; they then have to choose whether they want to use an already existing blockchain platform or if they want to create their platform. Developing a new platform can be slightly more costly and time-consuming; however, it would be more personalized to the requirements.

Public vs. Private: There are two significant kinds of blockchain platforms, either private or public. Both public and private networks have advantages and disadvantages; while public networks are more secure, they are slightly slower. Private networks have fewer nodes, so they process transactions much faster, but they need to be more secure since it is easier for hackers to access fewer nodes.

Security: Security is of great concern when considering the blockchain platform, especially for firms dealing with sensitive information. One should look at the peer reviews of the forum they are choosing.

CHAPTER 8

Investing in Cryptocurrencies

The cryptocurrency market has been relatively shorter than other traditional markets. However, it has expanded widely. This is solely because of the features cryptocurrencies have to offer. Bitcoin and every other cryptocurrency are known for their high volatility, giving massive gain opportunities for investors if they can digest the risk.

Cryptocurrency is an online market, and several digital platforms have simplified people to invest in this market. However, comparatively, it is much more complicated than acquiring traditional currencies. If you're new to this domain and willing to invest in cryptos, here's everything you need to know.

Cryptocurrency and Investing - The Basics

There are thousands of cryptocurrencies present market, and figuring out where to put your money becomes intimidating. From a broader perspective, every cryptocurrency is highly encrypted, and most are decentralized. But Bitcoin is the first cryptocurrency most recognized in the market on blockchain technology. Hence, this makes Bitcoin one of the most reliable coins out there.

Many investors are inclined towards investing in only Bitcoin and a few other popular currencies. For instance, people are keen on investing in Ethereum, where they attempt to buy low and sell high, believing it can be the next Bitcoin.

In any cryptocurrency you invest in, there is a common denominator – volatility. A fact with cryptocurrencies is that they have value as long as people comprehend it to have value. Though technically accurate with any currency, cryptos are more significant as they are not backed by the government or precious metals, like other traditional currencies. Therefore, investing in cryptos comes with added risks.

Getting Started

Investing in cryptocurrency means buying them and keeping them stored. So, to invest in cryptocurrency, we need to research where to buy and store the coins. Cryptocurrency exchanges are the places cryptocurrency can be purchased. They are online platforms that allow exchanging coins with fiat currencies or other digital assets.

There are several cryptocurrency exchanges out there on the internet. It is necessary to choose the right one as it is where you will buy, sell, trade, and store digital assets. Some popular crypto exchanges include Coinbase, Gemini, Binance, Kucoin, Kraken, Bybit, and Bitfinex. Apart from being popular, they are the most reliable exchanges available. There are exchanges where you can buy cryptocurrencies like Bitcoin and Ethereum using your bank account or a debit card. These are fiat-to-crypto exchanges, which allow the buying and selling of cryptos using only fiat currencies. In other words, you cannot buy a cryptocurrency with the help of another cryptocurrency.

The best site to research cryptocurrencies and exchanges is https://coinmarketcap.com; if you have yet to go to this site, go there now and set up an account to do some detailed research.

If you live in the US, you must approach one of the exchanges that can convert your USD to Crypto, like Gemini or Coinbase. But they may not support and hold all the Crypto you want to buy and save. Then you might have to use another cryptocurrency exchange that allows cryptocurrency trading with other cryptocurrencies; you have to use an exchange like Kucoin, Kraken, or Binance.

Some exchanges facilitate traders to buy and sell cryptocurrencies for other cryptocurrencies. Technically, you can trade pairs like ETH/BTC and XRP/BTC rather than just BTC/USD or ETH/USD. Thus, you need not involve traditional currencies in buying and selling cryptocurrency.

Besides these two types of exchanges, another type allows participants to buy and sell their cryptocurrencies directly. LocalBitcoins was one of the oldest and most popular portals for direct one-to-one transactions of cryptocurrencies. In early 2023 they stopped providing Bitcoin trading services. The three largest peer-to-peer exchanges have closed, so be careful and never leave your funds on these or any sales. There are other sites, like Paxful, where the sellers set prices, not the exchange. However, this is the least preferred route to buy and invest in cryptocurrencies as it involves direct transactions with a stranger whose currency cannot be verified. So, if you're new to cryptocurrency investing, starting with an exchange like Coinbase is recommended to exchange your USD to ETH or BTC to get started in Crypto.

Another option that's recently getting more prevalent is Bitcoin ATMs. As per sources, there are over 4,000 cryptocurrencies ATM locations in seventy-six countries presently. These can be used to purchase Bitcoin and send it to your cryptocurrency wallet.

The term 'cryptocurrency wallet' is often used when storing coins. And that is because a cryptocurrency wallet is a device or software that allows users to store and retrieve their digital assets. And this wallet represents your portfolio. For instance, when you create an account with Coinbase, you automatically get a software wallet for yourself. If you purchase any cryptocurrency, it will be reflected in your Coinbase wallet. This amount can be used to send to other exchanges for crypto-to-crypto trading.

From the launch of Bitcoin, we have observed a bell curve movement in prices. Initially, it started slow, skyrocketed to $20,000 in 2017, couldn't sustain, and dropped to around $3500. And this represents the volatility of Bitcoin.

So, investing in cryptocurrency is quite different from that of traditional investments. However, the risk analysis can be performed the same way. Like any other investment, you must weigh your potential profits against the risk you are willing to take. Investing in cryptocurrency comes from the type of trader you are. If you are a conservative investor looking to minimize risk and grow profits over time, cryptocurrency might not be the right choice for investment. Conversely, if you can bear the high risk to considerably maximize your earnings, you could try your hand in this market.

Bitcoin and altcoins are markets with inconsistent growth and significant volatility. Thus, 'speculation' goes more accurately with the above description than 'investing.'

How To Invest?

For a beginner just turning to the world of investing, the task behind actually starting to invest might seem daunting, even though it is pretty simple and easy to learn. Since purchasing cryptocurrencies is unlike investing in other assets available on stock exchanges or through your local banks, it takes a different approach. However, doing so only requires a minor procedure the investor can complete in a few steps. By just following these basic steps and complementing them with the necessary research, a person can start his journey into investing in Crypto Currencies. The steps are:

- Preliminary research
- Choosing the crypto-exchange
- Creating an account on the crypto exchange
- Choosing the cryptocurrency
- Placing the order
- Storing your Crypto investment

Preliminary Research

The first step, and one of the most important before making any investment decision, is preliminary research on the prospective assets or investments one will be looking into. This rule holds value in terms of crypto investments as well.

Regarding cryptocurrencies, the prospective investor should look forward to getting information on various topics such as the kind of market that is prevalent right now, the different types of cryptocurrencies that are being offered on the market, the rules and regulations regarding investments in cryptocurrencies, and crypto assets in the countries and territories they are staying in, how much they are willing to invest and finally but most importantly the various kind of risks that are evolved around supporting in this still a burgeoning sector of cryptocurrencies.

It is unnecessary, but a person investing in cryptocurrency should also have a basic knowledge of the technology behind it - Blockchain. Investors should know how Blockchain works and how it secures their crypto transactions. The investor also should be aware of how cryptocurrency mining occurs.

The person should also know what kind of patterns the particular cryptocurrency they plan to buy and the news and information regarding the company that has issued them. Also, knowing what kind of portfolio one wants to create is essential. It is usually intelligent to purchase several different cryptocurrencies to reduce the risk involved in this increasingly volatile market.

Choosing the Crypto-Exchange

The next step toward owning cryptocurrencies is choosing the correct crypto exchange. We know cryptocurrencies are unavailable on regular stock exchanges or through your banks, although some have started offering cryptocurrencies. So, to trade or purchase crypto-currencies, the investor must approach a crypto exchange instead.

Apart from crypto exchanges, it is possible to purchase cryptocurrency through crypto brokers such as Robinhood and SoFi. The decision to choose a crypto broker depends on various factors, such as the authenticity and security of the crypto exchange. These coins are being offered on that particular platform, the fee that the business will be charging, the method of payment that is available on the exchange such as - PayPal, bank transfer, credit card, debit card, and other crypto-currencies, and the user interface (UI) and user experience (UX) of the particular crypto exchange.

Some of the major crypto exchanges in the world are Coinbase And Coinbase Pro, Cash App, Binance, Bisq, eToro, Gemini, and Kraken. One doesn't have to stick to a particular crypto exchange since all the cryptocurrencies one wants to invest in might not be available at a single sale. One can have accounts on various crypto exchanges.

Creating an Account on the Crypto Exchange

After deciding on a crypto exchange, the next logical step is to create your account on the said crypto exchange. A person needs to have a budget to make purchases of various crypto assets and keep track of their previous purchases. Although it depends from platform to platform, one usually must provide proof of their identification to fully set up their account before making any purchases per the various anti-money laundering (AML) and Know Your Customer (KYC) norms. This process is done to reduce the risk of fraud and fulfill the regulatory requirements of the country the person is residing.

Once such formalities are completed, one may be able to sell or buy cryptocurrencies on the crypto exchange. The person might be asked to provide a government-issued ID proof to the business, and since all of this process takes place online, they might even ask for a current photograph to match the details with the documents provided.

Choosing the Cryptocurrency

Choosing cryptocurrency is the most crucial step in purchasing cryptocurrencies and the investment decision. There are hundreds and hundreds of different cryptocurrencies that are available for purchase.

Some of the major cryptocurrencies that are currently being traded around the world are:

- Bitcoin (BTC)
- Ethereum (ETH)
- Polkadot (DOT)
- Cardano (ADA)
- Ripple (XRP)
- Binance Coin (BNB)
- Litecoin (LTC)
- Chainlink (LINK)
- Stellar (XLM)
- Internet Computer (ISP)
- Filecoin (FIL)
- Aave (AAVE)
- Hedera (HBAR)

- Algorand (ALGO)
- Uniswap (UNI)
- Near Protocol (NEAR)
- Crypto Adoption Token (CAT)

One should decide on the cryptocurrency based on various parameters such as:

- One should look at the coin's total market capitalization and cannot accessits supply and circulation. It helps you understand the cryptocurrency's size and a hint towards the stability it might offer.
- High fluctuations in the price of a cryptocurrency are not usually seen as a good sign. One should avoid coins that only climb in value because of one person or company endorsing them.
- It is crucial that before buying a cryptocurrency, you study the persons and companies that have issued the said cryptocurrency. The kind of business the company is in, and the person's reputation can impact the coin's future value.
- The white paper is the plan forward. It is created for every coin, and it contains the purpose of the particular cryptocurrency and the vision for the same. The investor should look at the white paper and compare what has been accomplished to what was promised.
- **Technology:** The underlying technology on which the cryptocurrency is based is also essential; disruptive technologies with a brighter future provide better value in coins, such as the innovative contract technology that Ethereum initiated.

Further, it must be understood that investing in just a single cryptocurrency is not the wisest decision. Hence it is necessary to build a portfolio of various cryptocurrencies based on your needs and what they offer to the investors. Ideally, an investor should have a healthy balance between the riskier but high-yielding coins and the stable but low-yielding coins. Initially, having your portfolio tilted more toward safer options is considered a better option. When one becomes more experienced, one can start investing in riskier coins.

A good portfolio would have the following segments:

- **Store of Value:** Bitcoin, Ethereum
- **Digital currency:** Litecoin, XRP, XLM, dash, etc
- **Distributed applications:** Polkadot, Cardano, Tron, Waves, etc
- **New tech:** ADA, Tezos, Nano
- **Private coins:** Monero, Verge, etc
- **Exchange tokens:** Binance coin, Uniswap, etc
- **Stablecoins:** Tether, DAI, USD coin

A healthy mix of the above shall give the investor an excellent risk-to-yield ratio, which shall be suitable for a long-term investment.

Trading Platforms

There are several places Manage and track your digital wallets, but experience the unparalleled trading experience with Coinigy. https://www.coinigy.com/. The most popular trading platform in the market. Since their inception in 2014, they have experienced steady growth. Experience seamless trading across 45+ exchanges with our top-notch support and advanced trading charts. With 45+ exchanges, Coinigy users have a clear edge over those who don't use the platform.

Charting Tools

Besides CoinMarketCap, you should invest some time with other tools like https://www.tradingview.com. Experience the power of visualizing trading indicators and market trends with our charting tool. Draw trend lines and gain valuable insights into the market like never before. Enhance your technical analysis (TA) skills and stay ahead of the curve by honing your expertise with these trading indicators and trend lines. Maximize your earnings as a TA expert with the help of cutting-edge crypto analytics tools—experience real-time trading charts for cryptocurrency and stocks with Tradingview, a leading company in the industry. Discover the unparalleled expertise of one of the biggest charting providers in the industry. With an extensive range of technical indicators, you'll have everything you need to make informed decisions. Unlock a world of possibilities with our versatile platform offering free and premium features. Discover the preferred cryptocurrency charting tool of top traders: Tradingview.

Market Data

Discover the ultimate go-to platform for checking the latest prices, volume, and supply of coins – Coinmarketcap, https://coinmarketcap.com. Join the millions of users who trust this market-leading site for all their cryptocurrency needs. In addition, their API is highly reliable and can seamlessly integrate with your user interface to retrieve data. Gain a competitive edge by understanding the market's perspective.

Discover a wealth of data beyond Coinmarketcap with Messarios exclusive statistics. Discover the latest trends in the cryptocurrency market with our innovative platform. Explore our comprehensive selection of coins, including those categorized as scams, top gainers, and top losers. Plus, get exclusive access to our advanced market analysis tools, which can predict future market cap in the year 2050. Join us today and stay ahead of the game! Create a personalized dashboard that suits your unique needs! Discover why this site quickly becomes the go-to destination for reliable market data. Please take advantage of the opportunity to check it out! https://messari.io

Calendar Tools

Discover how to buy the rumor and sell the news with CoinMarketCal - the ultimate crypto trading tool. Join the ranks of successful traders who rely on this powerful platform to maximize their profits. Discover the latest and greatest in the world of cryptocurrency with our exceptional calendar, showcasing all the upcoming events across various coins. Discover the power of searching for your very own coin! Maximize your profits by leveraging the power of market speculation. Buy the rumor and sell the news with ease using our platform. https://coinmarketcal.com

Placing the Order

After the investor has decided what cryptocurrency combination they want to invest in, the next step is placing the order on the crypto exchange for the said coin. However, you must first have money to place the order. Depending on the platform, the crypto exchange or the holder shall allow you to transfer money into the narrative through cards, wire transfers, or PayPal.

In some cases, you will need to use other cryptocurrencies to make purchases, in which case, you will have to deposit them into your account. Sometimes it can take a while for the money to be credited into your account, so you must wait before purchasing your choice of cryptocurrencies.

Once the investor has the money in their account, they can place the orders. For placing the order, the person must choose the coin by clicking on its ticker (depending on the user interface), for example, BTC for Bitcoin, and then select the quantity they want to purchase. Most crypto exchanges even allow you to buy a fraction of cryptocurrency, such as Bitcoin, which is too expensive. After completing this, the cryptocurrency is deposited into the holder's account, and the corresponding money is debited. The exchanges and brokers charge a commission or fee for every transaction, depending on the quantum of the trade.

Storing your Crypto Investment

The last step is safely storing the cryptocurrency you have purchased since it is a precious investment. Since most exchanges do not provide much protection to the coins, they can be highly susceptible to hacks and thefts. There have been thefts worth millions of dollars in cryptocurrencies in the past.

For this purpose, one needs to store their crypto investments in crypto wallets. Crypto wallets can be of different types, such as wallets linked to the exchanges, software wallets, hardware wallets, cold wallets, and hot wallets. Depending on their needs, one can choose what kind of wallet they want as different wallets have different features, security, and costs.

Alternate Methods

In case one is skeptical about directly investing in cryptocurrencies through the process mentioned above, it is still possible to invest indirectly in the growth that the crypto world is having. For this, firstly, it is possible to wait for and then invest in Crypto exchange funds, which are linked to the value of a whole exchange. Hence they provide for automatic diversification of your profile. There are no Crypto-ETFs currently, but there are plans to launch some soon.

Another option is to invest in a company that works with cryptocurrencies, such as Nvidia, which creates the processing units essential for mining cryptocurrencies, or PayPal, which has become the go-to payment option for those wanting to purchase and sell their cryptocurrencies.

Crypto Exchanges - What Are They?

One of the few issues one can face while investing in cryptocurrencies is that they are not available on your regular exchanges, and the banks usually do not offer the trade. So for this purpose, the investor needs to create an account on a separate platform dedicated to selling and purchasing cryptocurrencies. These platforms are essential for the trade of these coins. This platform is what we call a crypto exchange.

A crypto exchange is a platform where the people who want to sell their cryptocurrencies and those who wish to purchase cryptocurrencies can meet, and then the deal for the same can occur. Crypto exchanges charge a nominal fee for every purchase, which can vary from business to sale and from one cryptocurrency to another. In effect, they work similarly to the regular currency exchanges.

Different crypto exchanges can have different types of user interfaces and user experiences. Usually, they can be a bit confusing for a novice to understand; hence they also provide a beginner-friendly platform, but it usually charges a higher rate than usual.

On a crypto exchange, the trader or investor must set up an account, and only then can he start purchasing or selling cryptocurrencies. To set up this account, one has to go through the required process and fulfill the various regulations, such as KYC or AML. Once made, the bill functions like any other trading account, where you can store the coins or tokens and then make exchanges with the same.

Payment Options

To make trades on a crypto exchange, one first needs to have funds in his account in business for which one can purchase the cryptocurrencies. You can get money in the report through different methods. Every crypto exchange allows for its payment methods, including Credit cards, debit cards, bank transfers, or PayPal. These methods use traditional fiat currencies for the purchase of cryptocurrencies. Thus you pay an exchange rate that the market has decided, i.e., you can convert your paper currency into a digital currency.

However, some crypto exchanges do not allow fiat currencies to purchase cryptocurrencies. On these exchanges, to buy a cryptocurrency, you need to exchange another cryptocurrency for it. Mostly this means that one has to use the usually common coins such as Bitcoin or Ethereum to buy the otherwise less common cryptocurrencies. The exchange decides the exchange rate for the same based on market forces.

The kind of payment options available on the crypto exchange is essential when deciding which crypto exchange one would choose for their trade.

Types of Crypto Exchanges

As discussed above, the crypto exchange platforms function differently and have additional features. Every crypto exchange has its features, advantages, and disadvantages. The primary type of crypto exchanges are:

Centralized Crypto Exchanges - As the name suggests, a centralized crypto exchange has a central authority figure. This authority acts as a third party between the seller and the buyer of the cryptocurrencies. These third parties are called exchange operators. The centralized crypto exchanges are used more commonly for trades since they are easier to use, and thus, even beginners can easily trade on these exchanges. Further, centralized exchanges also allow one to exchange fiat or traditional currencies for cryptocurrencies. However, since all their data is stored in a single space, they are more susceptible to hacks and data leaks and usually have significantly more regulations to be followed. Some of the common centralized crypto exchanges are Coinbase, Bittrex, and Kraken.

Decentralized Crypto Exchanges - A decentralized crypto exchange is sometimes called a direct trading platform. In this kind of exchange, there are only two parties to a transaction, and no third party overlooks the trades; this system is also called a peer-to-peer exchange. In such a situation, the seller decides the price, not the third party. When cryptocurrencies were created, they aimed to have a decentralized currency system with no central oversight. Hence these exchanges carry the true essence of crypto exchanges. Although they are safer than centralized crypto exchanges since data is not stored in a single space in different servers worldwide, they are harder to use and are not recommended for beginners. Another issue with Decentralised crypto exchanges is that they currently do not allow the purchase of cryptocurrencies with fiat currencies. Some common decentralized crypto exchanges are IDEX, Waves DEX, and Stellar DEX.

Hybrid Crypto Exchanges - Hybrid crypto exchanges have emerged and are said to be the future of crypto trading. They want to get the advantages of centralized and decentralized exchanges and reduce their disadvantages. Qurrex was the first hybrid crypto exchange.

How to Choose a Crypto Exchange?

Choosing the correct crypto exchange is an integral part of the investment decision. The choice can depend on different factors, such as:

- **Coins offered:** The most important thing to check before selecting a crypto exchange is what the business provides all coins. All currencies are not available on all platforms. Hence, going for a venue with more coins is advisable since that would allow one to quickly diversify their portfolio without signing up on multiple crypto exchanges.

- **Fees:** The crypto exchanges vary in the quantum of fees they charge the traders on the platform. Generally, centralized systems charge a higher price than decentralized ones. Similarly, businesses with more straightforward beginner-friendly user interfaces and user experiences charge higher transaction fees marginally. People trading daily are affected by the prices more than those who only purchase the cryptocurrency once as a way to store value.

- **Payment method:** The kind of payment methods offered by the exchanges can also impact the choice of crypto exchange. As already discussed, if one wants to pay for cryptocurrency using a fiat currency, they only have to choose from one of the centralized crypto exchanges. Further, if one only wants to use a specific payment method, such as bank transfers, they must select their crypto exchange accordingly.

- **Type:** As we have seen, there are three different kinds of crypto exchanges; now, choosing the crypto exchange depends on the crypto exchange you want. A person might wish for a decentralized crypto exchange because of its additional security. In contrast, another might wish for an easier-to-use platform on centralized crypto exchanges.

- **Country-based regulations:** Cryptocurrency regulations vary from country to country and territory to territory. Hence there is a possibility that some crypto exchanges do not work in certain regions. So before choosing a crypto exchange, one must see if it complies with their country's regulations.

- **KYC:** The Know Your Customer regulations also depend on crypto exchange to crypto exchange. Some have slightly relaxed rules, while others can be stringent. The person can choose the business based on his privacy concerns.

- **Security:** Researching a crypto exchange's security regulations is essential before choosing it. As we saw during the hack of Mt Gox, one can lose millions if the crypto exchange is itself not secure. Since many people keep their cryptocurrencies in the wallets attached to their accounts on the crypto exchange, they can be at risk.

Cryptocurrency Broker

Understanding the crypto exchange platforms can sometimes take work, especially in the beginning. Hence they can trade via a broker, which is easier to use. These brokers charge nominal brokerage fees for carrying out the investors' transactions. However, it must be considered before using a broker that some brokers do not allow the investor to endure the cryptocurrency out of their wallet with the brokerage firm. This can lead to the risk of a security breach as they are more theft-prone than other wallets, such as cold wallets. Robin Hood and Sifi are currently two of the most common cryptocurrency brokers in the market.

Popular Crypto Exchanges In The Market

Even though there are several crypto exchange platforms available to people, a few common ones are being used by mostly everyone. Some of these common and popular crypto exchanges are :

- **Coinbase:** Coinbase was founded in 2012 and is one of the largest and most used crypto exchanges in the world currently. Coinbase is a regulated, centralized crypto exchange. It has a very easy-to-use interface and is hence recommended to most beginners. However, it has a comparatively higher transaction fee. It also has a platform called Coinbase Earn, where one can earn cryptocurrencies by learning about them through videos.

- **Binance:** This is another viral crypto exchange that runs as Binance.com globally and on Binance.us in the USA. It is a slightly more advanced crypto exchange but charges a lower fee, so people can use it once they are more comfortable in crypto investing. Binance also lets you purchase cryptocurrencies through your debit or credit card. Via Binance, one can easily purchase cryptocurrencies for fiat currencies.

- **Kraken:** Kraken is another one of the early crypto exchanges, and it was set up in 2013. Kraken allows for investors worldwide and is hence more open than some country-specific crypto exchanges. Kraken is known for its good security for crypto wallets. Kraken is also meant for slightly advanced crypto investors.

- **Uniswap:** Uniswap is one of the most popular decentralized crypto exchange platforms. It was set up in 2018. Uniswap provides automated transactions between cryptocurrencies on the Blockchain set up by Ethereum through smart contracts.

- **eToro:** eToro is an advanced trading platform for cryptocurrencies. It even allows you to replicate the strategies of other top traders using a feature called the CopyTrader technology. Further, it also allows you to virtually trade cryptocurrencies to learn the process without investing your own money.

Crypto Investing Strategies

Investing is not just a game of luck, as many people have started to believe now. Investing takes a lot of analytics, decision-making, and asking the right questions. As Ben Graham, the father of value investing, as he is often called, once said, "The individual investor should act consistently as an investor and not as a speculator." So just putting money in a particular coin or currency because it is trendy is not smart investing. To become a better investor, you need to learn the game and start investing with specific ideas and goals; this means you must follow a particular set of strategies. There is, of course, still much leeway within these strategies and individual decisions to make, but they provide you with a guiding path you can follow.

Cost Averaging

This is one of the most commonly used investing strategies. Depending on the currency used, it is sometimes called Dollar Cost Averaging. The main idea behind this strategy is to average the cost of your investment over a more extended period, primarily when investing in a highly volatile market or where the price of the said investment is high.

Under the cost averaging method, the investor does, instead of purchasing all of the investment in one go at a single point, the purchases are spread over time. They can be done every week or every month at the same time. Thereby it reduces the risk of the investment's price falling drastically over a short time, and one is left with cryptocurrencies that were bought at a high price, reducing the possible profits.

For example, If investor A wishes to purchase a cryptocurrency worth 100 dollars and the current price is 10 dollars, then he can buy ten such coins at a go; however, if he invests 40 dollars at first and gets four coins. Then next week, when the price is 11 dollars, he gets 2.7 coins for 30 dollars; the week after that, when the price is 8 dollars, he gets 3.75 coins for 30 dollars. So by the end of three weeks, he has 10.45 coins at 9.56 dollars per coin. So we see that, on average, despite the fluctuations, the cost of each currency is lower than what would have happened had invested all of them in one go. If the price rises significantly, the investor can hold back on the subsequent investments if he wishes to.

HODL

HODL Means HODLing, which is a deliberate misspelling of the word holding, and it was created when an investor on a Bitcoin forum saw the fall in the price of Bitcoin and said, "I am HOLDING." It is easy to understand the concept behind this strategy. This is one of the most straightforward strategies, and most beginners try to use it. It is a way to invest the money you know you won't need for a few years to earn a sleeping income. One should follow the golden rule: Only invest the money you can afford to lose.

The point is to invest in blue-chip cryptocurrencies such as Bitcoin or Ethereum and then leave the investment for at least a few years. This strategy is, in fact, not only limited to just cryptocurrencies; it is generally accepted that holding on to blue-chip stocks gives better long-term results than other volatile riskier investments. The strategy is based on the fact that Blockchain and cryptocurrency are expected to be the next big thing and are still nascent. Even though the market might dip a bit right now, it will only grow over the coming years.

HODLing also lets you earn passive income through yields, which are cryptocurrency dividends. If you stake your cryptocurrencies, you can profit about 5-15% annually. Of course, it includes a certain amount of risk since not all hard wallets allow for staking.

Balanced Portfolio Diversification

Diversification is one of the oldest strategies in the world of investing, and it is equally applicable to crypto investing. As mentioned earlier, portfolio diversification is hedging your risks onto several different cryptocurrencies. If even one fails, you still have profited from other cryptocurrencies to balance the losses. Of course, the reward in this system is slightly lower, but so is the risk.

In a balanced portfolio, the investor puts an equal amount of money into all of his investments; e.g., if he has 500 dollars and is investing in 5 cryptocurrencies, it will be as follows:

1. **Bitcoin -** 100 dollars (20%)
2. **Ethereum -** 100 dollars (20%)
3. **Polkadot -** 100 dollars (20%)
4. **Other ALT -** 100 dollars (20%)
5. **Tether or other Stable Coin-** 100 dollars (20%)

The exact amount is being invested in the different cryptocurrencies. The value being invested is not dependent on the market of the crypto, the prospects of a single currency, or any other kind of research. A beginner can adopt this strategy if he needs to learn more about crypto. This means that if you do not know which cryptocurrency will give you the best gains or which is the riskiest, you invest equally in all of them.

Unbalanced Portfolio Diversification

The strategy of unbalanced portfolio diversification is, in fact, just a slightly more advanced way of diversification. While beginners maintain balanced portfolios, most of the more experienced crypto investors have unbalanced portfolios, which allows them to be much more flexible with their money.

For example, if a person has 500 dollars and he wants to invest in four different coins, then depending on their prospects, he may support as follows:

1. **Bitcoin -** 300 dollars (60%)
2. **Ethereum -** 100 dollars (20%)
3. **Tether or other Stable Coin -** 75 dollars (15%)
4. **Other Alt Coin -** 25 dollars (5%)

In such cases, we usually see that a more significant portion of the portfolio is invested in the more meaningful, more common, and slightly more stable cryptocurrencies such as Bitcoin. This allows the person to have a fixed investment that he can hold and also allows them to play with the market on the more volatile coins to earn faster gains.

Profit Re-Investing

It is generally agreed that one should only invest the money they do not need into crypto, but that might mean that a person who wants to earn more is low on capital. For this purpose, one can re-invest the profit made from previous investments. For example, if A bought three coins at the cost of 50 dollars and then sold them at the price of 450 dollars, then the total profit earned by A is 1200 dollars (400 dollars per coin). Instead of using that money as an income, A can invest the 1200 dollars earned as profit back into crypto. This provides A with additional capital without digging back into its resources.

Profit re-investing might mean limited immediate gains since the money is being returned to the market. Still, it also means that the long-term progress of the investor can grow exponentially.

Golden Cross/Death Cross

The golden cross/death cross strategy is slightly technical and uses statistics. The fundamental values that we need in this strategy are the 50-day moving average and the 200-day moving average of the value of the cryptocurrency over a long time frame. When we juxtapose the two charts over one another, we see two kinds of points, the convergence point, or the golden cross, and the divergence point, or the death cross.

In the convergence point, we see that the 50-day moving average crosses the 200-day moving average, which means there is a buyer's market, and the price in the short term is moving above a long time. Hence one should buy cryptocurrency. In the divergence point, the 50-day moving average goes below the 200-day moving average, which shows that it is a seller's market and the prices are falling below the long-time average, and one should sell his coin.

This method works best in the more volatile markets. Of course, these are not full-proof methods, but they give you a general momentum of the price and whether you should purchase or sell the cryptocurrencies.

These are the various strategies an investor can use to make better investments. The designs are not mutually exclusive, and a person can use multiple systems simultaneously to maximize the gains they can earn over a more extended period.

How To Safely Store Your Cryptocurrencies?

Cryptocurrencies are precious assets, and people can have portfolios worth millions of dollars in cryptocurrencies. Hence, like any other item of value, one must take care of the security of their cryptocurrencies. Cryptocurrencies are susceptible to thefts, fraud, and hacks; one of the largest hacks occurred when around 850,000 Bitcoins, valued at about 45 million then, were stolen from Mt. Gox, a Japan-based crypto exchange. At the time, Mt. Gox was the most significant Bitcoin intermediary. Hence it becomes necessary that instead of trusting the crypto deals unthinkingly, one takes care of the security of their assets by themselves.

When you purchase cryptocurrency on a crypto exchange, you get the coins or tokens; however, they are still on sale, which means that if somehow the exchange was hacked into or, say, your account was deleted by the business, you could lose all of your investment in the blink of an eye. Hence it becomes necessary that instead of trusting the crypto exchanges unthinkingly, one takes care of the security of their assets by themselves. For this purpose, we have Crypto wallets.

What are Crypto Wallets?

Crypto wallets are software or devices where you can securely keep your cryptocurrencies. You can easily track, send and receive cryptocurrencies using crypto wallets. Just like you need a bank account for your fiat currency, you need a crypto wallet for your cryptocurrencies.

Technically speaking, the crypto wallets don't store the cryptocurrency by themselves. Instead, they keep the private and the public keys that enable one to access the blockchains on which the cryptocurrencies are. These keys are essential, and the loss of them can mean the loss of your entire investment.

A public key is part of the wallet that is visible to the public and the other parties of a transaction, and it can be seen as something like your account number or email address. This is what the other party puts in to send the cryptocurrency to you. On the other hand, the private key provides access to the account and is known only to the user or the wallet owner. It is an encrypted alphanumeric code that unlocks the Blockchain.

To make it easier to understand, think of the public key as a box with a slit on it; people can put their suggestions and letters of donations inside the box. However, only the person with the key, or the private key, can open the box to retrieve these objects.

Crypto wallets can also provide other features such as crypto conversion, a list of your crypto transaction, and your current balance of cryptocurrencies, along with storing your public and private keys.

Types of Crypto Wallets

Several different types of wallets are available in the market. Some of the major types are:

- **Hardware Wallet:** A hardware wallet is also called a cold or offline wallet because it is not connected to the internet. Due to its offline nature, it is usually considered a much more secure crypto wallet. Hardware wallets can exist as USB sticks or hard drives attached to the computer. Once you connect them to your industry, you can use the private key to access your cryptocurrencies. Due to their more secure nature, they are generally pricier than their software counterparts. Ledger and Trezor are two of the most common hardware wallets.

- **Software Wallet:** A Software wallet is also called a hot wallet. They don't physically exist. These can further be of different types, such as:

- **Desktop Wallet**: A desktop wallet is an application or software on your laptop or desktop. They can be compatible with different operating systems like Mac or Windows. Some desktop wallets can also be accessed when not connected to the internet. They have a slightly more technical user experience than more straightforward mobile wallets. Exodus and Electrum are considered the leading desktop wallets.

- **Mobile Wallet**: The wallets can be downloaded on your mobile as an application. Different mobiles have different compatible mobile wallets. A mobile wallet allows you to connect to cryptocurrencies through your mobile phone and is thus considered more mobile than desktop wallets. Mobile wallets are also usually easier to use. Exodus mobile app and Atomic mobile app are two commonly used mobile wallets.

- **Online Wallet**: Online wallets exist only on the internet or the cloud. This makes it easier to access them from no matter any computer, which means higher mobility. However, since the private key for the wallet is stored online and secured by a third, these online wallets need to be more secure and can be hacked into. They are only recommended if the person is risk-averse and cannot afford a better, more secure wallet.

- **Paper Wallets:** Paper wallets are nothing but, as the name suggests, just papers with public and private keys printed. The keys can be published in the form of a QR code. They are considered a type of cold wallet since someone cannot access them online. Paper wallets are controversial since they are both secure, as only the paper holder can have the keys, but at the same time, if the paper is itself lost, then the keys can be compromised. Also, if the form is damaged, it can cause many issues. Bitaddress.org, Verge paper wallet generator, and Walletgenerator.net are the frequently used paper wallet generators that one can use.

How to Choose a Crypto Wallet?

As we have seen, there are many different types of crypto wallets, and further, each type has wallets being offered by many other companies. This cannot be very clear to a person. So to better choose the correct crypto wallet, one should look at the following factors:

Price: The price or the cost of the crypt wallet is the first factor to look into. Many online wallets are available on the web for free, but they are less secure; one could get them if one cannot afford a better wallet. Meanwhile, the hardware wallets from companies such as Ledger can cost a bit more, but they are very secure and should be used with some with an extensive portfolio.

Security: Different crypto wallets offer varying amounts of protection. The entire reason behind getting a crypto wallet is to provide a secure gateway to your crypto assets. One should carefully assess the risks associated with the different wallets before selecting one. Hardware wallets generally offer more security than hot wallets; however, some are more secure than others, even between software wallets. If a person is risk-averse, they can purchase a software wallet.

User interface: The user interface is integral to the investor's experience. A beginner usually starts with an easier-to-use crypto wallet before getting more technical. Mobile wallets, just mobile applications, offer the most easy-to-use platforms. Paper wallets are also considered easy to use, especially for those not keen on using digital software.

Flexibility and Compatibility: The compatibility and mobility offered by crypto wallets are also important factors. If one wants to use the wallet on the fly and access it from any computer or device, then an online wallet or even a mobile wallet is recommended. Desktop and hardware wallets are less mobile since the person can only carry them sometimes. A wallet is considered good if it can be used on multiple devices such as phones, desktops, laptops, and operating software like Windows, Mac, Linux, iOS, Android, etc.

Currencies offered: The number of cryptocurrencies the wallet supports must also be considered. If a person plans on having a portfolio containing many different cryptocurrencies, it is best to get a wallet supporting multiple currencies. However, if a person only invests in a single currency, they may get a dedicated wallet only made for that cryptocurrency.

Backup: The backup to a wallet is necessary. There have been instances where one loses their purse due to its corruption and cannot access their crypto assets. This can be a cause of significant concern. Even in the case of backups, there are multiple prices that the wallet creators may charge.

Multisig: Multisig is a new function available on specific crypto wallets. Multisig means that multiple people hold private keys to a particular crypto wallet. To make a transaction, all of the private keys are required. This makes the wallet much more secure since even if one of the private keys gets leaked or hacked, the transaction will still not go through. This is a feature that is ideal for family members and business partners.

Transparency: A wallet provider must be as transparent as the technology to secure the crypto wallets. A transparent open-source-based wallet provider is usually the safest option.

Privacy: The user's privacy is of utmost importance; when choosing the wallet, one should see all the data being asked, especially during the KYC process, and ensure that the crypto wallets do not leak such data.

These are the significant factors that one must consider; however, a person may decide according to their choice depending on their constraints and what they do or do not want in their crypto wallet.

It is also possible to not have a specific cryptocurrency wallet for oneself. Most crypto exchange platforms have their wallets attached to the account; however, they are significantly more risky than a proper cryptocurrency wallet.

Top Crypto Wallets In The Market

Now that we have seen the factors one must consider before deciding on the crypto wallet, let's look at the top crypto wallets available in the market.

Ledger X: Ledger X is the top-of-the-line crypto wallet from the company Ledger. It is a hardware wallet. It can connect with devices through either Bluetooth or USB. It is considered the most secure crypto wallet but has a significant price tag. The user interface is straightforward to use. It can hold multiple cryptocurrencies. Although it is primarily a cold wallet, one can also use the Ledger Live software.

Ledger S: Ledger S is the other cold wallet the French company offers. It comes at a price point that is slightly easier to digest for newer investors than Ledger X. Since it is cheaper, it has certain features, such as Bluetooth connectivity. However, one still has to use the Ledger Live software. It is an affordable yet secure crypto wallet that is suggested for beginners.

Trezor: Trezor is another company that offers hardware or cold wallets. They also have two lines of wallets, the entry-level wallet is called the Trezor One, and the flagship model is called the Trezor Model T. The model T comes with added functionalities and supports more currencies

Exodus: Exodus is one of the most popular online wallets. It is available on almost all operating software. It is easy to use and understand and is recommended for beginners as it is also free. In the early days of cryptocurrency, a different wallet was required for every type of coin in your possession. Exodus has revolutionized the situation. Experience the convenience of accessing over 100 coins with ease, purchasing coins seamlessly, and enjoying the peace of mind that comes with effortless backup functionality. Experience the effortless comfort of our product - it boasts a user-friendly interface and has gained immense popularity. Experience a hassle-free experience by choosing Exodus.

Atomic: Atomic wallet is available on both desktops and mobile devices. It supports over 500 different cryptocurrencies and has a simple user interface.

Electrum: Electrum is another free-to-use online wallet. The wallet is secure and open-sourced, but it only works for Bitcoins.

Verge Paper Wallet Generator: Verge is a cryptocurrency; However, it also provides a paper wallet generator. One needs to visit the site, and they generate a paper wallet, which one can print, fold and keep.

Gaming

Discover a world of possibilities with cryptocurrencies, where you can now earn while enjoying yourself through the innovative play-to-earn gaming model. Experience the buzz of the crypto world's latest hot topic - a concept captivating individuals worldwide with its inclusive, fair, and sound system.

Experience the future of gaming with play-to-earn games powered by blockchain technology. This innovative decentralized ledger system ensures unparalleled fairness and transparency, setting it apart from traditional gaming developers. Experience a revolutionary shift in the gaming industry with play-to-earn games. Thanks to their advanced technological infrastructure, players can now enjoy a new level of ownership and monetization opportunities within gaming economies.

Unlock a world of possibilities with our cutting-edge model that allows players to earn coveted in-game assets such as weapons, armor, and unique characters, all represented by Non-Fungible Tokens (NFTs). Discover the unparalleled value of NFTs - the digital assets that stand out. Unlike other digital assets, each NFT holds a unique information set, making every token one-of-a-kind and irreplaceable. Experience actual ownership of in-game purchases that extends beyond the game's ecosystem, thanks to their storage on the blockchain.

Discover the true essence of ownership in this context. Own your in-game assets and trade, sell, or lease them as you please. Unlock exclusive NFTs through gameplay and trade them on open marketplaces for other digital assets or cryptocurrencies. Each gameplay offers profit potential, making it an enriching experience.

We talked about NFTs and how they integrate well into gaming, but there are more ways to earn with gaming in cryptocurrencies. Experience the thrill of earning rewards in the form of native tokens with many exciting play-to-earn games. Experience the excitement of anticipating rewards while enjoying the direct monetary benefits that can fuel the real-world economy with this exceptional model. Earn native tokens that can be used for in-game purchases or traded on multiple cryptocurrency exchanges for other digital assets.

Experience the thrilling intersection of gaming and digital finance with play-to-earn games. I use my STEPN app every day. It is a move-to-earn app where you buy shoes and then walk, jog, or run to earn coins, tokens, and money. Discover a unique and exciting form of entertainment that provides endless fun and the potential to earn income. With their innovative approach to gaming, players can experience the best of both worlds. With the rapid development of the space and the emergence of new play-to-earn games, early adopters stand to reap the maximum potential benefits.

Discover the immense potential of this model by exploring some of the hottest Play-to-Earn (P2E) projects that are captivating investors and gamers.

Discover the latest and greatest P2E games that take the gaming world by storm. From thrilling adventures to strategic challenges, these games offer endless hours of entertainment and the chance to earn real rewards. Join the millions of players hooked on these exciting games and experience the ultimate gaming experience.

The play-to-earn model in the gaming industry holds great potential, as evidenced by our findings. Experience a new and exciting way to generate wealth while immersing yourself in a constantly evolving platform. Experience the thrilling adventure where gaming meets finance. It's the perfect start to an exciting journey for many.

Experience the thrill of Play-to-Earn games and earn in-game rewards that can be easily converted into cryptocurrency. Experience a new level of gaming with our blockchain-based platform. Earn exclusive non-fungible tokens (NFTs) and in-game assets that can be easily traded or sold on popular online marketplaces. Discover the thrilling world of blockchain gaming with popular titles like Axie Infinity, Decentraland, and The Sandbox.

Game Mining is the innovative approach to earning cryptocurrency tokens by completing tasks or levels. It's like the Play-to-Earn model but with a focus on mining. Experience the thrill of making crypto tokens by playing popular games such as Alien Worlds and RollerCoin. These games allow players to use their tickets within the game ecosystem or trade them on top crypto exchanges.

Unlock exclusive in-game assets like rare items, characters, and even real estate while playing your favorite games. Unlock the potential of your digital assets by representing them as NFTs. Trade or sell them on various platforms and watch your profits soar. Experience this phenomenon in popular games such as CryptoKitties and CryptoPunks.

Unlock the potential of your game development and design skills and earn cryptocurrency by crafting and marketing your very own games or game assets. Blockchain platforms incentivize developers to create on their platforms by providing financial rewards. Enjin offers a cutting-edge platform that empowers developers to design and monetize games and assets on the Ethereum blockchain.

Experience the thrill of Esports and Tournaments! Join the ranks of skilled players in popular games like Fortnite and League of Legends and compete for the chance to win big cryptocurrency prizes. Take advantage of the excitement and rewards of these thrilling competitions. Moreover, specific platforms provide the opportunity to wager using cryptocurrency in Esports competitions, presenting a potentially profitable yet precarious pursuit.

Please keep in mind that although these techniques have the potential to generate profits, they also come with a certain level of risk. Before investing, conduct thorough research and equip yourself to handle any potential outcome. Experience the thrill of gaming and consider any winnings as a bonus.

Book #2

Bitcoin & Blockchain Technology Explained For Beginners

How Bitcoin (BTC), Cryptocurrency (+ Altcoins) & The Blockchain Works & Why They Will Revolutionize Everyone's Life.

Introduction

Imagine a world where money isn't carried around in a wallet. Imagine a world where you can buy and sell things with just a simple tap of a button. Imagine a world where you never have to visit a bank or any other mainstream, traditional financial institution.

Now imagine a world where this new money-making system affects more than just how you spend and save. Imagine that this new world also alters how politics work, how people and customers are treated, and how poor citizens are treated. Imagine a world where money is wholly changed but acts as a domino and soon transforms everything associated with and tied to it.

It might sound like something out of a novel or the pipe dreams of someone who is all too hopeful about the future of our world. But a world like this can exist. We are *this* close to a world like this being the one we live in. We are on the verge of living in a society where we make, save, and spend money differently. While the changes could seem minor to some, they are massive and consequential.

We are also on the verge of a society where the status quo is radically shaken and changed - for the better. For generations, the people who have been considered at the bottom of the totem pole have yet to be treated as well as those at the top. It has resulted in a massive financial disparity between classes and a world where things are unfair. This system favored the rich, who only got richer, over the poor, who stayed poorer. But this newly proposed finance system can do away with a lot of that and create a level playing field. It can genuinely help lift people and keep things even and fair.

Again, these ideas are plausible. They are more than possible. To some, they are actually in development, in the works, and coming soon. Many people think that changing how money is made and spent won't have such a profound effect, but they are wrong. A change that is as seemingly simple as that really can set off a chain reaction that radically transforms the world around us. Not only is it possible, but it's also likely.

What will be the catalyst that does all of this? What is this major missing puzzle piece that has the power to alter the world as we know it? How can it do this? Who is in charge of it? What powers it?

The answer is you. This new financial system's power to revolutionize industries, businesses, and people is in your hands. That's because the key to unlocking all of this is cryptocurrency. And the key to powering cryptocurrency is blockchain. And both cryptocurrency and blockchain are powered by, maintained by, and used by the people. It's not at the whim of major financial institutions like banks, mortgage lenders, and brokerage firms. No, it's used by the people who will benefit from it: regular citizens looking to get in the game and help make it fairer for everyone.

It's very accurate that cryptocurrency and blockchain technologies can change the world. Why is that true? Because it's already happening.

You may not know it, but blockchain and crypto are already transforming how things are done, both big and small. You might not have noticed it, but it's very accurate. All over the world and throughout countless businesses, these two powerful electronic tools of the future are becoming benefits of the present and shaking things up.

Once you understand cryptocurrency and its blockchain engine, you will see how impressive it is. You will also know why investing in, believing in, and using it is so intelligent. You will see that cryptocurrency is about more than just buying and selling products. It's also about way more than trading crypto, like people trade commodities on Wall Street. No, cryptocurrency is about so, so much more than that. It's the largest, most powerful, and possibly most consequential silent protest in the history of the world.

You will also see that blockchain is about so much more than millions of people worldwide "mining" coins to make money off of them. Blockchain is about more than just powering various cryptocurrencies. No, blockchain is about helping businesses and entire massive industries perform better, faster, and safer. Blockchain is about updating and enhancing systems that have been stuck in time and outdated without even knowing it.

You will hear the terms cryptocurrency and blockchain used together often. To some, they are interchangeable. That's because they are so closely linked; they do work hand-in-hand. The truth is that one doesn't exist without the other. But while they are still very majorly linked and used together in all they do, they are also separated and working in great, impressive ways. Both cryptocurrency and blockchain are doing their things and branching out into other parts of the world, no longer forced to walk hand-in-hand across the globe. Seeing how they evolve and grow is fantastic, exciting, and impressive. And it's exciting to know that the sky is the limit for both of them.

It's no exaggeration to say that blockchain and cryptocurrency can change the world - and your life. They really can, and, in some ways, they already are. But you must truly understand how they work before you can comprehend what they have in store for you. You need to know what they are doing, why they are doing it, and *how* they are doing it before you can see the impact that will have on you.

Once you understand all those things, you will see how cryptocurrency and blockchain can help you and revolutionize your life in some radical ways. You can use it to your advantage for investing, spending, saving, and navigating a brand-new financial landscape that is making millions of dollars and improving businesses worldwide.

First, you need to know what cryptocurrency is. More importantly, you need to understand why it came to be. There is a deep, rich history of cryptocurrency and blockchain, even though both are only a bit over a decade old. Let's return to where it all started and find out how it began. More importantly, let's find out *why* it started.

What will be the catalyst that does all of this? What is this major missing puzzle piece that has the power to alter the world as we know it? How can it do this? Who is in charge of it? What powers it?

The answer is you. This new financial system's power to revolutionize industries, businesses, and people is in your hands. That's because the key to unlocking all of this is cryptocurrency. And the key to powering cryptocurrency is blockchain. And both cryptocurrency and blockchain are powered by, maintained by, and used by the people. It's not at the whim of major financial institutions like banks, mortgage lenders, and brokerage firms. No, it's used by the people who will benefit from it: regular citizens looking to get in the game and help make it fairer for everyone.

It's very accurate that cryptocurrency and blockchain technologies can change the world. Why is that true? Because it's already happening. You may not know it, but blockchain and crypto are already transforming how things are done, both big and small. You might not have noticed it, but it's very accurate. All over the world and throughout countless businesses, these two powerful electronic tools of the future are becoming benefits of the present and shaking things up.

Once you understand cryptocurrency and the blockchain engine behind it, you will see just how impressive it is. You will also know why investing in, believing in, and using it is so intelligent. You will see that cryptocurrency is about more than just buying and selling products. It's also about way more than trading crypto, like people trade commodities on Wall Street. No, cryptocurrency is about so, so much more than that. It's the largest, most powerful, and possibly most consequential silent protest in the history of the world.

You will also see that blockchain is about so much more than millions of people worldwide "mining" coins to make money off of them. Blockchain is about more than just powering various cryptocurrencies. No, blockchain is about helping businesses and entire massive industries perform better, faster, and safer. Blockchain is about updating and enhancing systems that have been stuck in time and outdated without even knowing it.

You will hear the terms cryptocurrency and blockchain used together often. To some, they are interchangeable. That's because they are so closely linked; they do work hand-in-hand. The truth is that one doesn't exist without the other. But while they are still very majorly linked and used together in all they do, they are also separated and working in great, impressive ways. Both cryptocurrency and blockchain are doing their things and branching out into other parts of the world, no longer forced to walk hand-in-hand across the globe. Seeing how they evolve and grow is fantastic, exciting, and impressive. And it's exciting to know that the sky is the limit for both of them.

It's no exaggeration to say that blockchain and cryptocurrency can change the world - and your life. They really can, and, in some ways, they already are. But you must truly understand how they work before you can comprehend what they have in store for you. You need to know what they are doing, why they are doing it, and *how* they are doing it before you can see the impact that will have on you.

Once you understand all those things, you will see how cryptocurrency and blockchain can help you and revolutionize your life in some radical ways. You can use it to your advantage for investing, spending, saving, and navigating a brand-new financial landscape that is making millions of dollars and improving businesses worldwide.

First, you need to know what cryptocurrency is. More importantly, you need to understand why it came to be. There is a deep, rich history of cryptocurrency and blockchain, even though both are only a bit over a decade old. Let's return to where it all started and find out how it began. More importantly, let's find out *why* it started.

What is Bitcoin

I don't know what level of experience you have with cryptocurrency or Bitcoin, but maybe we should start this book and end this introduction with a definition of what Bitcoin is... *Bitcoin is the first limited resource that can be confirmed entirely digitally.*

Discover the cryptocurrency world with Bitcoin, the digital currency that utilizes cryptography to ensure top-notch security. Experience the convenience of a purely digital currency with bitcoins. Unlike traditional currencies, bitcoins have no physical form. Instead, they are represented by balances associated with public and private keys, which can be explained as long numbers and letters linked through a sophisticated mathematical encryption algorithm.

The "limited resource" that is Bitcoin has captured the attention of investors and technologically savvy people worldwide. With a hard cap of 21 million bitcoins, the potential for scarcity has driven demand to new heights. Satoshi Nakamoto, the brilliant mind behind Bitcoin, embedded this restriction into the code. Mining new Bitcoins is becoming increasingly challenging and resource-intensive due to the growing number of mined bitcoins. Similarly, Bitcoin's behavior resembles a scarce commodity, like gold and silver.

Discover the seamless process of verifying transactions on the Bitcoin Blockchain, where confirmation is achieved entirely through digital means. Experience the secure and transparent world of Bitcoin transactions. The Network of "miners" tirelessly verifies each transaction through complex mathematical problem-solving. Once verified, the transaction is added to the unalterable Bitcoin blockchain, ensuring security and transparency.

Mining is a fully digital process that enables the Bitcoin network to confirm transactions and prevent duplicate spending without needing a trusted third party. Mining is also the term for the method through which Bitcoins are created. Bitcoin is an unprecedented development since it is an entirely digital, finite resource that utilizes a decentralized verification system.

CHAPTER 1

Cryptocurrency 101 - What is It?

What, how, where, when, and why? You have indeed been told in the past that those are the most important questions to ask when you are trying to figure something out and wrap your head around it and truly understand it. Those are the basic building blocks to genuinely comprehending a subject or event. With those, you will be aware of something.

That is true for cryptocurrency, which has proven very complicated for millions. Just the word alone is enough to scare people away and not entice them to learn more. Scores and scores of people think cryptocurrency is a super-advanced, complex, intimidating system that is too tricky to wrap their heads around. While cryptocurrency is very deep and its strategy is difficult, nothing should scare anyone. Cryptocurrency is simple when you break it down, especially when examining its principles, beliefs, and concepts.

Who? What? Where? When and why? Much of that information about cryptocurrency will reveal itself as we tell its tale, but it is best to start by asking why—the why is so valuable when it comes to cryptocurrency. Unlike many other markets ' assets, cryptocurrency wasn't created simply so people could make millions of dollars.

Initially, cryptocurrency was a way for protesters to speak out. Those in power were being sent a message. The importance of this cannot be overstated. One of the reasons cryptocurrency started - and still does - was the power of its meaning and message. Many people believe in cryptocurrency because it is not just about making money. What it stands for, what it represents, is what they believe in.

Those who created cryptocurrency and championed it from the beginning are unique investors, as you will see when studying cryptocurrency. Their goal is to make a point and have a voice. A message is being sent, and a system is being changed. Making money is one of many goals. In truth, these people started Bitcoin and cryptocurrency for a righteous cause and belief.

Many of these invigorated and committed traders are still involved in the crypto market to this day, which is why it's so crucial that you understand why they made the decisions they did. Since the marketplace they crafted was created in their image, you will be better able to understand them. You can better navigate cryptocurrency once you know what the pioneers thought. Perhaps you even hold the same principles they do.

What is Cryptocurrency?

Here is the million-dollar question that confuses many, even though it is simple and the answer is plain. As easy as it is, you need to master it before you can master anything else, especially since so many people still ask for it even as cryptocurrency takes hold and becomes more and more successful.

So, here is the question that consumes and confuses so many: what is cryptocurrency? How many people have asked that? And how many have been able actually to answer accurately?

It's a digital currency. Doesn't that seem straightforward? Crypto has so much more to offer than that, but that's the main point. Unlike conventional currencies, such as debit cards, credit cards, or cash in your wallet, all cryptocurrencies are digital money that can be spent to buy goods and services. Cryptocurrency can be used to buy anything, despite what some might think. Certain places allow you to purchase plane tickets, home furnishing, food, and even cars with cryptocurrency. When you think of what cryptocurrency can do, look at it as no different from the Dollar, Yen, or any other form of payment you see worldwide.

What sets cryptocurrency apart is two things: how it is held and how it is kept safe. Those are two radically different approaches to money and two of the main reasons why people don't understand it or, worse yet, fear it. When you hear people talk about cryptocurrency, many will talk about its safety. Millions think that cryptocurrency isn't safe, but that's because they don't know how it works. If they were to learn the truth, like you will, they would see that cryptocurrency is far safer than almost any other currency in the world.

But aside from the safety, a prominent attractive selling point about crypto is its nature and how it is stored. This crypto area confuses you; you can't blame people for being in the dark about it. It's a valid question: how do you physically keep your hands on Bitcoin or cryptocurrency? But you don't. Unlike traditional forms of currency, you will never have a Bitcoin in your hands or your wallet. You will never hold cryptocurrency. It does not exist that way. It is purely digital, only living online in every way. For many, that needs to be clarified, something they cannot wrap their heads around. If there is value in cryptocurrency - and there is - how can you not keep it with you and keep it safe that way? How do you pay for goods and services with an item you cannot physically hand over to someone? How does that make any sense? How is their value in things that you cannot see?

But there is value in your credit card transactions. The same is true with your debit card transactions too. When you write a check, no one questions the value of your review. Therefore, when you think about it, it makes sense that cryptocurrency can hold plenty of weight without ever being something you have in your hands. Still, many people need help getting into the idea of cryptocurrency because it will never be something they fold into their wallets or hand to a cashier.

The other radical and different thing about cryptocurrency is how it is kept safe. That is what brings us to the concept of blockchain. Blockchain is a massive, ever-changing online ledger system supporting every cryptocurrency transaction in check. Spread across computers worldwide, the blockchain is a living and breathing thing, a gigantic code that keeps every transaction visible and accountable. It is a wildly different way of keeping track of the world of cryptocurrency, and we will get into it much more later. But rest assured that no matter how complicated and different blockchain is, it is also one of cryptocurrency's most critical and revolutionary aspects and makes it safe and secure.

Far too many people view cryptocurrency as fake money, as something that isn't real and shouldn't be looked at in the same ways as traditional currencies. But that is such a short-sighted way to view it. Is cryptocurrency different? Yes. Does it still have much room to grow before it is as powerful as the dollar? Yes. But does it have just as much potential and promise as any other currency? It sure does. Even though something is new and radically different, it must still be more critical than its peers. There was a time when the television seemed radical, as did the airplane, the internet, and more.

Right now, millions still view cryptocurrency as a bizarre little currency that only a select few people use online. That is wildly inaccurate. Not only do millions of people worldwide invest in and use cryptocurrency, but it is now minor. It has grown so much over the last decade. If people knew how it started and how little value it once had, they would no longer call cryptocurrency little.

Why Cryptocurrency?

Why should I use cryptocurrency? You will hear that question again and again. Even you might be asking yourself. Why should I even read about it, learn about it, or give it a second thought? Why not use the forms of money I am used to, the traditional currencies I have known all my life? Why risk cryptocurrency when I already have it so good with what I have?

These are valid questions and ones that many people will ask. The answer is different for everyone, and there are many legitimate and proper reasons why people dive into crypto. However, the typical response is that cryptocurrency holds more potential, promise, and power than any other form of currency worldwide. It also has value in more ways than one, making it attractive to both people looking to perfect their approach to wealth management and people looking to invest.

Some people buy into cryptocurrency because they believe in its cause and what it stands for. That is why so many people jumped into the crypto world when it first launched. It was a form of protest, saying something and taking a stand. Other people use cryptocurrency because they think it has the chance to be the future currency. They see when people can walk into their corner store and pay with their crypto wallet instead of traditional money. Then others invest in crypto because they want to ride the market and make a profit. Like the stock market, some people buy into cryptocurrency to ride the market's wave, cash out at the right time, and walk away with more money than when they started. It's a wise investment, as made evident by the millions of people who have made lots of money off it.

For these reasons, modern cryptocurrencies should be considered a currency and a commodity. That means it is something you can spend, like cash, and invest and trade in. Essentially if you own any cryptocurrency, you are holding stock in that crypto. The market that it's a part of has proven, again and again, that it can create significant gains for those involved.

Unlike so many other assets and industries, there are so many reasons why people should get into cryptocurrency. There is more than one solid, definitive reason but dozens and dozens. Each is valid, can stand independently, and is enough to sway even the most cautious and uncertain investor. Cryptocurrency has many different possible uses and so many attractive features, and so many exciting aspects that the reasons why are countless and seemingly constantly growing.

The truth is that investing in *anything* is a risk. Investing in something as common and useful as milk could still be risky because you cannot control the world around you or prevent other investors or the market. If you are looking for something risk-free, investing in crypto - or anything - isn't for you.

But beginning a cryptocurrency journey isn't about abandoning traditional money. It is about expanding your abilities and financial horizons. It is about being ahead of the curve and realizing that industries can and will change. The future will catch up with us; it always has. There have been many examples of something we thought was steadfast and eternal changing. People never thought anyone would see a motion picture because the radio was the preferred method of entertainment. Then theaters became a massive entertainment enterprise. Then people thought that no one would stream movies from home because they preferred theaters, and using so much bandwidth was unreliable and expensive. Now entire movie studios pour their films at home before they even hit theaters. This is just one example of how times change. Accepting and understanding cryptocurrency is about your desire to be a part of what is ahead. It isn't about abandoning or getting rid of traditional currencies. It's about saying there can be more options for everyone - and you want a part of that.

You certainly have to be careful when you begin using cryptocurrency. Just like physical money, it can evaporate when careless and reckless. But using it successfully and smartly can lead to expanding your wealth tenfold. It can also ween you off the traditional banking methods and schemes that have helped and hurt many more.

Cryptocurrencies exist solely in a safe digital environment thanks to cutting-edge technology. Your finances will stay secure and off-limits to unruly hackers, greedy governments, and money-hungry banks. Thanks to robust and reliable encryption, fraud and interference are not a part of the cryptocurrency system. Cryptocurrency provides a safe, anonymous, and completely personalized financial system that is modern and completely digital. It feels like the future wave because it *is* the coming wave.

Cryptocurrency and blockchain have existed for over ten years, still shrouded in mystery and confusion. Even those who think they know it best really do not. And those who know little are fed misinformation or false facts. This book seeks to change so everyone, from a new investor to an old pro, understands Bitcoin and how it can change the world.

Does Cryptocurrency Have Potential?

Cryptocurrency causes more confusion than any other word in the modern age. People hear and see the word constantly, in the media and even among friends and family. Yet, nearly every time it is mentioned, it is met with multiple questions and utter suspicion. Even as cryptocurrency has become more popular over the years, the confusion has reigned even harder and has been more challenging to escape.

That's a shame because few products of the 21st century have more potential and promise than cryptocurrency. Indeed, the people who have paid close attention to the cryptocurrency industry have seen significant growth. It has been growth that needs to be consistent, of course. No one is going to argue that. But it has been growth that has led to terrific financial success and stability for many people. It is also the sort of potential that has invited people new to investing and those who have, until now, never put their money into any market.

Additionally, cryptocurrency has been a great disruptor. More than anything, cryptocurrency has sent a message to many who have long been a part of the investing world. Cryptocurrency has sent a shot across the bow, shaken things up, and shown the young and old world that the status quo doesn't have to be the only way things are. Things can change, and items can be altered, even after generations.

Cryptocurrency has been more than a way for people to make millions of dollars. It has been a way to show the world the potential of technology and new ways of thinking. Make no mistake: cryptocurrency has been more than an asset trading on a radically free market. It has been a message, a silent protest that has still spoken loudly. Anyone who doesn't recognize that ignores cryptocurrency's general concept and ideals.

You would think something as promising and groundbreaking as cryptocurrency would have nothing but fans worldwide. Yet that is not the case. People need help understanding it. Even the most studied and well-versed traders have basic questions. Yes, even those who have studied Wall Street for decades and have made vast fortunes investing, buying, selling, and trading can't even really express what cryptocurrency is.

There are so many legions and legions of people, both professional and not, who need to learn how crypto works, why it works, and what it is about. Confusion reigns, and so does mindless speculation, rumor, and suspicion. Many see cryptocurrency as a fluke, something that isn't real, or some major scam that will steal your money like a pyramid scheme. Indeed, even though the opinions are based on factually incorrect assumptions and a lack of knowledge and research, nearly every belief about cryptocurrency is firm and set in its way.

Despite what people say, cryptocurrency isn't a shady scam created by criminals looking to use the internet to line their pocketbooks or do something horrible. That couldn't be further from the truth. The truth is much more exciting for anyone willing to put money into the market. The truth is that cryptocurrency is one of the best ways to invest, a thoughtful approach to entering a market that is still young and fresh and needs to be adequately valued by many. While scores of people need help understanding cryptocurrency accurately, that is okay for those looking to make money. That is a benefit to you if you are looking to become an active and successful cryptocurrency trader. The more knowledge you have about cryptocurrency, the more power you have. Once you truly understand how it works, why it works, and how it may work in the future, the better your chances to make much money.

You would have been laughed away by experts a decade ago if you asked them whether to invest in a virtual currency. Now, things have turned around. The digitally-coded currency, cryptocurrency, is undisputed and known as the next frontier in the global financial order. Cryptocurrencies will continue to thrive and exist for a very long time because there are over 5000 types in circulation.

Cryptocurrencies are regarded as the most profitable assets within the realm of investments. Cryptocurrency has gradually taken over as the top choice for investors to store their capital, even though it began as a decentralized alternative to the conventional financial system driven by fiat money. Cryptocurrencies such as Bitcoin and Ethereum have established a good reputation. For a currency to be robust, its supply, functionality, security protocol, and acceptability must be in place. One can assess whether cryptocurrency is a good investment by looking into these aspects.

Yes, cryptocurrency has much potential. Some argue that it has more potential than most traditional forms of currency. That is because of what it stands for, its functionality and how it can perform, and the system built to power and protect it.

Yes, the engine behind cryptocurrency is one of the biggest reasons people believe in and invest in cryptocurrency. That engine creates and maintains checks and balances like a well-oiled machine. And that engine, like cryptocurrency itself, is powered by and for the people. The people who use and believe in cryptocurrency are the same people who keep an eye on it and ensure everything is performing smoothly and just like it should.

A significant part of the engine behind cryptocurrency is something called blockchain. In some ways, blockchain is more complicated than cryptocurrency itself. Indeed, it's impossible to deny that blockchain is a massive system that runs like a living and breathing organism that never sleeps and never rests. There are many moving parts - millions of them. However, like cryptocurrency, blockchain's basic premise and concepts aren't that hard to understand. And once you do grasp them and truly see how and why they work, it will open up avenues of investment, saving, and trading that can make you a small fortune.

But blockchain is about more than that, which is precisely why it has so much potential. From healthcare companies to automation to elections to transportation, shipping, and more, blockchain is finding ways to touch upon industries all over the globe. Blockchain is proving what it can do - and how it can alter entire businesses with ease and efficiency. For that reason and many others, blockchain has more potential than can be summarized. It does have the power to change the world ultimately.

CHAPTER 2

The History of Cryptocurrency

How Did It Start?

Cryptocurrency - and the blockchain system that powers it - has come a long way since it was conceived many years ago. Like all of the greatest inventions of the 21st century and before, these two things started as thoughts, ideas that seemed unachievable but carried great promise from the very beginning. It was later refined, crafted, and created before being put into action. But where did they come from? Why were they made? And why have they always been thought of as revolutionary and radical thoughts and ideas since the beginning?

Desperate times call for desperate measures. If you were alive during the early-to-mid 2000s, you know just how desperate those times were. Sure enough, the chaotic and troubling age of the late 2000s called for the creation of cryptocurrency after years and years of just speculating about it. The status quo had reached a point that was no longer safe or stable, and people were looking to shake it up in some significant, startling ways. That shake-up would lead to the actual implementation of cryptocurrency. In short, it would change the world.

It is essential to remember where things stood economically during that time. Every action is a reaction. The inception of Bitcoin, altcoins, the trading market, and all of the cryptocurrency was a reaction to a system going wildly off the rails.

The US and global economies boomed in the 1990s. The stock market rose, millions of jobs were created, and the internet changed money-making and spending. Millions were happiest. The economy boomed after the late 1980s and early 1990s recession. For the first time in generations, 2000 was exciting and hopeful.

In 2000, many people's finances improved. Global trade was increasing, banks were freed from numerous financial rules that limited their capacity to lend, and the Internet was becoming solid and new. No significant conflicts allowed oil and trade between multiple superpowers.

The internet has grown constantly. Websites grew overnight. Amazon and Google started well. They have redefined reality. Many couldn't imagine life before such sites.

Internet success helped several major companies. Things escalated. Good things end. After a few years, the dot-com bubble crashed, and many promising sites failed. Early internet businesses evaluated every idea. Many continue. Many perished. Investors stunned. Even in good times, the market was kind to only some companies. Lows follow highs. Goodness fades.

Homeowners and loan applicants prospered as the internet faltered—years of bank loan difficulties. You required good credit. Due to solid government constraints, US banks must make intelligent decisions with limited lending. Banks battled with 1980s excess. These restrictions prohibited millions of Americans from getting their dream homes. With capital, a bank would accept them.

The early 2000s were different. Washington, DC, made life easier for lenders and bank loan applicants across multiple administrations.

Conservative Americans changed regulations. Structures disappeared ten years ago. The new mindset encouraged rule-breaking and unrestrained enterprise. After years of adjusting, bank lending standards eased in the late 90s and early 00s. Many banks had complete control over lending and amounts. In a significant legislative change, anyone might find a home. Banks lent to many previously unaffordable people. Banks now discounted and repaid hostile credit clients. Nationwide, under-$30,000 buyers bought two-bedroom dwellings.

The cause? Because old rules were removed. Banks have more freedom to boost the economy. Banks signed billions in loans and leases. Americans bought homes and spent to profit. They were still expanding.

Banks profited from mortgages and borrowers in new ways while making more money. Debt benefited them. They sold mortgage debts to other banks when clients defaulted. Banks bought debts. One bank would buy client debt, knowing the consumer or third party would pay it. Debt-buying banks gain anyway. Lending and buying receivables made banks money.

It was an intelligent system that made banks and loan companies unlimited money from others' sorrow. New homeowners' hardship benefited banks. The system collapsed. The corrupted and connected system did it in.

Millions received fraudulent loans and mortgages. Why not? Banks won. They might collect mortgage payments or sell faulty lending and debt to other banks for profit. More chickens returned than expected. New homeowners who couldn't afford their mortgages kept defaulting. Many owed. Late millions due trillions.

The banks lost money since they quickly sold these debts to various financial institutions. Many couldn't pay, and mortgage-based funding needed to be more adequate. Debt sales fell short. Worse, banks and financial institutions buying those debts also suffered. They bought lender debt expecting payment. Bad lenders and borrowers should have paid. Banks lost money.

A financial web exchanged consumer debts. Banks worldwide collaborated, so the idea of one failing was unthinkable. Why so unlikely? Because this had been done for millennia, and if one component of this web disappeared, others would too. Dominoes would crash the financial world—network outage. Greed and money-making have established a community. The single ship sank the fleet. An apocalyptic collapse seemed unfathomable.

Unchecked, it crumbled. The housing bubble burst catastrophically. Homebuyers stopped. Banks and mortgage companies went bankrupt, lending to everyone. After debts, they had nothing. Bad loans and debt purchases cost billions. They couldn't wait. Big banks and companies needed to collect.

This was a series of economic tremors that kept coming. Weekly, monthly. Bad financial news piled up, harming the US and global economies. A thousand cuts killed the American economy. They continued. All fell. Things worsened.

Wall Street's biggest names were ensnared in this enormous disaster after trading debt like a commodity. Wall Street Titans struggled. All connected. Banks, brokerages, mortgage lenders, etc. Everyone died instantly.

Loans stopped, affecting more businesses worldwide. Business stops without money. Banks needed to be more vital to lend or take risks. After banks stopped financing, companies worldwide cut spending, hours, and staff. All froze. Many successful enterprises failed because banks wouldn't lend them money. During an exceptional recession, some big corporations sacked employees at an alarming rate. Money disappeared. No one could borrow, lend, work, or depend on banks.

Media and the economy wreaked havoc daily. In the fall of 2008, a major retailer, bank, or corporation failed daily. Each story was wrecked. Some decades-old brands closed and laid off workers. Unemployment skyrocketed. Many American cities featured tent villages as families were evicted at alarming rates. Influential individuals looked afraid. The same bureaucrats who had relaxed limitations and permitted banks to change laws for their benefit were now fixing everything. Historians witnessed the 1920s Great Depression began. Only this crisis might worsen things beyond that historic low.

Understandable global and American fury. Most people were innocent. Therefore, they felt cheated. Most avoided problematic loans and expensive residences. Most worked and saved. Meanwhile, influential banks and politicians modified the system to generate more money—an unprecedented economic collapse. Most people followed the rules, but the plan was rigged, and its crooked laws put people in dangerous situations.

Political conditions should be known to non-attendees. Banks and other financial institutions fell, the economy crumbled, and worry and uncertainty loomed throughout the most excellent American presidential election history. The election cost millions before Wall Street and Main Street crashed. The two leading candidates, Arizona Senator John McCain and Illinois Senator Barack Obama were trying to adapt to this new reality and prove they could restore the economy and instability. George W. Bush cautioned the November 2008 winner of a unique problem. Long-term crisis. It survived the new presidency.

His composure and dedication helped Senator Obama win a landslide victory in November 2008. This historic candidate faced decades-long storms. The president later predicted a deeper economic downturn and shortages not seen since the 1930s. Obama's optimism didn't help.

In 2008, more unmatched institutions failed. CEOs and Washington power brokers' incompetence and shadiness broke these massive corporations. Many other businesses would follow if they failed, destroying the economy for decades. The spider web was unraveling, the dominoes were falling, and the US government had a choice: let them all collapse and wreck the global economy, reducing the US into a third-world country overnight, or keep these businesses propped up with American tax dollars. The government chose the latter in one of the most controversial American moments.

Many were unhappy that the government bailed out big banks, lenders, and Wall Street titans. Most Americans realized that the world would have entered a dark financial age if nothing were done, yet many were dissatisfied with Congress and the president's choice. Why support Wall Street when Main Street suffers more? Why were bankers and lenders hired while others waited in unemployment lines? Betrayed, approval ratings dropped. These enormous firms breached the regulations and got away with gluttonous, greedy deeds, yet they were paid abundantly while struggling workers lost their jobs for something they didn't do.

No one was convicted. The economy revived after millions of jobs and businesses closed. Wall Street and big banks were exempt. Congress called witnesses, and some lost high-paying careers, but nothing changed. They were breaking the rules. Hedge fund managers and CEOs flaunted their wealth and lawlessness while making millions. No judges or juries saw them. They got off. The corruption that produced the most significant recession since the 1930s was still present.

The Great Recession raised questions. Many discussed our system. System creators profited. Why? Why did citizens need authorities? Profiting how? Millionaires benefitting from homebuyers' pain? Why wasn't anyone safeguarding the tiny family promised a mortgage by a bank that knew they shouldn't? How did the system become so corrupt? The chaos caused a financial catastrophe. Worst hit? US citizen. Criminals exploited them. Criminals ran Wall Street and banks. As indicated, the crooks didn't care and kept power as the average American struggled.

Millions raged. Washington's politics and system were detested. Corruption increased. Many witnessed unpunished crimes but felt helpless. How do you change a vast, embedded system? They couldn't leave. They rejected a financial plan that rewarded the undeserving.

They'd escape how? Alternatives to American and global banks were impossible. The establishment seemed to have the upper hand against innovation. Restarting looked hard. It was like acquiring a DMV license to use a different currency. Nobody knew how.

Suddenly, ideas that had existed in the deepest reaches of the internet for ages took on new life and had new interest shined on them. There had been talking of an alternative to traditional currency and the system that used it, this talk had existed for years and years, but it never amounted to more than gossip and speculation, the sort of thing message boards online specialized in. In certain internet circles, people had spoken and written about an all-digital form of money that would only be used online. It wouldn't be printed; it couldn't be held. It would break free from the powerful, restrictive, corrupt system that caused many problems. It would be a currency that was for the people, by the people. If someone could figure out how to create and implement a system like this, they could introduce millions to a whole new way to make, save, spend, and buy.

But how could that be done? How could anyone create a system of an all-digital currency? How could anyone monitor it and ensure it wasn't taken advantage of and misused? No one was under the impression that only the rich and powerful on Wall Street were the ones who could grow corrupt. Great power and wealth create a desire for more, often leading to people breaking the rules, breaking the law, and doing everything to advance their means.

It was plain that an all-digital currency would be worthwhile if it could be practical. Yet, despite all the talk of this online currency, no one knew how to create and make it work. All the presented options relied upon old institutions many were trying to move away from, such as banks and the government. Those who proposed a digital currency didn't want anything to do with those powers, so they created this idea in the first place.

Then, in 2008, everything changed when one man, or a group of people, proposed what would become Bitcoin. With just some simple keystrokes and a few new ideas, fantasy became a reality that has changed our world for the better.

The Birth of Bitcoin

The concept of a digital currency has been talked about before by many different people all over the internet. However, the central ideas that would eventually transform into Bitcoin and cryptocurrency were introduced on October 31, 2008, days before the presidential election and amid the Great Recession. These thoughts and solid plans were submitted by a person or group named Satoshi Nakamoto. You may be asking yourself, who is Satoshi Nakamoto? The simple answer is that no one knows. Since Nakamoto would never reveal their or their identity, the name remains shrouded in true mystery. One person or group could use a single word to produce their content. Many assume that Satoshi Nakamoto was a pseudonym used by individuals who shared the single, strong idea to overhaul the banking system with the working concept of cryptocurrency. It doesn't matter who Nakamoto was because the thoughts they created speak louder than an identity; they are far more significant than just one person or one name.

Nakamoto started a movement with just the click of his mouse. He created a post on a cryptography mailing list called "Bitcoin P2P e-cash paper." The title was bland, but the information therein was revolutionary. A link took readers to a paper called "Bitcoin: A Peer-to-Peer Electronic Cash System." That substantial paper laid out the plans and the functionality of what would become Bitcoin. Unlike many other online debates, Nakamoto's paper was written with original, thought-out concepts mixed with hard facts. It poses questions - and answers - that hadn't been heard or thought of before. It wasn't just some out-of-this-world idea; it showed how cryptocurrency could be implemented, monitored, and run safely and effectively. To those who had spoken of this vague idea of cryptocurrency for a long time, Nakamoto's paper was akin to the creation of the wheel or the discovery of fire.

Nakamoto's plan was based on a series of "coins" or "tokens." These coins could be sent across the network from user to user without employing a single administrator to keep tabs on them. No banks, governments, or financial powerhouses run or use the system to their advantage.

The paper also brought another brand new concept to the table, one that changed everything: blockchain. To make this radical, all-digital system work, the system would need some all-digital ledger to keep things in line. Without banks doing the paperwork, there stood a chance that people could game the system or otherwise not keep track of who was sending whom money and how much that money was worth. It had been done before with traditional currency; why wouldn't it happen with Bitcoin if it wasn't kept in check?

That led to the inclusion of blockchain. Like a hard-bound paper book you would find in a bank, blockchain is an online ledger used across an entire network of computers participating in the system. It is not owned or run by one group or person. Instead, blockchain runs itself and constantly updates all transactions' history. It is impossible to be tampered with and is a safe, secure, and anonymous way for the cryptocurrency world to keep moving. Everyone who participates owns the blockchain, which is spread worldwide, making it safer than one centralized history of all the Bitcoin transactions.

Blockchain was almost as revolutionary as Bitcoin and cryptocurrency itself. It was a new technology, a way to tie transactions together and turn them into a series of blocks. The way that every transaction is secured together (hence the word "chain") means that if you change one trade, you change them all. That means you cannot modify any block without altering the rest of the chain. This is terrible news for anyone trying to hack or tweak the system for their advantage. Essentially all Bitcoin users expand upon an incredibly long line of code every time they make a transaction. Every piece of the chain, known as hashes, relies on one another; they are all linked in ways that cannot be pulled apart. They work together in a way that makes them more secure and impossible to be tweaked after the fact. It is one long chain and cannot exist without another. Each chain piece is shared; every computer with the blockchain code has *all* of it.

As stated, the blockchain is not stored in one central location, like a vault in a bank. Instead, it is distributed among all the users of the system. Everyone has a copy of this blockchain and spreads and refreshes it whenever a new transaction is added to the network. Instead of one bank vault, think of it as millions of lockers applying worldwide. But unless you can access all of them unnoticed and simultaneously, none will be worth it. The web of computers running the blockchain made it nearly impossible to be hacked or toyed with.

Blockchain is a reliable and safe way of recording any transactions. It does away with the need for external authority, which is one of the reasons why so many people were attracted to the idea. Bitcoin users did not need to report to a third party every time they made a transaction. Instead, they relied upon the ever-evolving blockchain and other Bitcoin users to keep everything robust, healthy, and safe. This concept was new and revolutionary, taking the idea of cryptocurrency and making it realistic and even possible. With these secure checkpoints, the cryptocurrency could be established and flourish.

Blockchain was the missing puzzle piece that tied everything together and took Bitcoin into a realm previously possible cryptocurrencies never achieved. A plan and a real cryptocurrency with a blueprint for success could now be followed. Blockchain did away with the worries that cryptocurrency would be unregulated and completely unsafe; it was no longer considered a Wild West landscape for the modern age. Instead, it was now safer than traditional money. If implemented, this plan would rely upon the people using Bitcoin. They would be the enforcers, the vanguards, the safety that kept the entire system honest and robust. This was a brilliant idea, turning the champions and most significant fans of cryptocurrency into the guardians and protectors of it. Who better than them to run things and ensure everything went smoothly and safely? These people had the most skin in the game; it only made sense that they were the most involved.

Nakamoto's concepts of Bitcoin, especially the inclusion of blockchain, made many people all over the globe excited. Finally, written in precise detail and understandable language, was the definitive idea that so many people had rallied behind for years: the premise of a digitized currency that was for the people and by the people and did not rely on banks. The safety installed by blockchain made the belief even more tantalizing for so many. Digital currency proponents would finally have a strong, tested concept that could stand independently. They took to the critics and showed them that not only was cryptocurrency safe, but it was also possible.

And then, Bitcoin was born, and cryptocurrency was introduced to the world. On January 3, 2009, the Bitcoin network officially started when Nakamoto created, or "mined," the first block of Bitcoin, block 0. Australian programmer Hal Finley was the first person to receive any bitcoins. He downloaded the Bitcoin software on the first day and received ten bitcoins from Nakamoto for his troubles. That transaction, which occurred on January 12, 2009, was the first Bitcoin transaction ever. Little did the parties involved know just how historic that moment was.

As stated, the blockchain is not stored in one central location, like a vault in a bank. Instead, it is distributed among all the users of the system. Everyone has a copy of this blockchain and spreads and refreshes it whenever a new transaction is added to the network. Instead of one bank vault, think of it as millions of lockers applying worldwide. But unless you can access all of them unnoticed and simultaneously, none will be worth it. The web of computers running the blockchain made it nearly impossible to be hacked or toyed with.

Blockchain is a reliable and safe way of recording any transactions. It does away with the need for external authority, which is one of the reasons why so many people were attracted to the idea. Bitcoin users did not need to report to a third party every time they made a transaction. Instead, they relied upon the ever-evolving blockchain and other Bitcoin users to keep everything robust, healthy, and safe. This concept was new and revolutionary, taking the idea of cryptocurrency and making it realistic and even possible. With these secure checkpoints in place, cryptocurrency could be established and flourish.

Blockchain was the missing puzzle piece that tied everything together and took Bitcoin into a realm previously possible cryptocurrencies never achieved. A plan and a real cryptocurrency with a blueprint for success could now be followed. Blockchain did away with the worries that cryptocurrency would be unregulated and completely unsafe; it was no longer considered a Wild West landscape for the modern age. Instead, it was now safer than traditional money. If implemented, this plan would rely upon the people using Bitcoin. They would be the enforcers, the vanguards, the safety that kept the entire system honest and robust. This was a brilliant idea, turning the champions and most significant fans of cryptocurrency into the guardians and protectors of it. Who better than them to run things and ensure everything went smoothly and safely? These people had the most skin in the game; it only made sense that they were the most involved.

Nakamoto's concepts of Bitcoin, especially the inclusion of blockchain, made many people all over the globe excited. Finally, written in precise detail and understandable language, was the definitive idea that so many people had rallied behind for years: the premise of a digitized currency that was for the people and by the people and did not rely on banks. The safety installed by blockchain made the belief even more tantalizing for so many. Digital currency proponents would finally have a strong, tested concept that could stand independently. They took to the critics and showed them that not only was cryptocurrency safe, but it was also possible.

And then, Bitcoin was born, and with it, cryptocurrency was introduced to the world. On January 3, 2009, the Bitcoin network officially started when Nakamoto created, or "mined," the first block of Bitcoin, block 0. Australian programmer Hal Finley was the first person to receive any bitcoins. He downloaded the Bitcoin software on the first day and received ten bitcoins from Nakamoto for his troubles. That transaction, which occurred on January 12, 2009, was the first Bitcoin transaction ever. Little did the parties involved know just how historic that moment was.

How much was Bitcoin worth on its opening day? Very little, almost next to nothing. Yet, the amount was agreed on in a very democratic and fair way. The people using the Bitcoin forums decided and negotiated the value of these first Bitcoin transactions. They would debate, argue, agree, and come together with an appropriate amount everyone saw eye-to-eye on. Again, that proved that Bitcoin was and will always be a form of currency that kept the people using it front-and-center and always in control. Even from its start, Bitcoin strongly emphasized being a democratic and decentralized form of payment that would always put the people first.

Bitcoin was born, but its future was uncertain from the very start. In time, it would be repeatedly proven that its future would often remain uncertain. Where would it go next? The same power would dictate the future the past had been: the people who cared most about Bitcoin on both sides of the argument. The fight for and against Bitcoin had just begun.

Bitcoin was just a promising but unreadable idea when Satoshi Nakamoto published his paper on creating, managing, and maintaining Bitcoin. From there, things moved quickly, and the first coin was made on January 3, 2009.

After the creation of the first Bitcoin, the system began to come to life and live on its own, a system that would rise or fall based solely on the involvement of those championing it and participating in it.

For the first few years of Bitcoin, the value of Bitcoin has remained low. It was incredibly, incredibly low. In the beginning, a single Bitcoin was valued at only $0.003. The distance it has come since then is truly astronomical.

Though the cost of Bitcoin was meager in its early days, people didn't know how to use it. They didn't know how to obtain it. They didn't know how to determine the value of it. Although the person or group called Satoshi Nakamoto had laid out the blueprint for Bitcoin, he didn't stick around long to see how far it would go. In 2011, Nakamoto stepped away from Bitcoin to work on other projects. He has not been heard from since, and because of his anonymous true identity, he has never been found. The creator of Bitcoin disappeared right as his baby was becoming a toddler.

The early days of Bitcoin were wild and most casual. People who could get Bitcoins would trade them or use them to buy commodities from others in the community. In May 2010, a Florida programmer named Laszlo Hanyec offered 10,000 Bitcoins in exchange for some Papa John's pizza. A British Bitcoin fan took him up on the offer and sent two pizzas to Hanyec's home. That date, May 22, 2010, is now called Bitcoin Pizza Day. To many, it is believed to be the first time Bitcoin was ever used to make an actual purchase. The Bitcoins didn't buy the pizzas; the British fan's credit card did. But it was the first time that Bitcoins were used to receive goods or services. In 2010, 10,000 Bitcoins were worth the value of two large pizzas. Times have changed dramatically since then.

Around the same time as Bitcoin Pizza Day, users online determined that they needed to establish some online exchange system to trade and easily buy Bitcoin honestly. They took note of techniques such as the stock market and trading sites that quickly allowed clients to buy, sell, and trade their stocks. If sites like these could be created for Bitcoin, proponents believed that you would see a significant number of people looking to buy and sell and grow the popularity of Bitcoin.

Bitcoinmarket.com was launched on January 15, 2010, by a user on a Bitcoin message board. The site was rudimentary at first, but it was also an incredible feat and a step forward for the future of Bitcoin. On the site, people could buy Bitcoin at a user-determined price. This would be the way that people decided upon the value of Bitcoin. It would use the most basic principles of capitalism and supply and demand. If people wanted to spend more on Bitcoins, they could. If people thought it didn't have as much value, their financial offer would express that.

This was a significant moment for Bitcoin. It was when things started moving forward, and the new currency's actual, easy-to-understand value was founded. By simply supply and demand and speculative opinion from users, Bitcoin was gaining a true sense of worth. As mentioned, it wasn't a lot. In the early days, a single Bitcoin cost less than a penny. But as time passed, the same fundamental ideas established at that early trading site would carry forward into others. There will be multiple other ways to buy, trade, and speculate on Bitcoin in just a few years. The value would only go up and up too. But it all started in those early days of 2010 when an anonymous user took it upon themself to create a site to dictate the Bitcoin market.

This was another example of Bitcoin being for and by the people. In the beginning, no one knew how much a Bitcoin was worth. No one knew if the man who received his pizzas and spent 10,000 Bitcoins to get them was being ripped off or receiving a great deal. No one knew if $0.003 was too high or too low for a Bitcoin. It was all up in the air, nothing was determined, and nothing was certain.

But the system worked itself out, not with the help of any government bank too. The people who believed in Bitcoin stepped forward and showed their faith in the ideas proposed just months before by creating a system that would keep the entire concept of Bitcoin alive. None of this would have happened if it weren't for the people. If it weren't for the people, the future of Bitcoin would have collapsed in such uncertainty. As it stands now, the people were the ones that believed in Bitcoin and pushed it forward.

In the weeks, months, and years after its creation, the value of Bitcoin continued to rise. As Bitcoin was now trading on an online exchange and consumers were selecting a price for the currency, it was finding a footing with others, not only those who had championed it before it existed.

If you look at the price history of Bitcoin, you can see the progress it has made. The excitement of its buyers has always influenced Bitcoin's value, but there was a time when that enthusiasm needed to translate into a high value. When Bitcoin was first introduced, it was worth less than a penny. Eventually, it was worth more than that, but only by a little.

Bitcoin was just $1 in April 2011, a few years ago. That was a significant moment for the cryptocurrency, proving it was competitive with the dollar. Bitcoins were meant to grow much more valuable than just a single dollar in the future. Some naysayers never imagined it would have progressed that far. It was a watershed moment when it equaled a dollar, but it was only the beginning.

It wasn't until 2011 that Bitcoin showed just how volatile it could be. Bitcoin's wild fluctuations in value are a recurring theme. When you look at a chart of the price of Bitcoin over time, you will see highs as high as the sky and lows as steep as the earth. There have been a lot of ups and downs, ups and downs, and ups and downs since creation. In general, its volatility is much greater than that of most other currencies. This was also true in 2011 when Bitcoin experienced enormous gains...and losses.

It was a big deal when Bitcoin reached $1 in April 2011. Only after Bitcoin's price increased this became a bigger deal. When Bitcoin hit $32 in June of that year, the value was almost three times what it was in January. The gain in a few months was nearly 3,200%. Bitcoin enthusiasts were ecstatic, seeing this as a sign that cryptocurrency was catching on faster than expected and their ground-floor investments would pay off big. The timing was right for many of them, they felt. It was only upwards, upwards.

However, those familiar with trading markets, and those who recognize that there are peaks and valleys in trading any commodity, assumed that this ascent would only last for a while. Bitcon's price would likely plummet shockingly fast. Sure enough, Bitcoin's value dropped to $2 in November 2011, just a few months after reaching its high of $32. At the beginning of that year, Bitcoin was worth $1. By the summer, it was worth $32; at the end of the year, it was worth just $2. For investors, this was quite the wild ride and the moment that stood out for those who thought Bitcoin's prices would only rise. The exchange rate reminded us that currency values change quickly, only sometimes in your favor. This lesson was an important wake-up call to the many Bitcoin fans investing for the first time: don't assume anything is a sure thing, and only sometimes expect success. Even with something you genuinely believe in, investing is not guaranteed.

This was when I opened my account at Coinbase. If I had funded it in 2012, I would not have had to write books about it to make money.

As the year 2012 wore on, Bitcoin's value steadily rose. It reached nearly $5 in May and then $13.20 by the summer of that year. The Bitcoin community agreed that the cryptocurrency was headed in the right direction. Would the drops become more rapid in the future?

Many online exchanges, message boards, and stories have been written about cryptocurrency, especially Bitcoin, as it grew in popularity. Bitcoin was becoming widespread worldwide, and its early adoption was considered helpful in getting in on it as soon as possible. In Bitcoin's early years, there were substantial and often reliable gains. Bitcoin was getting more and more popular.

CHAPTER 3

Blockchain 101 - What Is It?

Blockchain in Simple Terms

If you are trying to wrap your head around cryptocurrency and blockchain, it is essential that you break it down to its basic components, its base ideas, and concepts. This knowledge will be very valued if you attempt to carve a path for yourself in the investing world or want to explain blockchain and cryptocurrency to others who don't understand it.

Knowing how to summarize concepts in simple, basic terms is essential when educating others and yourself. Even the most complex ideas and institutions can be broken down into simple terms and conveyed in ways everyone can understand. The same is true for blockchain and its system: cryptocurrency.

The truth is that many people don't venture into the world of cryptocurrency because they are afraid of it. Why are they scared of it? Simply because they don't know how to wrap their heads around it. They don't understand it. They don't see how it works, why it works, or why it would be worth their time and effort.

It may seem not very easy, and it can be, but its core concept is quite simple. An example of a blockchain is a database. To understand blockchain, one must first understand what a database is.

An electronic database is a collection of information stored on a computer system. Databases typically contain information in table form so that searching for specific information is more accessible. Is it different from using a spreadsheet instead of a database to store data?

A spreadsheet is designed to store and make access to the limited information available to one person or a small group. By contrast, a database is designed to hold a significant amount of data multiple users can access, filter, and manipulate simultaneously.

The data is stored on powerful computers in large databases. For an extensive database to be accessible simultaneously, these servers may use hundreds of computers to provide the computational power and storage capacity. Usually, a spreadsheet or database is owned by a business and managed by a specific individual with access to all the data.

What is the difference between a blockchain and a database?

Well, there are, in fact, many differences. One key difference between a typical database and a blockchain is how the data is structured. A blockchain collects information together in groups, also known as blocks, that hold sets of information. Blocks have specific storage capacities and, when filled, are chained onto the previously served block, forming a data chain known as the "blockchain." All new information that follows that freshly added block is compiled into a newly formed block that will be added to the chain once filled.

Unlike a database that structures data into tables, a blockchain, as its name implies, structures its data into chunks (blocks) linked together. In other words, not all databases are blockchains, but all blockchains are databases. When implemented in a decentralized manner, this system creates an irreversible timeline of data. Once a block is filled, it is set in stone and becomes part of this timeline. A partnership is given an exact timestamp when added to the chain.

The implementation of blockchain by Bitcoin provides a helpful context to comprehend blockchain. Bitcoin's blockchain is stored on a collection of computers, just like a database. The blockchain in Bitcoin acts as a database for saving every Bitcoin transaction ever made. This is not the case with most databases, and in Bitcoin's case, each compute node is controlled by an individual or a small group of individuals.

Assume a company owns a server with 10,000 computers and a database with all its clients' account information. They have a warehouse with all of these computers under one roof and complete control over each of them and the data stored on them. Like Bitcoin, Bitcoin includes thousands of computers, each of which holds a blockchain in a different geographic location and is operated by an individual or group of individuals. Bitcoin's network is composed of computers called nodes.

Using Bitcoin's blockchain as a decentralized database is part of this model. It is possible for private, centralized blockchains, which are made up of computers owned and controlled by one entity, to exist.

Each node records the data stored on a blockchain since it began. The data for Bitcoin consists of the entire history of all Bitcoin transactions. Thousands of other nodes can be a reference if one node has an error in its data.o, correct it. The network is thus protected from being altered by any one node within it. This means that every transaction in a block of the Bitcoin blockchain cannot be reversed.

One user could tamper with Bitcoin's history of transactions, and all the other nodes would quickly identify the node with incorrect data. We can establish a transparent and precise order of events using this system. Blockchains can hold a myriad of information, including transactions for Bitcoin, state identifications, and company inventories.

A majority of the decentralized network's computing power would be required to change how the system operates or the information it contains. Whenever changes do occur, it is in the majority's best interests.

Due to the decentralized nature of Bitcoin's blockchain, all transactions can be viewed transparently by using an individual node or blockchain explorers that allow anyone to see the live transactions. Each node gets its copy as new blocks are confirmed and added to the chain. Therefore, bitcoin could be tracked wherever it goes.

For example, exchanges have been hacked, resulting in Bitcoin holders losing everything they had. Despite the hacker's anonymity, the Bitcoins they extracted are easily traceable. It would be known where some of the Bitcoins stolen in some of these hacks went if they were moved or spent.

In several ways, blockchain technology addresses issues of security and trust. First of all, new blocks are always stored linearly and chronologically. Therefore, they are always tacked onto the end of the blockchain. As of November 2020, the block's height had reached 656,197. Each block on Bitcoin's blockchain has a position on the chain called a "height."

Unless the majority reaches a consensus to change the contents of an added block, it is nearly impossible to go back in time and alter a previously added block. This is because each block has its hash, the previous block, and a time stamp. Digital information is converted to a string of numbers and letters using a mathematical function. Whenever the data is altered, the hash code also changes.

That's why security depends on it. Let us imagine that a hacker wants to steal Bitcoin from everyone by modifying the blockchain. They would have to change their copy, or everyone else's copy would be out of alignment. The rest of the world would see this one copy stand out when they cross-reference their documents, making that hacker's version look rubbish.

The hacker would need to simultaneously control and alter 51% of the blockchain copies so that their copy becomes the majority and, thus, the agreed-upon chain. In addition to the time and resources needed to orchestrate an attack, they would have to rewrite the code for all the blocks since the timestamps and hashes would differ.

Due to the size of Bitcoin's network and its fast-growing, the cost to pull off such a feat would probably be insurmountable. Not only would this be extremely expensive, but it would also likely be fruitless. Doing such a thing would not go unnoticed, as network members would see such drastic alterations to the blockchain. The network members would then fork off to a new chain version unaffected.

This would cause the attacked version of Bitcoin to plummet in value, making the attack ultimately pointless as the lousy actor has control of a worthless asset. The same would occur if the awful actor attacked the new Bitcoin fork. It is built this way so that participating in the network is far more economically incentivized than attacking it.

The Origins of Blockchain

Blockchain aims to allow digital information to be recorded and distributed, but not edited. Blockchain technology was first outlined in 1991 by Stuart Haber and W. Scott Stornetta, two researchers who wanted to implement a system where document timestamps could not be tampered with. But After almost 20 years, Bitcoin's launch in January 2009 was the first time blockchain was used for real-life purposes.

A blockchain is the foundation of the Bitcoin protocol. Satoshi Nakamoto, the pseudonymous creator of Bitcoin, called the digital currency "a new electronic cash system that is fully peer-to-peer and without any trusted third parties."

Bitcoin uses blockchain to record payments transparently, but theoretically, it can record any number of quantities immutably. This may be a transaction, a vote in an election, a product inventory, a state identification, a deed for a home, and more.

Several blockchain-based projects are exploring using blockchain for more than just recording transactions. A good example is the use of blockchains for democratized elections. As a result of blockchain's immutability, fraudulent voting would become much less likely.

For instance, each country's citizen could be issued a cryptocurrency or token as a voting system. Upon receiving a wallet address, each candidate would be given their own, and their tokens or cryptocurrency would then be sent to that address. Due to blockchain's transparent and traceable nature, voting would no longer require human intervention, and no physical ballots could be tampered with.

Advantages and Disadvantages of Blockchain

Blockchain is a revolutionary creation that powers cryptocurrencies and can transform other industries for the better.

Even with its upsides and advantages, blockchain has some disadvantages. Knowing both is necessary to grasp blockchain's potential and abilities fully.

It is important to note that many people rail against blockchain and all cryptocurrency and think it is dangerous and should be illegal. We will discuss that are more length soon. But it is also vital to understand that many issues people have with blockchain and cryptocurrency, valid or not, are overblown. And more importantly, many things that bother people about these two technological marvels can be found in just about any other form of currency on Earth. As you see all the annoying things about blockchain, you will see that that can be applied to the Dollar, the Yen, and so much more.

The truth is that there are advantages and disadvantages to all forms of currency and the systems that run them. That is not unique solely to blockchain and cryptocurrency. That can be admitted and addressed without completely discounting the importance of both. So while blockchain does indeed have many good *and* bad things, they are not the big, scary deal breakers that some people in power make them out to be.

The Advantages of Blockchain

Accuracy of the Chain

A network of thousands of computers approves transactions on the blockchain network. Almost all human input is removed during verification, resulting in less human error and more accurate data. A computational mistake made by one computer on the network would only affect some of the blockchains. It would take at least 51 percent of the computers on the web to make that mistake, which would be nearly impossible on a rapidly expanding network like Bitcoin's.

Cost Reductions

Customers typically pay a bank for a transactional confirmation, a notary for a document signature, or a minister for a marriage ceremony. By eliminating third-party verification, blockchain eliminates associated costs. A small fee is charged to business owners when they accept credit card payments, for example, since banks and payment processing companies handle these transactions. In contrast, Bitcoin is decentralized and offers low transaction fees.

Decentralization

There is no central location for storing blockchain information. An electronic network of computers copies and distributes the blockchain. Any change to the blockchain is reflected on each computer on the web. Blockchain is more difficult to tamper with because the information is spread across several networks rather than centralized. A hacker could only access one copy of the blockchain rather than the entire network if they received a copy.

Efficient Transactions

It can take a few days for transactions completed through a central authority to settle. If you attempt to deposit a check on Friday, it could take until Monday morning to see the funds in your account. Blockchain works 24 hours a day, seven days a week, 365 days a year, unlike financial institutions, which operate five days a week during business hours. The transaction can be completed in as little as ten minutes and considered secure after only a few hours. A benefit of this is that it can be used in cross-border trades, which typically take longer due to time zone differences, and all parties must confirm payment processing.

Private Transactions

The transaction history of some blockchain networks is accessible to anyone with an internet connection because they function as public databases. Users can access transaction information but cannot see an individual's identity. There is a common misconception that blockchain networks like Bitcoin are anonymous. They are not, but at the same time, they still mostly are.

When users make public transactions, their unique code, called a public key, is recorded on the blockchain rather than their personal information. If a person has made a Bitcoin purchase on an exchange requiring identification, their identity is still linked to their blockchain address. Still, a transaction, even when tied to a person's name, does not reveal personal information.

Secure Transactions

The blockchain network must verify the authenticity of a transaction once it has been recorded. On the blockchain, thousands of computers confirm the correct purchase details. Computers validate transactions and add them to the blockchain. In a blockchain, each block has its unique hash and the previous block's hash. Editing information on a block will affect the hashcode of that block but not the hashcode of a block after that. This discrepancy can only change Information on the blockchain with prior notice.

Transparency

Most blockchains are entirely open-source software. This means that anyone and everyone can view its code. This gives auditors the ability to review cryptocurrencies like Bitcoin for security. This also means there is no absolute authority on who controls Bitcoin's code or how it is edited. Because of this, anyone can suggest changes or upgrades to the system. If most network users agree that the new version of the code with the promotion is sound and worthwhile, then Bitcoin can be updated.

Banking the Unbanked

Perhaps the most profound facet of blockchain and Bitcoin is the ability for anyone, regardless of ethnicity, gender, or cultural background, to use it. According to the world bank, nearly 2 billion adults do not have bank accounts or any means of storing their money or wealth.[5] Nearly all of these individuals live in developing countries where the economy is in its infancy and entirely dependent on cash.

These people often earn little money that is paid in physical cash. They then need to store this physical cash in hidden locations in their homes or places of living, subjecting them to robbery or unnecessary violence. Keys to a Bitcoin wallet can be stored on paper, a cheap cell phone, or even memorized if necessary. For most people, these options are likely more easily hidden than a small pile of cash under a mattress.

Blockchains of the future are also looking for solutions to not only be a unit of account for wealth storage but also to store medical records, property rights, and a variety of other legal contracts.

Disadvantages of Blockchain

While there are significant upsides to the blockchain, there are also significant challenges to its adoption. The roadblocks to applying blockchain technology today are more than just technical. The real challenges are political and regulatory, mostly to say nothing of the thousands of hours (read: money) of custom software design and back-end programming required to integrate blockchain into current business networks. Here are some of the challenges standing in the way of widespread blockchain adoption.

The Costs

Although blockchain can save users money on transaction fees, the technology is far from free. For example, Bitcoin's "proof of work" system to validate transactions consumes vast computational power. In the real world, the energy from the millions of computers on the Bitcoin network is close to what Denmark consumes annually. Assuming electricity costs of $0.03~$0.05 per kilowatt-hour, mining costs, excluding hardware expenses, are about $5,000~$7,000 per coin.

Despite the costs of mining Bitcoin, users continue to drive up their electricity bills to validate blockchain transactions. That's because when miners add a block to the Bitcoin blockchain, they are rewarded with enough Bitcoin to make their time and energy worthwhile. However, miners must be paid or otherwise incentivized to validate transactions regarding blockchains that do not use cryptocurrency.

Some solutions to these issues are beginning to arise. For example, bitcoin mining farms have been set up to use solar power, excess natural gas from fracking sites, or energy from wind farms.

The Speed

Bitcoin is a perfect case study for the possible inefficiencies of blockchain. Bitcoin's "proof of work" system takes about ten minutes to add a new block to the blockchain. At that rate, it's estimated that the blockchain network can only manage about seven transactions per second (TPS). Although other cryptocurrencies, such as Ethereum, perform better than Bitcoin, blockchain still limits them. Legacy brand Visa, for context, can process 24,000 TPS.

Solutions to this issue have been in development for years. There are currently blockchains that boast over 30,000 transactions per second.

Illegal Activity

While confidentiality on the blockchain network protects users from hacks and preserves privacy, it also allows for illegal trading and activity on the blockchain network. The most cited example of blockchain being used for illicit transactions is probably the Silk Road, an online "dark web" drug marketplace operating from February 2011 until October 2013, when the FBI shut it down.

The website allowed users to browse without being tracked using the Tor browser and make illegal purchases in Bitcoin or other cryptocurrencies. Current U.S. regulations require financial service providers to obtain information about their customers when they open an account, verify the identity of each customer, and confirm that customers do not appear on any list of known or suspected terrorist organizations. This system can be seen as both a pro and a con. It gives anyone access to financial accounts and allows criminals to transact more efficiently. Many have argued that the good uses of crypto, like banking the unbanked world, outweigh cryptocurrency's inadequate benefits, primarily when most illegal activity is still accomplished through untraceable cash.

Regulation

Many in the crypto space have expressed concerns about government regulation over cryptocurrencies. While it is getting increasingly tricky and near impossible to end something like Bitcoin as its decentralized network grows, governments could theoretically make it illegal to own cryptocurrencies or participate in their networks.

Over time this concern has grown smaller as large companies like PayPal begin to allow the ownership and use of cryptocurrencies on its platform.

Is Blockchain Safe?

Like everything related to cryptocurrency, many people ask: is it safe? Is blockchain a secure system that delivers on its promise? Or is it too good to be accurate and ready to be hacked and toyed with by criminals looking to make extra money?

The answer is yes, blockchain is safe. It is incredibly safe. What makes it that way? It is a fact that the entire system is entirely decentralized. That means it is located in more than one part of the world. As stated, the computers that run the blockchain system are in homes and businesses across the globe. That is a massive benefit because hackers attempting to access computers must travel worldwide to find them virtually.

This is additionally beneficial because you need to access all of the computers running the blockchain database simultaneously if you hope to break into the system and alter things. Why? Because every computer using blockchain is seeing all the same data in real-time as it evolves and develops and grows. If someone were attempting to break into the system and change it in their favor, they would need to enter somehow every computer running the system and change the growing database so that no other computer would have even a slight variation. If that isn't just about impossible, nothing is.

The blockchain system is safer than safe; it is a Fort Knox vault that will not be broken into or tweaked. It would require the sort of technological magic that isn't possible, nor will it ever be.

What makes blockchain safe is that it is run and monitored, and championed by the same people using it to build their wealth. No one is a bigger fan of blockchain than those looking over it. They need blockchain to invest and trade and buy and sell. They need it to work safely and flawlessly at all times. These people are the system's guardians, using their impressive computer rigs to power the system. They are the ones who need blockchain the most, so they are the ones who will make sure it goes smoothly and smoothly.

Blockchain is a reliable and safe way of recording any transactions. It does away with the need for external authority, which is one of the reasons why so many people were attracted to the idea. Bitcoin users did not need to report to a third party every time they made a transaction. Instead, they relied upon the ever-evolving blockchain and other Bitcoin users to keep everything robust, healthy, and safe. With just a few exceptions, this system worked like a charm.

Nakamoto's idea behind Bitcoin and the inclusion of blockchain made many people all over the globe excited. Finally, written in precise detail and realistic terms, was the idea that so many people had rallied behind for years: the idea of a digitized currency that was for the people and by the people and did not rely on banks. The safety installed by blockchain made the premise even more tantalizing for so many.

Is Cryptocurrency Safe?

This is the question you will be asked again and again. It is one that you will definitely learn the answer to and will believe wholeheartedly. Still, its solution is one to convince some people.

It is worth mentioning repeatedly that cryptocurrency is looked at with suspicion, rumor, and often fear. People don't understand it, and, worst of all, many people seem to fear it. They must learn how something as new and different as cryptocurrency could be safe. The fact that it existed online doesn't help its cause, either. Many investors, including older ones who cut their teeth before the web and were a significant market contributing factor, must see how something solely online can be safe. Isn't it just a big scam? Won't it just steal all your money and leave you nothing?

So, back to the question at hand, the one that will be asked to you repeatedly: are cryptocurrencies safe? The answer to that is a resounding and hearty yes. You can confidently say this and utter the truth whenever you speak it. Cryptocurrencies are incredibly safe. They are often far safer than traditional currencies like the ones we all use currently. Is there a threat of hacking that will rob you of your personal information from the sites you trust most? If we are being honest, we have to say that, yes, there is. However, that is true for any form of money: any bank or institution risks having your information stolen away from them. You do not exist in a world without risks. How often have you heard stories of banks and other major financial institutions falling victim to a significant security breach that gives away millions and millions of customers' information? It happens often. We live in a world where it is a standard part of doing business.

So there is risk in all things regarding money; every company, agency, or firm that accepts and stores your money is in the crosshairs of hackers.

However, the idea of cryptocurrency being easily hacked is ludicrous and patently false. As described in the previous section, blockchain technology powering cryptocurrency is nearly impenetrable to almost all hacking schemes. Yes, you may lose your information in a heist, but the overall chance of you losing your valued Bitcoin or another form of cryptocurrency is nearly nonexistent.

Cryptocurrency is safe; it has always been safe and will always be safe. It was created with one of the safest and most secure systems in place: the blockchain. With that, cryptocurrency is not something that can easily be tinkered with. Nor can it easily be stolen away in the dead of night. You may never hold cryptocurrency in your hand, and it may exist only online, but it still needs to be one of Earth's most secure and protected forms of currency.

The fear many people have about the safety of cryptocurrency is unfounded, spurred on by speculation, confusion, ignorance, and sometimes greed by those trying to discredit cryptocurrency. Few things on this earth are safer than holding cryptocurrency.

While cryptocurrency is safe and buying cryptocurrency is too, some risk factors are involved based upon whom you purchase and trade your crypto with. You are investing in and securing your cryptocurrency through online exchanges and websites that act as online marketplaces for buying, trading, and storing your cryptocurrency. When you purchase your share of crypto, you are given a "private key, " a complicated and private string of code used to authorize all outgoing transactions on the blockchain network. Think of your key as a unique ID associated with your cryptocurrency account. It's like your cryptocurrency DNA, only you have it, and it has access to your most valuable information.

We cannot say that your cryptocurrency is safe in every situation because there have been rare times when poorly-made and poorly-regulated online exchanges have allowed themselves to open doors to dangerous schemes.

Unfortunately, hackers have intruded on several online exchanges over the years and have stolen millions of dollars worth of cryptocurrency. This has yet to happen with the more high-end online businesses because they take extra steps to ensure their security is more challenging than their competitors. But it happened at lower-level talks, leading some people to lose valuable investments. It's a rare event that doesn't happen nearly as often as cryptocurrency critics would have you believe. And while some online exchanges cannot get your crypto back for you, others are insured to ensure you are taken care of after a hack. Therefore, while the threat of hacks looms its ugly head occasionally in cryptocurrency, it is okay if you choose a reputable and reliable online exchange. That gives you even more reason to make sure you put your money into a business you can trust, which has repeatedly proven itself to other consumers.

Safety is a significant feature of cryptocurrency. There is the safety of not being tracked by the government and not relying on their outdated system. The safety of the blockchain also ensures that all transactions are accounted for, legitimate, and honest. Then there is the added safety of online exchanges, which have built-in measures to ensure your money doesn't get into the hands of others. Safety is built throughout the cryptocurrency ecosystem; it is downright essential. The cryptocurrency was formed and released into the world when its security and safety were tested, proven, and tested again. The most diehard fans and supporters of cryptocurrency will tell you to be innovative and to make the right choices when it comes to investing and buying. The system will do a lot to keep you safe, but you must do your work too.

CHAPTER 4

Blockchain & The Market

How Blockchain Changes and Powers the Market

Over the past decade, marketing has undergone many changes; now, it will undergo another revolution, mainly due to blockchain technology. Although most of us associate digital marketing with things like AI and analytics, blockchain might be the most disruptive technology to hit marketers across all industries. You might be surprised at who will benefit from blockchain in digital marketing.

With blockchain technology, two parties can conduct transactions without requiring a third party to verify anything. In finance and cryptocurrencies, blockchain technology has mainly been used, but it could also be used for marketing.

Blockchain allows consumers to regain control of their personal information and thus level the playing field. Here are some ways blockchain is changing digital marketing forever and for the better.

The most exciting aspect of blockchain is that it returns data value to consumers. In the past, many companies had the advantage of gaining information about their customers. Almost everyone asks for our phone number, email address, and address, as well as our firstborn's name, even when we make a simple purchase in-store or online. This helps the consumer, as it allows them to be targeted by companies. Yet it's also an invasive practice because companies can make money from collecting and sometimes selling the personal data of anyone interacting with their products.

This is simple but revolutionary in terms of digital marketing. The free-for-all data grab is over.

Indeed, if you're in the marketing business, you may not love this concept. In many ways, it's like going back to ground zero—relying on customers to give you the information you want and need to serve them better. Maybe not the best news for digital marketing—but a necessary step forward in terms of consumer protection.

Blockchain technology can do much more than change how people approach and market. Blockchain promises to enable the smooth exchange of information between parties and streamline business processes. Enterprise blockchain can guarantee the accuracy and quality of information, goods, and services and automate contracts.

In a business network, blockchain enhances trust, which allows participants to collaborate without additional guarantees. Companies within the same industry tend to trust one another since they all work towards the same goal of helping the business succeed. It is rare to find that trust between individuals representing different companies, which makes collaboration challenging. A blockchain can build trust and improve processes across multiple organizations.

Eastman Kodak, the legendary camera maker, is an excellent example of how Blockchain can impact businesses. With the introduction of smartphones, the company has struggled to stay competitive. The legacy company was able to reinvent itself with the help of blockchain technology. To create a digital ledger of copyright ownership, the company announced the launch of KODAKOne. Photographers can use the platform to register their old and new work and license it for sale. Through this system, professionals can participate in the new economy of photography by receiving instant, secure payments for their photos.

Accounting can also be radically changed by it. Blockchain technology can be highly beneficial to the field of accounting. Accountancy is filled with challenges - from the overly complex tax code to the need for accuracy and precision. The blockchain can address all of these issues.

The blockchain can reduce auditors' time sampling and validating transactions by providing transparency. Auditors could focus on controls and other vital tasks with more time available.

Blockchain-based systems can also affect pay in multinational corporations and businesses across borders. It simplifies and standardizes payments in different currencies, changing how companies pay their employees. Changing how workers save for retirement can improve employer care.

Workchain, a decentralized protocol for the work economy, presented a tremendous blockchain-based payroll system. Using Workchain, employees can get their paycheck as soon as they complete their work. At the same time, employers can reduce costs and improve efficiency with an automated payroll solution.

A worker is another example of an HR use case; a multi-chain validated data protocol for application creation that simplifies the design and management of applications based on verified data and reputation scores. As a result of Aworker's flexibility, public blockchains can be customized for various applications.

What Is Cryptography?

Cryptography is the study of secure communications techniques that allow only the sender and intended recipient to see the content of a message. The term derives from the Greek word Kryptos, which means hidden. Cryptography involves scrambling ordinary text into what is known as ciphertext, then converting it back to plain text upon delivery. Also included in cryptography is the obfuscation of information in images using microdots or merging. One of the first modern ciphers is credited to Julius Caesar for using one of these methods in complex hieroglyphics.

Most commonly, cryptography is used to encrypt and decrypt plain-text emails and other electronic data. An asymmetric or "secret key" system is the simplest method. A secret key encrypts data, and the encoded message and key are sent to the recipient for decryption. What's the problem? When a message is intercepted, a third party has access to everything they need to decrypt and read the news. Therefore, asymmetric critical systems were invented by cryptologists. Each user has two keys: a public and a private key. Senders encrypt messages and send them along with the recipient's public key. When the message arrives, only the recipient's private key can decode it - which means theft is ineffective without the corresponding private key.

Despite malicious third parties–known as adversaries–cryptography offers secure communication. Combining an algorithm and key can transform an input (plaintext) into an encrypted output. When the same key is used with a given algorithm, the plaintext will continually be transformed into the same ciphertext.

Algorithms are considered secure if an attacker cannot determine any properties of the plaintext or key, given the ciphertext. An attacker should not be able to determine anything about a key, given many plaintext/ciphertext combinations that use the key.

There are two different types of cryptography: symmetric and asymmetric. What are they, how do they work, and why do they matter?

With symmetric cryptography, the same key is used for encryption and decryption. A sender and a recipient must already have a shared key known to both. Key distribution is a tricky problem and was the impetus for developing asymmetric cryptography.

With asymmetric crypto, two different keys are used for encryption and decryption. Every user in an asymmetric cryptosystem has a public and private key. The private key is always kept secret, but the public key may be freely distributed.

Data encrypted with a public key may only be decrypted with the corresponding private key. So, sending a message to John requires encrypting that message with John's public key. Only John can interpret the news, as only John has his private key. Any data encrypted with a private key can only be solved with the corresponding public key. Similarly, Jane could digitally sign a message with her private key, and anyone with Jane's public key could decrypt the signed message and verify that it was, in fact, Jane who sent it.

Symmetric is generally very fast and ideal for encrypting large amounts of data. Asymmetric is much slower and can only encrypt pieces of data smaller than the critical size (typically 2048 bits or smaller). Thus, asymmetric crypto is generally used to encrypt symmetric encryption keys, which are then used to encrypt much larger data blocks. For digital signatures, asymmetric crypto is usually used to encrypt the hashes of messages rather than entire messages.

A cryptosystem provides for managing cryptographic keys, including generation, exchange, storage, use, revocation, and replacement of the keys.

A secure system should provide several assurances, such as confidentiality, integrity, and availability of data as well as authenticity and non-repudiation. When used correctly, crypto helps to give these assurances. Cryptography can ensure the confidentiality and integrity of data in transit and at rest. It can also authenticate senders and recipients to one another and protect against repudiation.

Software systems often have multiple endpoints, typically multiple clients, and one or more back-end servers. These client/server communications occur over networks that cannot be trusted. Contact occurs over open, public networks such as the Internet, or private networks, which external attackers or malicious insiders may compromise.

It can protect communications that traverse untrusted networks. An adversary may attempt to carry out two main types of attacks on a network. Passive attacks involve an attacker simply listening to a network segment and trying to read sensitive information as it travels. Passive attacks may be online (in which an attacker reads traffic in real-time) or offline (in which an attacker captures traffic in real-time and views it later—perhaps after spending some time decrypting it). Active attacks involve an attacker impersonating a client or server, intercepting communications in transit, and viewing and modifying the contents before passing them on to their intended destination (or dropping them entirely).

The confidentiality and integrity protections offered by cryptographic protocols such as SSL/TLS can protect communications from malicious eavesdropping and` tampering. Authenticity protections ensure that users are communicating with the systems as intended. For example, are you sending your online banking password to your bank or someone else?

It can also be used to protect data at rest. Data on a removable disk or database can be encrypted to prevent disclosing sensitive data should the physical media be lost or stolen. In addition, it can also provide integrity protection of data at rest to detect malicious tampering.

Different Types of Cryptography

Numerous cryptographic algorithms are in use, but in general, they can be broken into three categories: secret key cryptography, public key cryptography, and hash functions. Each has its role to play within the cryptographic landscape.

Secret key cryptography: The Caesar cipher discussed above is an excellent example of private key cryptography. In the model we used, if encrypted messages were being exchanged between Caesar and one of his centurions, both parties would have to know the key — in this case, how many letters forward or backward in the alphabet you need to move to transform plaintext to ciphertext or vice versa. But the essential needs to stay a secret between the two of them. You couldn't send the key along with the message, for instance, because if both fell into enemy hands, the message would be straightforward for them to decipher, defeating the whole purpose of encrypting it in the first place. Caesar and his centurion would presumably have to discuss the key when they saw each other in person, though this is less than ideal when wars are being fought over long distances.

Secret key cryptography, sometimes a symmetric key, is widely used to keep data confidential. It can be beneficial for maintaining a local hard drive private; for instance, since the same user generally encrypts and decrypts the protected data, sharing the secret key is not an issue. Secret key cryptography can also be used to keep messages transmitted across the internet confidential; however, to successfully make this happen, you need to deploy our following form of cryptography in tandem with it.

Public key cryptography: Caesar may have been able to confer with his centurions in person, but you don't want to go into your bank and talk to the teller to learn what the private key is for encrypting your electronic communication with the bank — that would defeat the purpose of online banking. In general, to function securely, the internet needs a way for communicating parties to establish a secure communications channel while only talking to each other across an inherently insecure network. The way this works is via public key cryptography.

Each participant has two keys in public key cryptography, sometimes called an asymmetric key. One is shared and sent to anyone the party wishes to communicate with. That's the key used to encrypt messages. But the other key is private, shared with nobody, and it's necessary to decrypt those messages. To use a metaphor: think of the public key as opening a slot in a mailbox just wide enough to drop a letter in. Give those dimensions to anyone you feel might send you a letter. The private key is what you use to open the mailbox so you can get the letters out.

The mathematics of how you can use one key to encrypt a message and another to decrypt it is much less intuitive than how the key to the Caesar cipher works. The Infosec Institute has a deep dive if you're interested. The core principle that makes the process work is that the two keys are related mathematically, so it's easy to derive the public key from the private key but not vice versa. For instance, the private key might be two huge prime numbers, which you'd multiply to get the public key.

The computations needed for public key cryptography are much more complex and resource intensive than those behind secret critical infrastructure. Fortunately, you don't need to use it to protect every message you send online. Instead, what usually happens is that one party will use public key cryptography to encrypt a message containing yet another cryptographic key. Having been safely transmitted across the insecure internet, this key will become the private key that encodes a much longer communications session encrypted via secret key encryption.

In this way, public key cryptography assists the cause of confidentiality. But these public keys are also part of a more extensive set of functions known as public critical infrastructure, or PKI. PKI provides ways to be sure that any public key is associated with a specific person or institution. A message encrypted with a public key thus confirms the identity of the sender, establishing authentication and non-repudiation.

Hash functions: Public and private key cryptographic algorithms transform plaintext into ciphertext and back into plaintext. By contrast, a hash function is a one-way encryption algorithm: once you've encrypted your plaintext, you can't recover it from the resulting ciphertext (a hash).

This might make hash functions seem like a somewhat pointless exercise. But the key to their usefulness is that no two plaintexts will produce the same hash for any given hash function. (Mathematically, this needs to be corrected, but for any hash function in use, the chances of it happening are generally vanishingly small and can be safely ignored.)

This makes hashing algorithms an excellent tool for ensuring data integrity. For instance, a message can be sent along with its hash. Upon receiving the message, you can run the same hashing algorithm on the text; if the hash you produce differs from the one accompanying the news, you know the message has been modified in transit.

Hashing is also used to ensure the confidentiality of passwords. Storing passwords as plaintext is a big security no-no because that makes users prone to account and identity theft in the wake of data breaches (which sadly doesn't stop big players from doing it). If, instead, you store a hashed version of a user's password, hackers won't be able to decrypt it and use it elsewhere, even if they do manage to breach your defenses. When a legitimate user logs in with their password, you can hash it and check against the hash you have on file.

Cryptography and Crypto

A large draw of cryptocurrencies is their security and transparency on the blockchain. All of that relies on cryptographic mechanisms. That is how most blockchain-based cryptocurrencies maintain security; therefore, it constitutes the very nature of cryptocurrencies.

It was on a cryptography message board back in 2009 that Bitcoin creator Satoshi Nakamoto suggested a way to solve the double-spend problem that had long been the Achilles heel of digital currencies. The double-spend problem occurs when the same crypto unit has the potential to be spent twice, which would destroy trust in them as an online payment solution and make them essentially worthless.

Nakamoto proposed using a peer-to-peer distributed ledger that was timestamped and secured cryptographically. That led to the creation of the blockchain as we know it today. As with all technology, cryptography will evolve to keep up with the demands of a secure digital environment. This is especially true with the growing adoption of blockchains and cryptocurrencies across industries and borders.

Ethereum & Cardano

Ethereum

Ethereum is a blockchain platform with its cryptocurrency, called Ether (ETH) or Ethereum, and its programming language, Solidity.

As a blockchain network, Ethereum is a decentralized public ledger for verifying and recording transactions. The network's users can create, publish, monetize, and use applications on the platform, using its Ether cryptocurrency as payment. Insiders call the decentralized applications on the network "dApps."

Ethereum was created to enable developers to build and publish intelligent contracts and distributed applications that can be used without the risks of downtime, fraud, or interference from a third party.

Ethereum describes itself as "the world's programmable blockchain." It distinguishes itself from Bitcoin as a programmable network that serves as a marketplace for financial services, games, and apps, all of which can be paid for in Ether cryptocurrency and are safe from fraud, theft, or censorship.

Ethereum was launched in July 2015 by a small group of blockchain enthusiasts. They included Joe Lubin, founder of ConsenSys, a blockchain applications developer that uses the Ethereum network. Another co-founder, Vitalik Buterin, is credited with originating the Ethereum concept and now serves as its CEO and public face. Buterin is sometimes described as the world's youngest crypto billionaire.

The Ether cryptocurrency was designed to be used within the Ethereum network. However, like Bitcoin, Ether is now an accepted form of payment by some merchants and service vendors. Overstock, Shopify, and CheapAir are online sites accepting Ether as payment.

The founders of Ethereum were among the first to consider the potential of blockchain technology for uses beyond the secure trading of virtual currency. Its ETH cryptocurrency was created primarily as a payment medium for apps built on its platform.

Its invulnerability to hackers and other snoopers has opened up possibilities for storing private information, from healthcare records to voting systems. Its reliance on cryptocurrency opened up opportunities for programmers to create and market games and business applications on the network.

A blockchain may be invulnerable to hacker attacks, but it's not for lack of trying. In 2016, a malicious actor stole over $50 million worth of Ether that had been raised for a project called The DAO, a set of smart contracts created by a third party and originating from Ethereum's software platform. The successful raid was blamed on a third-party developer.

The Ethereum community opted to reverse the theft by creating a "hard fork," invalidating the existing blockchain and creating a second Ethereum blockchain. The original is known as Ethereum Classic.

As of May 2021, Ethereum was the second-largest virtual currency on the market, behind only Bitcoin. The number of ETHs in circulation crossed the 100 million mark in 2018.

Unlike Bitcoin, there is no limit to the number of ETHs that can be created.

Ethereum is currently undergoing a long-awaited upgrade known as Ethereum 2.0, which is intended to allow the network to scale up while addressing congestion problems that have slowed it down in the past.

How would you explain Ethereum to someone in the simplest of terms? It's relatively easy. Ethereum, like any blockchain, is a database of information designed to be unhackable. Ether, or ETH, is the cryptocurrency used to complete transactions on the blockchain.

Unlike in a traditional database, information in a blockchain is organized as a chronological "chain" made up of "blocks" of data. For instance, every Ether coin transaction must be verified and recorded as an additional block on that coin's unique blockchain. This process of recording every transaction in a sequence is why a blockchain is often compared to a ledger.

The Ethereum blockchain stores more than transaction records for Ether currency. It allows software developers to create games and business applications, called dApps, and market them to users. Those users want to take advantage of the relative lack of risks that come with storing sensitive information on the World Wide Web.

But is it better than Bitcoin and its competitors? In some ways, it is. Unlike the Bitcoin blockchain, Ethereum was not created to support a cryptocurrency. The Ether cryptocurrency was created to provide an in-house currency for applications built on the Ethereum blockchain.

In other words, Ethereum has broader ambitions. It wants to be a platform for all applications that can safely store information.

Despite their differences, the two are the creators of virtual currencies that have become rivals in the investing world. And virtual currencies are just that: They are coins that have no physical existence but are represented by a string of codes that can be exchanged at a price agreed upon by a buyer and a seller.

And what's next for Ethereum? It's worth noting that Ethereum has been met with healthy skepticism. For one, Ethereum is far from scalable, meaning it can't support many users right now, throwing a wrench in the idea of a "world computer" that disrupts Google, Facebook, and other centralized platforms.

Ethereum 2.0, launched Dec. 1, 2020, aims to fix some of these issues. Other scaling technologies, such as Raiden – which has been in the works for years – could also help with the scalability problem.

Cardano

Cardano is a third-generation, decentralized proof-of-stake (PoS) blockchain platform designed to be a more efficient alternative to proof-of-work (PoW) networks. The infrastructure burden of growing costs, energy use, and slow transaction times limit scalability, interoperability, and sustainability on PoW networks like Ethereum.

Charles Hoskinson, the co-founder of the proof-of-work (PoW) blockchain Ethereum, understood the implications of these challenges to blockchain networks and began developing Cardano and its primary cryptocurrency, named ada, in 2015, launching the platform and the ADA token in 2017.

The Cardano platform runs on the Ouroboros consensus protocol. Ouroboros, created by Cardano in its foundation phase, is the first PoS protocol that not only was proved to be secure but also was the first to be informed by scholarly academic research. Each development phase, or era, in the Cardano roadmap is anchored by the research-based framework, incorporating peer-reviewed insights with evidence-based methods to progress toward and achieve the milestones related to the future directions of the use applications of the blockchain network and the ADA token.

Some back story on Cardano and its origins and purpose. It is closely related to Ethereum, and its separation shows how divided the cryptocurrency market and industry can become.

Charles Hoskinson started Cardano with his former Ethereum colleague Jerry Wood in 2014 after leaving Ethereum, following a difference in opinion with the team running the Ethereum Foundation over governance and the role of venture capital. In the early days of Ethereum, Hoskinson saw the need for a more standardized and scalable blockchain. With his mathematics background, Hoskinson began thinking about more scientific ways to build a blockchain. During this time, Hoskinson connected with Jeremy Wood, a former Ethereum co-worker looking to create a better blockchain and smart contracts platform. The two began to pursue Cardano as it exists today.

Cardano is supported by the same-named foundation that aids the research and development of the protocol and its community. The Cardano project's development is spearheaded by the for-profit company Input Output Hong Kong, also called IOHK. It comes as no surprise that Hoskinson also heads IOHK. The project signed up leading academics in several universities worldwide to review their work before announcing Cardano. It was peer-tested and approved and crafted with functionality and a democratic aspect heavily built into it. From the beginning, Hoskinson wanted Cardano to be community-driven because he knew that would keep it strong and viable throughout the years. A strong base of users who truly believed in the system would go a long way to keep it alive, healthy, and safe.

2017 Cardano launched its native cryptocurrency ADA after famous and celebrated 19th-century mathematician Ada Lovelace. Lovelace is credited as being one of the world's first computer programmers by being the first to publish her idea of a machine algorithm for a computer-like "analytical engine." The Cardano project itself is named after the Italian polymath Gerolamo Cardano. The homages to Lovelace and Cardano are just other examples of the team behind this promising blockchain and altcoin tipping their hats to those who came before them and made the entire project and system possible.

Cardano's main applications are in identity management and traceability. The former application can be used to streamline and simplify processes that require the collection of data from multiple sources. The latter application can track and audit a product's manufacturing processes from provenance to finished goods and, potentially, eliminate the market for counterfeit goods.

Oversight of the advancement of the Cardano protocol ecosystem is decentralized, and Cardano's partners share responsibilities: The Cardano Foundation, IOHK, and EMURGO. The Cardano Foundation, a not-for-profit organization, is the legal custodian responsible for the primary oversight and supervision of the Cardano brand. The foundation advances the visibility of the protocol on the global stage, cultivates use-case opportunities, and connects with policymakers, regulators, and academia.

IOHK is the software engineering and technology company responsible for building Cardano, with a research arm dedicated to promoting blockchain education. IOHK works closely with academic partners to not only further its educational mission but also improve the long-term scalability of the Cardano protocol by using the most recent peer-reviewed scientific research to inform platform updates before implementation. EMURGO is the global technology partner responsible for driving the commercial adoption of the Cardano protocol, integrating businesses across a wide range of sectors into their blockchain system.

The organizations behind Cardano have released three products: Atala PRISM, Atala SCAN, and Atala Trace. The first product is marketed as an identity management tool that can provide access to services. For example, it can be used to verify credentials to open a bank account or eligibility for government aid. The other two products trace a product's journey through a supply chain.

Cardano is also developing an innovative contract platform that will be stable and secure for developing enterprise-level decentralized apps. Shortly, the team at Cardano plans to use a democratic on-chain governance system called Project Catalyst to manage the development and execution of projects. They will also revamp their treasury management system to fund future costs using Project Catalyst.

The Cardano blockchain is stratified into the Cardano Settlement Layer (CSL) and the Cardano Computational Layer (CCL), which separates Cardano from the regular innovative contract platform. Ethereum runs a single-layer architecture, which has seen it experience network congestion, slow transaction speed, and high gas fees.

Cardano seeks to address these issues through the CSL and CCL. Its CSL layer facilitates peer-to-peer transactions such as tokens transfer between users. The CSL is Cardano's balance ledger. Using a proof-of-stake consensus algorithm (Ouroboros protocol) to generate new blocks and confirm transactions, Cardano wants to improve Bitcoin's proof-of-work protocol.

The CCL layer is where Cardano truly distinguishes itself. The CCL powers the computational needs of the blockchain, enabling the execution of smart contracts.

This layer is operated separately from the settlement layer to afford flexibility if the need for changes arises. Its off-chain protocol offers greater data storage flexibility and an access model that lets users create customized rules when validating transactions.

High fees have been a limiting factor for the DeFi space. As the appeal for these projects increases with record values locked up, Ethereum's gas fees have made them an expensive endeavor. Cardano is aiming to fix this and more with its Mary upgrade.

Cardano developers can now create custom tokens or import projects from other blockchains into the Cardano network. This could benefit exciting projects like the DeFi and NFT ecosystems.

Will Cardano's Mary upgrade finally position the one-time underdog as a serious challenger to Ethereum? While Cardano is innovating, other blockchain platforms — including Ethereum — are in a race to work out issues like scalability and sustainability.

But in the world of technology, it's not necessarily the best technology that wins, but the one with the better business strategy. Time will tell whether Cardano's Africa and Fortune 500 strategy will prevail.

What about Cardano has raised the level of interest in popularity around it? On its surface, it appears much like many other altcoins on the market. It has a volatile nature and its fair share of ups and downs; it can be traded on many online exchanges, just like Ethereum and plenty of other coins that rival and try to challenge Bitcoin. So what is it that makes Cardano so unique?

Its name recognition, the people behind it, and the science and technology that drives Cardano are the main features that should draw investors to it. Just because it was assembled and launched by the same people who got Ethereum up and running is a significant draw for many. Then the blockchain technology that runs Cardano is just icing on the cake of these promising altcoins.

But there are drawbacks, too, things to consider when you put your money into Cardano. Firstly, its system and technique, and functionality are limited. Cardano is indeed built upon an open-source blockchain that can be adapted and improved by others in the community. That is a vital feature, a huge benefit that makes Cardano even more attractive. However, it is also hard to master and isn't the most accessible technology to adapt to enterprises and businesses. It takes much work and is challenging for new programmers. The nuts and bolts that run Cardano are complicated, complex and have a steep learning curve. It is unlikely that you won't see the Cardano system in many businesses and other altcoins soon because it is challenging to master, even though it is open to anyone who wants to take a shot at it.

Still, despite its drawbacks, Cardano is one of the most promising altcoins. There is a reason so many people are putting their money into Cardano, and it's more than just the team behind it. Cardano has a back-end functionality that is strong, cutting-edge, and can improve and grow. Plus, the community that buys into Cardano is the same community that runs, changes, adjusts, and benefits from it. Many people are drawn to cryptocurrency because of the feeling of society that can come with it. Cardano has a strong community feel to it, and that is just one of the significant reasons why it has proven to be resilient and enticing again and again and again.

CHAPTER 5

Altcoins

You have now learned about cryptocurrency generally and its most popular and well-known offspring: Bitcoin. Indeed, when people talk about crypto, they are almost always going to mention Bitcoin because it is the coin that has taken the world by storm and shown even the most stubborn naysayers that there is potential in cryptocurrencies of all types.

In the beginning, there was only Bitcoin. It was the only form of cryptocurrency that people cared to have. But, over time, the crypto world has evolved, and what was once only one has now become hundreds upon hundreds. There are countless ways to invest in cryptocurrency; you do not have to be beholden to solely Bitcoin.

What are these other forms of cryptocurrency? They are called altcoins - and they are plenty. But what are they? How do they work? Why do they exist? Let's dive in.

Why Do Altcoins Exist?

Altcoins are an alternative to Bitcoin and exist to expand the field of cryptocurrency and allow investors and buyers more options when they are looking to enter the booming marketplace of crypto. That is why altcoins exist and the most polite way of saying it. There are other reasons why altcoins have come to be - and even more reasons why they have become so popular.

Essentially, altcoins were made because there is an opportunity for others to experience financial growth. The concept behind all cryptocurrency is that people can buy and sell goods and pay for them with a new form of digital payment. That is very much the truth. However, there are other reasons why cryptocurrency has become so popular. For one, it is an investment opportunity, a way for people to put money into the market and ride the following success. If you play your cards right, you can invest several hundred dollars into cryptocurrencies and walk away with thousands. This is exciting for many people. The businesses and entrepreneurs who started altcoins all over the world saw a chance to make money, much money. They knew that if they got in on the ground floor and offered something that stood a chance of making a lot of financial gains for many, they would find fans and people willing to accept the opportunity to turn a profit.

Yes, altcoins exist so people can make money. There is no shame in that fact. However, why don't people invest in Bitcoin, especially since it has proven to be the most popular and successful form of crypto? For one, these people think that there is a chance that the altcoin they are starting or buying into can become the next big thing, a cryptocurrency that threatens Bitcoin's place at the top of the food chain. There is always room for expansion and success in cryptocurrency; who is to say the next altcoin might not be the biggest yet?

Additionally, many people look to altcoins because they may feature something that Bitcoin does not. For example, because of the processing it goes through, it takes time to spend or receive Bitcoin successfully. The coin needs to be sent; it must go through the entire crypto-mining process, verifying that everything is accurate and legitimate. This takes much longer than it takes to slide a debit card through a machine at a local business. Certain altcoins, however, have sped up the process. With specific altcoins on the market, you can make a purchase and have it paid for quickly. That is a massive benefit to some of these coins and a significant reason why some people are drawn to them. There is also the fact that some altcoins are even more anonymous than Bitcoin. While most of the people buying things with cryptocurrency are entirely above the board and not doing anything scandalous or criminal, some people are using crypto pay for illegal goods and services. Why not use an altcoin that cannot track your identity or location? Some altcoins appeal to people for that very reason alone.

Altcoins exist because the world of cryptocurrency is a booming marketplace full of many potential buyers, investors, inventors, and more. It is an area of industry that is looking to expand continually, and there are people from all over the world looking to get into that. They are searching for alternatives, the next breakthrough, or just a chance for them to make some money. That is why altcoins exist. The potential in the cryptocurrency world is so vast and endless that altcoins began to capitalize on that.

While the field of altcoins is now crowded and still constantly growing, it is sometimes different. There was a time when there was just one single altcoin to compete against Bitcoin. Even though, back then, it wasn't much of a competition at all.

The first altcoin was an experiment, a quest to see if the possible idea of altcoins was even possible or if it was just a hope and a dream that would never get off the ground. However, like cryptocurrency, altcoins eventually grew stronger and became an entire industry rivaling Bitcoin's popularity and potential growth.

The world of altcoins began in 2010, just a couple of years after Bitcoin was up and running. On the BitcoinTalk forums, a discussion about Bitcoin and cryptocurrency was in full swing. From these conversations about alternative cryptocurrencies and what they could achieve, Namecoin was born. It was the first altcoin, and, like Bitcoin itself, it was more than just a cryptocurrency. With Namecoin, the construction and functionality were tied to a decentralized DNS system. It was a complicated system, but the Namecoin system would have value in multiple ways, both by acting as a currency and as being tied to domain name creation.

When a Namecoin block is created, it is tied to a unique domain name that can be sold for money. Therefore, each coin has a monetary value but also has value because it is related to a domain name, which can also raise money for the owner.

In almost every way, Namecoin is a Bitcoin clone. It was so closely related to Bitcoin that Bitcoin miners could also mine Namecoin simultaneously. This method, called pooled mining, was another significant feature that invited and impressed many.

Namecoin was the first, but it only lasted for a while. Over time, Namecoin eventually faded and is now seen as a dead coin. However, its place in altcoin history was solidified long ago. Namecoin proved to millions that alternative currencies were possible, had potential, and could carry promise and purpose that stood on their own and were separate from Bitcoin. This was a significant moment in cryptocurrency history, the start of something massive.

The floodgates began to open after Namecoin. Other industries and creators began to craft their altcoins. Before investors knew it, the marketplace became increasingly filled with altcoins with different names, features, premises, and promises. Online exchanges started offering these altcoins, allowing users to invest, buy, and trade them just like with Bitcoin. None of these new coins would ever truly rival and surpass Bitcoin in terms of popularity and value, but they all made splashes in their ways.

One of the most attractive features of altcoins is the variety. Nowadays, there are indeed hundreds of altcoins for investors to choose from. This means there are many chances at finding the next big thing, some altcoin that floats right below the surface, looking to break big. An intelligent investor can do much research and digging and find something others have yet to notice.

A true investor will study the marketplace and find the altcoins that have the most potential and the most significant chance to make an impact. Someone who knows how the market works, what it wants, and what it reacts to will be able to decipher the wills and desires of the market. That way, they will know what altcoins will speak to investors and which have the most excellent chance of breaking through. Like all things cryptocurrency, the more knowledge you have, the more power you have.

Some people want to invest solely in Bitcoin when they enter cryptocurrency. They feel that Bitcoin is the only sure thing, an investment that will always pay off and has fewer risks than others. As stated before, countless people think that Bitcoin is the only cryptocurrency. Is that short-sighted? It sure is, but it's better for you in many ways. The fewer people seeking out altcoins, the better chance you have to be the one who stumbles upon the next altcoin that will create waves.

A limited view of the crypto market is all well and good for some people, but if you are looking to become a talented and successful trader, you should fill your portfolio with some altcoins. Why? Because altcoins give you more opportunities for success, variety, and potential. It's a simple investment approach that you would be taught in any investing class: the wider variety of cryptocurrencies you own, the bigger your chances for success. With more options, you have more possibilities for financial success. Why would you limit yourself only to Bitcoin? Yes, you could make your fortune with only Bitcoin; it limits you significantly. Ideally, you should find altcoins with great potential and study and understand them and the market. Once you comprehend how the cryptocurrency market functions and why it encounters its usual ups and downs, you will better handle which altcoins show promise, which could become hits, and which ones will become misses.

Altcoins are a terrific way to make more money and find options for success that others may have missed. But it would be best always to choose the altcoins you want to invest in. Instead, it would be best to make your choices based on understanding the market and the history of cryptocurrency, Bitcoin, and altcoins. Know what has driven other altcoins to great heights - and deep lows. You will begin to see patterns in the cryptocurrency world, certain features that appeal to investors and those that don't. This will inform your choices and lead you to find the right altcoin. With so many options out there and so many chances for great value and significant loss, it is essential that you take buying altcoin very seriously. Otherwise, it is just like you throwing your money away.

Investing in altcoins is a way to open up more possibilities to yourself and also a way to indeed be in touch with the nature and personality of the cryptocurrency landscape. There have been many altcoins over the years, and many more still to this day, and each of them has the potential to be something that could break the system wide open, rival Bitcoin in a major way, and create a significant financial windfall for investors. There is no reason to ignore altcoins. Not giving them proper attention is a surefire way to miss out on the chance to become an investor that others envy.

The Most Common Altcoins

While you may know about altcoins, how many are there? Did you know that there are not just dozens of options for you when investing in altcoins but hundreds, even thousands, of ways to spend and make money?

It's true; the world of altcoins has exploded over the last few years. Bitcoin is no longer alone, not by a long shot. Now plenty of cryptocurrency investors still need to buy into Bitcoin. Instead, they choose to find an altcoin that seems appealing to them. Certain businesses are also beginning to create their altcoins, sure they could create something powerful, modern, and cutting-edge.

There are so many altcoins out there that the thought of finding the one that is right for you is downright overwhelming. While you could spend days researching and looking into altcoins to find the one you want to invest in, it is best to know the top names in the game and the most significant coins that have made the biggest splashes. You have many more options than these, but here are some of the most impressive, robust, and reliable altcoins that have significantly changed the cryptocurrency world.

Litecoin

If we talk about altcoins, we might as well start by discussing the one that has created the most significant impact. Litecoin is not just a big altcoin, it is a vast altcoin, and many people feel that it has now surpassed Bitcoin in terms of power and potential. If anyone can take down Bitcoin as the most significant crypto in the world, it is undoubtedly Litecoin.

Created in 2011, Litecoin has quickly become the gold standard of altcoins. There is no doubt or question that Litecoin is the top of the top and the highest-rated and most sought-after altcoin on the market. Its popularity and success have steadily gained and, most impressively, stayed stable throughout its lifetime. In a marketplace that sees a lot of volatility and sudden change, Litecoin has remained consistent and strong over the years. This sort of consistency appeals to many buyers, especially new ones, and that only makes the Litecoin fanbase grow in size year after year.

Like all altcoins, Litecoin doesn't cost as much as Bitcoin. That is just one of the many benefits of it, one of the many reasons Litecoin continues to bring in new investors, even people who have yet to buy a slice of Bitcoin. You do not have to lose as much money when investing in Litecoin. However, other features make this altcoin attractive to all investors. The amount of Litecoin that exists - or will exist - is also incredibly appealing.

Regarding availability and the future of Litecoin, there are just so many more Litecoins to mine. That is surprising since Litecoin is much like Bitcoin and wants a manageable supply. This altcoin was started as a branch of Bitcoin initially. It now has a supply limit of about 84 million, which is far more than the limit Bitcoin will have. That means there is more of a supply of Litecoin, which means you have a better chance at buying cheaper because the demand doesn't affect supply as much as other altcoins, especially with Bitcoin. Some consider Litecoin the best altcoin to look into when starting your investing career.

Ethereum

Whenever you mention Litecoin as the gold standard for altcoins, you must say Ethereum, the silver to Litecoin's gold. It may not be *as* popular as Litecoin, but it still has a large, loyal fanbase that sings its praises often.

This altcoin has grown in popularity over the years and has shown how devoted it is to the future of all cryptocurrencies. In 2016, Ethereum split into two: Ethereum and Ethereum Classic. The price of Ethereum is relatively low compared to Bitcoin and some other altcoins, but many predict its value will only go up and up.

The most promising aspect of Ethereum is its speed. While it can take around 15 minutes for a Bitcoin to be encrypted, mined, and cleared, it only takes about 15 seconds for the same to be done with Ethereum. That isn't just fast; it is *blazingly* fast.

The speed is excellent; the price isn't as lovely. It will cost you a pretty penny to invest in Ethereum. But it has such promise and growth ahead that you would be silly to write off Ethereum. For serious investors, those who don't mind throwing down a large chunk of change on the promise of more, Ethereum is the way to go.

Bitcoin Cash

The name for this altcoin confuses many. Bitcoin Cash? So this is a form of Bitcoin? If that is the case, why don't people buy Bitcoin?

We understand the confusion and know an explanation is needed.

Bitcoin Cash is one of the earliest altcoins on the market and holds the distinction of being an oft-publicized hard fork from the original Bitcoin. A fork is when developers and miners cannot see eye-to-eye, and the decision is made to create vast differences in the code and branch off and complete a brand-new form of crypto.

When this happens, the original blockchain continues, and the new cryptocurrency and its chain "fork" off and go their own way. That is what happened with Bitcoin Cash, or BCH. In August 2017, it was created and took off on its own. Since then, it has not proven successful in its own and some people refer to it as Bitcoin Trash. However, its name and affiliation with Bitcoin have led to some confusion.

Cat

This 2023 Pro-Crypto Education, Adoption, and Public Awareness Token will revolutionize cryptocurrencies. Crypto Adoption Token's (CAT) unique advertising campaigns promote Crypto's immense potential. Join CAT's future! Join a thriving community of forward-thinking people who want to share cryptocurrency's benefits. We can change money and create a better future. These astonishing coins will transform political fundraising. These coins are improving the future by supporting pro-crypto politicians and regulatory reforms. Join the movement and change now! A revolutionary Bitcoin education and advocacy project. A new lobbying business will empower the next generation with strategic crypto knowledge. Introducing a unique project to popularize cryptocurrencies! CAT will empower people with crypto knowledge by making it widely accessible to the public. Adoption coins are changing how people view and participate in this exciting digital frontier through schools, libraries, independent lectures, seminars, and other engaging venues. Join us on this thrilling trip to unveil crypto's secrets and create a better, more informed future!

Celsius

Back in 2018, the Celsius Network earned $20 million via crowdfunding. That shows just how interested people were in Celsius before it officially launched. Since its creation and release, it has written over $6 million in loans and generated more than $11 million in interest.

The fact that Celsius has generated so much money in loans is surprising and encouraging and causes concern. We have seen numerous loaning giants fold over the years because of bad investments and loans that must be paid back. Celsius is too new to the loaning world and will make bad beds and offer loans to people who do not and should not get them. If that is the case, you can expect Celsius to face severe problems in the years ahead. However, there is a chance that Celsius will only continue to expand instead of collapse. And if you are still in Crypto, you know that Celsius has gone bankrupt, and clients with collateral stuck on the failed platform had to look to the bankruptcy courts and process for relief. And now we have another crypto technology with a fun name and yet another crypto that happened to be started by one of the creators behind Ethereum.

Polkadot.

It is fun to say, that's for sure. But Polkadot is far more than just a fun, playful name. It is a technology and system that wants to bring all sorts of other blockchains together for the better of all blockchains and all cryptocurrencies.

At its course, Polkadot is best described as a multi-chain network connecting different specialized blockchains into one unified network. These connected blockchains are called "para chains." These para chains come together to create a network that is uniform, easy to understand, easy to fix and tweak and further evolves. All of the para chains also run independently and parallel to one another. This is good because it prevents a network overload and lets each para chain run quickly and safely while still connected to the entire Polkadot network. Polkadot also created protocols allowing its network to interact with other blockchains. Since its blockchain network is flexible, it has an increased ability to pivot and serve more specific needs.

Why is this so important? What about Polkadot's revolutionary chain of blockchains makes it unique and worthy of your time and money? Its importance comes from Polkadot's ability to create a way for all developers to build blockchains with value, security, and a uniform system.

With Polkadot, blockchains can connect in the para chains. When placed together, these para chains create a so-called "relay chain" in which all transaction addresses are checked and verified, and all data is standardized to understand each system in the relay chain. Polkadot turns all blockchains into one extra-long, extra-safe blockchain.

But there is more to Polkadot than just its blockchain technology. Like Cardano and other cryptocurrency systems, Polkadot offers its coin, predictably named DOT. DOT is an internal cryptocurrency token that can directly influence the Polkadot network. Users who buy into DOT can vote on potential changes within Polkadot, meaning each purchased pass is also a vote and part of the democratic Polkadot process.

Polkadot is the creation of cryptocurrency mastermind Gavin Wood, an important figure in the history of rival coins, Ethereum. Wood was co-founder and one of the core developers of Ethereum, which would become one of the biggest names in the game and still proves to be one of the most popular coins in the marketplace. Wood was the man who coded the platform's first implementation, wrote its formal specification, and invented the Solidity contract programming language. He had long ago proven his worth and ability, giving crypto investors plenty of reasons to believe in him and follow his lead.

He moved on from Ethereum, and people were interested in what he would do next. He was satisfied with Polkadot's twist on blockchains and the idea behind connecting them into one giant, extra-safe chain.

On January 11, 2016, Wood moved on from Ethereum entirely and focused all his attention on Polkadot. In Wood's opinion, the new tech that would later be known as Polkadot would deliver on many of the promises that Ethereum still needs to achieve. He had high hopes and many goals in his mind. Wood has said that the original idea for Polkadot popped into his mind in the summer of 2016. Spurred on by fellow developer Marek Kotewicz, Wood began designing a sharded version of Ethereum that was as simple as possible. By October 2016, Wood had finished the first draft of the Polkadot White Paper, and he immediately knew he had something special.

Since launching on the market, Polkadot has hit many milestones, proving that many people did believe in Wood and followed him onto his new venture. It climbed to become the fourth largest cryptocurrency and achieved a peak market point of $18 billion.

It isn't just investors who believe in Polkadot. Other cryptocurrency companies and teams genuinely believe in the ideas and concepts behind Polkadot too. How is that known? Simply because there are now over 340 projects that are actively being developed on the Polkadot system. All of them will be connected via Polkadot's parchhain system. If so many people who create cryptocurrencies believe in Polkadot, it's no surprise that regular, everyday investors believe in it too.

Why Altcoin?

Some people want to invest solely in Bitcoin when they enter cryptocurrency. They feel that Bitcoin is the only sure thing, an investment that will always pay off and has fewer risks than others.

That's all good for those people, but you should fill your portfolio with some altcoins to become a talented and successful trader. Why? Because altcoins give you more opportunities for success, variety, and potential. Think of it this way: the wider variety of cryptocurrencies you own, the bigger your chances for success. Why limit yourself only to Bitcoin? While you could make your fortune with Bitcoin, it limits you significantly. Instead, you should study altcoins with great potential and research them and the market. Once you understand how the cryptocurrency market works and why it encounters the ups and downs it does, you will have a better handle on which altcoins show promise, which ones could become hits, and which ones will become misses.

Altcoins are a terrific way to make more money and find options for success that others may have missed. But it would be best always to choose the altcoins you want to invest in. Instead, it would be best to make your choices based on understanding the market and the history of cryptocurrency, Bitcoin, and altcoins. Know what has driven other altcoins to great heights - and deep lows. You will begin to see patterns in the cryptocurrency world, certain features that appeal to investors and those that don't. This will inform your choices and lead you to find the right altcoin. With so many options out there and so many chances for great value and significant loss, it is essential that you take buying altcoin very seriously. Otherwise, it is just like you throwing your money away.

How To Buy Bitcoin and Altcoin

Armed with more knowledge about how the market works the way it does, it is time to move onto another vital subject: just where on Earth do you buy crypto and start your trading career?

Thankfully, now you have quite a few options. In the early days of crypto, buying some was a challenging task. People needed to learn how to buy their share of cryptocurrency. Mainly because there were no rules or regulations, no set of guidance that told people where to go, how to buy, and what to look for. Remember, everything was created by people who wanted the system and longed for cryptocurrency for ages. They were both the ones dictating how the system worked and were also the ones using it.

In the early days, it was like many people wandering around in a pitch-black room looking for a light switch. They didn't know where to go, they didn't know what to do, and they didn't know the proper steps to take. Over time, a formal procedure began to formulate, and certain websites and message boards emerged. As cryptocurrency became more popular, even with a relatively small group of people, things became much more straightforward. The early days of crypto found people buying and selling coins on message boards, a primitive and complicated approach to trading that took too much time and effort and was far too confusing.

Boy, how times have changed. Today, you can buy cryptocurrency easily. It's as simple as logging into a website. In just a few moments, you can create a brand new account linked to your debit card and be capable of investing in the crypto of your choice.

The websites you can buy cryptocurrency from are called online exchanges, marketplaces for your crypto purchase. Depending on the site, you have specific options when making your purchase. There are many options for you, way more than there used to be even a few years ago. We will get into all these other types of cryptocurrencies, called altcoins, later. However, for our example, we will focus solely on the first and most popular form of cryptocurrency: Bitcoin.

It would be best to decide which online exchange will get your time, energy, and money. This is a crucial decision because a good rule of thumb is to stick with the same online business for all your crypto needs. Whomever you go with, try to stay with them throughout your trading career.

Who do you have to choose from when it comes to online exchanges? The options are varied and always promising. It's up to you to figure out who is your right fit.

Coinbase

Let's start with the biggest name in the game. Coinbase is, without question, the most popular online cryptocurrency exchange globally. It is the most widely-known exchange and is the go-to for many people, the gold standard of cryptocurrency exchanges. For both newcomers and long-term investors, Coinbase has set the bar high for its competitors. Unsurprisingly, Coinbase is investing much money into advertising and recruiting new traders as often as possible. They have made a name for themselves as the premier online exchange.

What attracts so many customers to Coinbase? It's simple, really: they make investing feel like a breeze. The site has proven itself as a safe and easy place to start your Bitcoin investing career. It only charges fees of $.99 to $2.99 depending on the value of your purchase. It also has a wide variety of coins, including some of the best altcoins on the market. Remember, the ability to buy altcoin is one of the most attractive features for some people looking to make their name in the world of cryptocurrency.

Coinbase offers insured wallets for investors. That means if something happens to your investment, Coinbase has you covered - to an extent. That coverage doesn't apply to *all* sorts of mishaps; restrictions apply. However, this is a vital sign that Coinbase takes its customers' satisfaction and safety seriously.

Coinbase also has something called Coinbase Pro, an upgraded version of their system with a different fee structure and more options for data and personalization. Coinbase Pro is another reason this site has become popular and is here to stay. They repeatedly show that they take Bitcoin investing seriously and continually upgrade the customer experience to reflect that.

Binance

Binance was founded in 2017. Since then, it has built an impressive and loyal following of Bitcoin and cryptocurrency investors who have succeeded with this online exchange and sing its praises. Binance is one of the market's most reliable and popular online exchanges. What has caused the explosion of popularity? The fact that this online exchange has a strong emphasis and focus on altcoins is what drives its loyalty among investors. Some say this site is better than even Coinbase if you want to build a portfolio consisting of lesser-known coins. Coinbase has access to 46 different cryptocurrencies, while Binance boasts over 50. That shows just how seriously Binance takes the concept of altcoins.

Binance also prides itself on its selection of essential data and charts. Top-quality analysis is integral to making intelligent investments, and Binance has many data points to help you navigate the market. You can find and make many different graphs with the site, which will help you become an even better crypto trader.

The consumer fees charged at Binance are neither too intense nor weighty. They are usually about .1% of each transaction. That will encourage new investors to trade and buy without fear and hesitation. It is easy to make a new buy when you are only charged the most minimal amount possible.

It could be better news. There are some things that Binance could improve. For example, the site is built for more advanced users with more experience in the market and using online exchanges. All of the data and analysis take work. It also doesn't work in 22 states in America, which means that if you live in one of those regions, you will be locked out of Binance. However, if you can get your hands on this online exchange and want to experience all that crypto offers - mainly if you invest heavily in altcoins.

KuCoin

Originally hailing from China, KuCoin is one of the most popular online exchanges, which has amassed a significant following with a great offering of cryptocurrencies.

One of the best things about KuCoin, and undoubtedly one of the things that draw in so many of its users, is that it has no deposit fees. And when it comes to the trading fee, it's relatively cheap, too, coming in at just .1%. KuCoin has also committed to having low prices in other aspects too. The withdrawal fees are next to nothing compared to other online exchanges.

But there is more to KuCoin than its cheap fees. It is a site that has a few things that others have done. For one, it offers its very own native cryptocurrency, called KuCoin Shares, also known as KCS. That is an offering you don't find everywhere in the crypto market. Then there is the fact that KuCoin offers many incentives to its users, such as financial rewards when they invite new members onto the site. KuCoin also offers exclusive promotions and bonuses for users actively using the site.

Now, KuCoin also has its downsides too. One of the most significant disadvantages of using the site is that it only works with traditional or fiat currency. That means you must use a different service to get Bitcoin or Ethereum before you can start trading on KuCoin.

KuCoin is an exciting, inventive online exchange for newcomers and seasoned traders. It is thinking outside the box, trying new things, and doing it differently, attempting to give further incentives and rewards that other sites don't offer. All in all, KuCoin will draw people in, and not only because it makes investing and trading coins easy.

eToro

eToro is another wildly popular cryptocurrency online exchange that has now established itself in over 100 countries. Coming out of Israel, eToro started by only offering Bitcoin trading but eventually opened up to accept more forms of crypto, including dozens of promising and below-the-radar altcoins. It now has a vast assortment of options for the most seasoned pro. But even if you're starting in the crypto world, eToro has much to offer you.

Firstly, eToro is an easy-to-use and functional site with many helpful features. These features make investing and trading painless and straightforward, whether you're embarking on your first or one-hundredth trade. The truth is that many online exchanges tend not to be very user-friendly. Sadly, many people have difficulty navigating through investing in crypto, but eToro makes it easy and will leave you feeling like you have a deep and solid understanding of things.

And some of their new ideas are downright brilliant. For example, the copy-trading technique. This stunning feature allows you to replicate the position of other traders in the network, even if you don't know them. That may seem more exciting and original, but it is helpful if you know other people on the site who have found the success you are looking for. Why not just copy their positions? There is no shame in attempting to be like those you respect. If you become a fan of a particular investor or want to mimic their success, the copy-trading feature will let you do just that.

eToro allows you to try your hand at more than just cryptocurrency. You can also buy and trade stocks, currencies, commodities, etc. You will notice that many online exchanges are starting to allow their clients to purchase other things to integrate Bitcoin with supplies and give them a true sense of normalcy.

Gemini

Gemini was started by Tyler and Cameron Winklevoss, the twin brother magnates who claimed they were the ones who created the idea for Facebook. Their foray into the cryptocurrency industry was met with speculation and attention; they had people ready to use Gemini before it fully launched. To some, it felt like a couple of tech start-up celebrities trying to climb aboard the next big thing without truly believing in it. Despite that, the Winklevoss twins put much effort into Gemini to turn it into something special that could stand on its own.

The look and feel of Gemini are slick and modern and look very hip; it makes investing in crypto feel cool. The entire site is incredibly user-friendly, too, and has a lot of intuitive controls that will make it a breeze for first-time users. Great emphasis has been put on creating an easy and painless investing process.

Gemini has a lot going for it but has a few downsides. For example, there aren't many currencies to choose from, and the community is still so tight-knit that it may feel small to some. It also might feel a bit too close-knit, a bit too close. That means making many personal connections with others on Gemini is hard. Others claim that Gemini feels sterile and cold, the opposite of inclusive. However, it works well and looks great too, and is accessible in many regions such as the US, Canada, Japan, the UK, and more. As for the aesthetic, that is a look that many other modern sites are going for because it gives off a hip, young, modern vibe.

But that's not all; other ways to purchase Bitcoin and cryptocurrency don't require you to log into a website. As the crypto craze has heated up over the years and all over the globe, a real-world alternative to buying your cryptocurrency has come to life.

Bitcoin ATMS

You may be perplexed by seeing the term "Bitcoin ATM" listed here because it has been told to you again and again that you cannot buy Bitcoins or cryptocurrency in the real world. That is still true; you can't purchase them like any tangible asset. But the times have changed, and you can buy crypto in person. Sort of.

Since the creation of Bitcoin ATMs, online exchanges aren't the only way for you to make a Bitcoin purchase. Investing has now become as easy as walking up to an ATM. That is because there are now Bitcoin ATMs in the world. Like a regular bank ATM, a Bitcoin ATM allows you to place your money in exchange for some Bitcoin. But since Bitcoin doesn't physically exist, placing your money in a Bitcoin ATM is like putting your fiat currency online. You will never see it again, but you know it is out there, making you money.

The concept behind Bitcoin ATMs could be more precise because, unlike traditional ATMs, you are not depositing or withdrawing cash at one of these machines. Yes, you are placing money into the machine. But it isn't going into your account. Instead, a Bitcoin ATM is used to buy and sell Bitcoin using fiat currency. So you walk up to the machine, enter your information, deposit your cash, and then choose the cryptocurrency you want to purchase. It is a way to enter the Bitcoin industry and invest without logging into the computer.

Buying or selling with a Bitcoin ATM is relatively simple and resembles the steps taken at a regular, traditional ATM. First, you approach the machine, and the first thing you have to do is verify your identity. Most Bitcoin ATMs will typically ask you to enter your mobile phone information. After entering that, you will be sent a text message to verify your identity before moving forward.

If you want to purchase Bitcoin at an ATM, you must deposit the appropriate amount of cash. After that, the automated teller machine will generate a unique QR code that your digital wallet app will scan on your phone. This way, the ATM tells your digital wallet that the transaction was a success and adds the digital funds to your wallet. Throughout the entire process, no money is ever changed hands aside from the initial deposit made into the machine. This may scare some people off since they need to get used to having an ATM *not* give them something. But this is a Bitcoin ATM, and, like all things cryptocurrency, it heavily emphasizes the Internet. Newcomers must be comfortable that they won't pull money out of the machine, only put it in.

The creation of Bitcoin ATMs shows just how popular cryptocurrency is becoming. Indeed, they wouldn't be installed worldwide if people weren't using them. No, Bitcoin ATMs offer that people are flocking to cryptocurrency, which is becoming increasingly popular and more mainstream. This is a sign of progress, that more people are adapting to cryptocurrency, and that you are getting in at the right time to start your investing career.

The fees these ATMs charge is outrageous and will only make sense for some people. At some point, these Bitcoin ATMs will merge with regular retail establishments. You should be able to go to any CVS and tell them you want to buy X amount of Bitcoin; they will tell you the fiat dollar amount you owe, you pay, and they deposit the amount in crypto to your wallet.

How Do I Store Cryptocurrency?

The safety of buying cryptocurrency was mentioned before, and the conclusion was made that, while it has risks, cryptocurrency is a safe commodity to invest in. The chances of any hacking or thievery stealing away your accumulated wealth are rare. It is rarer than rare. Although, the case is never zero. It could happen.

That is what leads some people to invest in a wallet. What is a wallet? A wallet is exactly what it sounds like a place for you to store your funds. However, since this is a cryptocurrency, a crypto wallet has a significant digital aspect tied to it. How do you keep something that doesn't exist, you may ask yourself? If it is all digital, what does the wallet hold inside it? This is a very stylish digital wallet since this is a modern digital currency.

A cryptocurrency wallet stores private keys that act as your specialized ID, the unique code allowing you to trade your crypto with others. The way that a crypto wallet works is that you gain access to it via a unique password that only you know. As with all passwords, you should never give away your crypto wallet. Otherwise, you open yourself up for severe pain and financial loss.

It is important to note that most online exchanges offer in-house crypto wallets. When you purchase crypto through these sites, they are stored in the area as well, and you can log into the website, monitor your crypto, and send, invest, and buy more directly through the site. This leads many people to ask why to go outside the area you purchased your crypto in. Why not just use the wallet that they provide you? The answer is that many people want extra security for their investments. They want to go above and beyond and buy a wallet that gives them even more safety. Many wallet and ledger companies worldwide have proven themselves to millions of customers, companies that go a step beyond online exchanges and promise more.

There are multiple types of crypto wallets in the marketplace today, all with their benefits and drawbacks. Depending on the type of trader you are, and the kind of safety you desire, there is a wallet that will feel perfect for you. For example, a web wallet, as you imagine, allows you to receive, send, and store your Bitcoin and cryptocurrency directly from a web browser. This basic form of a wallet is easy to use and has a little learning curve. Almost all online exchanges offering an account will also give you a free web wallet. However, it is usually advised that you research and invest in a different type of wallet, one with a few more robust safety measures that will bring you more comfort and security. While online exchanges are a great place to find, buy, and trade crypto, they are not always the best place to go when you want to store it.

There are also desktop wallets, which store your private keys directly onto a hard drive. This keeps all of your money in one central location. A desktop wallet turns your computer into a safe with your hard-earned cryptocurrency. And since it is only stored in that one location, you can only access this wallet if you can access the sole computer with the hard drive. This is a great benefit because you will always know where your money is, giving many users peace of mind. However, you must ensure that the computer you install your desktop wallet on is safer than safe and invulnerable to intrusion by outside parties.

Additionally, there are also mobile wallets as well. They are portable devices that you can take on the go on your smartphones. Using QR codes and other mobile technology, these mobile wallets allow you to access and monitor your funds often and with little work.

Hardware wallets are one of the most common types. They resemble the little USB drives you see in the hands of many students and business people, the little hard drives you can plug into a laptop and carry your information on the go. Like USB drives, the hardware wallet is a physical way to have a non-physical item: your cryptocurrency. With a hardware wallet, you can access your funds via a password only you know. As these hardware wallets become increasingly popular, they become more functional and easier to find and use. They now come with their apps, created specifically for them. The hardware wallet market is growing increasingly and is one of the most exciting industries in all cryptocurrency. It is also one of the safest.

The added security of a password you created for your hardware wallet is one of the many bonuses of owning one. The fact that you can take the wallet offline and disconnect it from the internet makes it safe from hackers, while the password makes it safe from anyone who gets their hands on your wallet. These layers of protection create the hardware wallet even safer, easier to use, and even more reliable.

CHAPTER 6

Blockchain Beyond Crypto

How is Blockchain Changing the World?

As you can see, blockchain technology is used by many companies in many other industries. It is a giant, global spreadsheet that is accessed by millions of people all over the world. It's open source so that anyone can change the underlying code, and they can see what's going on. It's genuinely peer-to-peer; it doesn't require powerful intermediaries to authenticate or settle transactions.

That idea alone is one of the ways that blockchain is so revolutionary and game-changing. It makes the little man just as powerful as those at the top.

But blockchain will change the world for more than just that. Take sending money, for example. Sending money abroad can take days. At best, this is frustrating; at worst, it could mean friends or family lacking necessities or waiting for emergency medical treatment.

Currently, banks hold foreign currencies in nostro/vostro accounts in other countries and use the SWIFT messaging system to arrange transfers. The transfer is usually done on the same business day if an agreement exists between the two banks. But in developing countries, where currencies are strictly controlled, your bank must use intermediaries or liquidity agents, which is more expensive, time-consuming, and labor-intensive.

Blockchain solutions dramatically reduce the time and cost of sending money abroad. With participating banks connected through a blockchain network, all the compliance and ID checks are fulfilled automatically and authenticated by cryptographic signatures. Once cleared, transactions are usually settled in just a few seconds, leaving an immutable, transparent record for both banks.

What about buying a home? Did you know blockchain will assist that age-old process too? The property market is a messy, tedious business. Buying a house can take months of grueling paperwork and costly lawyer fees. In the UK, things are even worse. Your seller can accept your offer but reject it later for a higher bid, a tactic known as gazumping (though officials are finally starting to regulate it).

Most property market issues stem from a need for more trust. Complex land registries backed by reams of signed paperwork make tracking difficult, and verification requires the coordination of banks, government agencies, and lawyers. The result is an expensive, time-consuming process that many of us dread.

Blockchain, however, is trustless, removing the need for complex verification processes carried out by intermediaries. With blockchain, there is a single, transparent version of the truth, and one party can't make changes without agreement from everyone else. It's effectively tamper-proof, cutting down on paperwork and reducing fraud risk.

Perhaps most importantly, blockchain will significantly improve the medical industry. Your medical history helps doctors treat you quickly and effectively, but chances are it's fragmented across multiple healthcare providers. Incompatibilities between providers' systems slow transfer records, often requiring manual intervention. Without your complete medical history, doctors could waste money and time on tests you don't need or be unable to give you the best treatment.

Blockchain could make it easier to treat health problems by radically improving the accuracy and availability of your medical history. By creating an accessible, permanent blockchain record you own, you could instantly reveal the ailments, allergies, and lifestyle factors that help doctors diagnose and treat you. It'll also verify your identity, ensuring you're not confused with the other John Smith in the waiting room.

Finally, blockchain will give you a stronger guarantee that the goods you buy are authentic.

Currently, the bulk of supply chain management is done through EDI, a messaging system first introduced in the 1970s. Although a big step up from paper, it's far from perfect. EDI is two-way only, leaving other interested parties out of the loop. If two parties commit to defrauding a third, their activities will remain hidden (e.g., fake goods manufacturers conspiring with distributors to sell products on Amazon).

That's not the case with blockchain. Every stage of a product's journey, from its manufacture to the serial of its shipping container, is recorded and available to all stakeholders, with no possibility of cutting corners or falsifying information. It also provides an open and transparent framework that eliminates confusion and disputes.

Blockchain ensures that it's the real deal when you buy something. It's the real deal when you purchase something.

Why Is Blockchain Becoming So Popular?

Undoubtedly, the science and technology behind blockchain are gaining steam and new fans worldwide in many companies, industries, and walks of life. Why? What is it that is driving this popularity?

Blockchain technology is becoming a big deal because it's associated with cryptocurrencies and tokenized solutions. Tokenization is splitting up units of value into ever smaller units so that more people can buy smaller units than would otherwise be possible.

This takes the existing Internet of information and communication and adds on the Internet of money and value transactions.

And the permutations that this can take are vast and varied, ranging from Bitcoin and other cryptocurrencies to Facebook's plans for an international payment system, banking, and finance, creating blockchain-based designs for faster and more secure international settlements, to real estate and other securities-based investments that allow for smaller investment into securities that used to have a high dollar value entry point, to autonomous invoicing and payments by IOT (Internet of Things) based sensors, to simply tipping online, in small amounts.

Blockchain takes the Internet - and adds money.

Money that is not controlled, regulated, or constrained by the existing national and international banking systems for fiat currencies.

And blockchain is just barely getting started. As with the Internet, as the technology matures and more easy-to-use consumer solutions appear - the more rapidly the new technology will be adopted and used.

NFTs

An NFT is, in essence, a collectible digital asset that holds value as a form of cryptocurrency and art or culture. Much like art is seen as a value-holding investment, so are NFTs. But how?

First, let's break down the term. NFT stands for a non-fungible token – a digital token that's a type of cryptocurrency, much like Bitcoin or Ethereum. But unlike a standard coin in the Bitcoin blockchain, an NFT is unique and can't be exchanged like-for-like (hence, non-fungible).

So what makes an NFT more special than a run-of-the-mill crypto coin? The file stores extra information, elevating it above pure currency and bringing it into the realm of anything. The types of NFTs are super-varied, but they could take the form of a piece of digital art or a music file – anything unique that could be stored digitally and be thought of to hold value. Essentially, they are like any other physical collector's item, but instead of receiving an oil painting on canvas to hang on your wall, for example, you get a JPG file.

NFTs are part of the Ethereum blockchain and are individual tokens with extra information. That additional information is crucial, allowing them to take the form of art, music, and video in JPG, MP3s, videos, GIFs, and more. Because they hold value, they can be bought and sold just like other types of art – and, like with physical skill; the value is set mainly by the market and demand.

However, that's not to say that only one digital version of an NFT art is available on the marketplace. In much the same way as art prints of an original are made, used, bought, and sold, copies of an NFT are still valid parts of the blockchain – but they will not hold the same value as the original.

And don't go thinking you've hacked the system by right-clicking and saving the image of an NFT, either. That won't make you a millionaire because your downloaded file won't hold the information that makes it part of the Ethereum blockchain. Make sense?

NFTs can be bought on a variety of platforms, and which you choose will depend on what it is you want to buy (for example, if you want to buy baseball cards, you're best heading to a site specifically made to sell and auction them, but other marketplaces sell more generalized pieces). You'll need a wallet specific to the platform you're buying on, and you'll need to fill that wallet with cryptocurrency.

Because of the high demand for many NFTs, they are often released as 'drops' (much like in events, when batches of tickets are often released at different times). This means a frenzied rush of eager buyers when the drop starts, so you must be registered and have your wallet topped up.

NFTs are having a moment with creators of NFT art, including artists, gamers, and brands across the spectrum of culture. Every day brings a new player to the NFT marketplace.

For artists, stepping into the NFT space adds another space and format to create and share art – and offers their admirers another way to support their work. With pieces ranging from small, quick-to-make GIFs (Rainbow Cat, above, was sold by NyanCat for $690,000) to more ambitious works, artists can offer the public a range of ways to buy art and make money.

We've talked about those making NFTs to include in video games, something that's shaking up the concept of buying assets in-game. Until now, any digital assets purchased inside a match still belonged to the game company – with gamers just buying them temporarily to use when playing the game. But NFTs mean that the ownership of assets has shifted to the actual buyer, meaning they can be bought and sold across the gaming platform with extra value based on who owns them. Games are beginning to be made that are based entirely around NFTs, proving how they are shaking up the industry.

NFTs are an attractive revenue stream for brands, as shown by all the recent brands jumping on the bandwagon. Taco Bell sold taco-themed GIFs and images (see one above) on one marketplace, and 25 sold out in just 30 minutes. Seriously. Each NFT held a $500 gift card, which the original owner could spend, which may explain their popularity initially. But these TacoCards are now selling on the secondary market, with the most expensive card selling for $3,500. And that doesn't include the gift card.

There's much money to be made in the NFT market. But you also may have heard some controversy surrounding NFTs, particularly about their impact on the climate. While NFTs are offering items in ways that are technologically advanced, the process of creating them could be more environmentally safe.

NFTs use a monster amount of energy in their creation. So much so that many protesters are worried about the genuine impact the craze could have on the environment. One piece called 'Coronavirus' consumed an incredible 192 kWh in its creation. That's equivalent to one European Union resident's total energy consumption for two weeks. But that must be a particularly huge piece, you ask? Nope, a 'simple' GIF can equate to the same consumption.

In a modern age where people are trying to be more and more green and pleasing to the planet, NFTs are providing controversy because of what they are doing to the environment.

CHAPTER 7

Crypto Mining

Crypto mining is a term you have heard many times if you are researching cryptocurrencies and looking to get into buying and trading. Indeed, mining is one of the most common things spoken about when people refer to crypto. It likely makes you think of an old gold miner using a pick axe to carve some gold or diamonds deep in a dark, dangerous cave.

Sure enough, mining can help you find some diamonds of your own in the form of Bitcoin. It can indeed put many cryptocurrencies in your pocket. And like the miners from the Gold Rush of the 1800s, mining can also have you walking away with nothing at all. There is indeed great reward related to mining. There is also significant risk.

So what is it? Just what is this mining thing that so many people are drawn to? Even among seasoned cryptocurrency fans, mining is a confusing sticking point that raises more questions than answers. People who have long studied crypto still do not attempt to get into mining because it is daunting and challenging. What makes it so hard? Also, is it worth it? Is it more hard work than it is worth, or is it a legitimate way to make extra money?

Crypto mining is complicated. Not only is the actual process itself complex, but so is the explanation of it. We will try to break it down as quickly and plainly as possible but do not be alarmed if it doesn't make sense.

Crypto mining is a slow, painstaking process that checks on the latest crypto transactions to verify them and ensure they are legitimate. The goal of mining is to avoid the dreaded idea of double-spending. Double spending is something that explicitly affects cryptocurrencies. It is when someone spends the same money in two places at once.

Double-spending isn't possible with physical money. If you walk into a store and spend $10 on a sandwich, you hand over the $10 bill to the employee, and it is no longer yours, and you cannot then spend it elsewhere. The same is true if you pay with a debit or credit card. Whichever financial institution you are a part of will immediately deduct the exact amount from your checking or credit card account, and that money is no longer yours to spend.

But when you pay with crypto, you can spend the money in two places simultaneously. You are paying with codes and specific keys made for each transaction. And you are doing all this without the regular checks and balances established by banks and other stable monetary systems. Cheating is possible if no one is looking.

That is where crypto mining comes into play. Mining is those checks and balances you need to ensure no one is being scammed. However, mining isn't done by an employee at your bank or an anonymous computer following a built-in procedure. Instead, mining is done by the very same people who invest in and trade crypto in the first place.

What is Mining?

Cryptocurrency mining is a process that validates Bitcoin transactions by adding them to the ledger or record of the currency, known as a blockchain. This is a challenging process. It is also a long process. Mining is not something you can casually pick up or run off of just any computer.

Miners use specialty hardware to complete the complex calculations confirming Bitcoin transactions. In simple terms, miners are trying to assemble a massive and ultra-hard puzzle. Thousands of miners are working simultaneously, trying to crack a code sent to them. They are anonymous auditors, all working towards the same goal. And whoever gets it first receives a prize: Bitcoins.

Mining continues the blockchain we spoke of before. Mining is taking important information, like all the Bitcoin transactions within the last 10 minutes, and verifying them. From there, a computer, known as the miner, must figure out a computational puzzle.

Once that miner encrypts that chunk of information or block, they can share it across the internet with other miners. Once it is verified, it is added to the existing chain. As for the computer and the user who solved the puzzle, they are rewarded with their very own Bitcoins.

Mining continues the blockchain we spoke of before. Mining is taking important information, like all the Bitcoin transactions within the last 10 minutes, and verifying them. From there, a computer, known as the miner, must figure out a computational puzzle.

Once that miner encrypts that chunk of information or block, they can share it across the internet with other miners. Once it is verified, it is added to the existing chain. As for the computer and the user who solved the puzzle, they are rewarded with their very own Bitcoins.

Can I Be A Miner?

Let's say that you have decided that you are going to take a chance and spend the time and money to build your very own cryptocurrency mining computer. You have researched the information and determined you could make a beautiful penny if your computer works.

It sure is much work, but it can and will pay off if done correctly. You stand to earn a huge profit if you have a mining rig at home, digging away at code and unlocking and encrypting blockchain.

But this isn't like buying a regular computer. You cannot walk into any retail or computer store and tell them you want to buy a mining rig. No, this takes a lot more work, and you need to know what you are doing to earn your Bitcoin reward.

It is time to determine what it takes to buy and build your mining computer. If you follow these steps, have patience, and do not expect immediate success overnight, great profit might await you.

But before we get into what you need and the steps you must take, you must be reminded again that you *could* make much money by crypto mining, but it is still being determined. You may not ever make a dime off of mining. Do not walk into the crypto mining world expecting a cash windfall. Not now, maybe not ever. If it pays out, it pays out well. But there is no promise that it will ever pay out.

Types of Rigs

What is a cryptocurrency mining rig? It is a computer. But it is not a computer like the one you have at home. No, a mining rig is a computer with many graphic cards but lacks a monitor. The computer case has GPU cards, a motherboard, a cooling system, and more.

And how does it work? The rig is hooked up to the internet, of course, and the blockchain network that it needs. The blockchain network works on its own 24 hours a day and is powered by the graphic cards in the computers connected to the network.

Mining rigs often work on their own once they get up and running. They take up more space than a standard computer because of some of the protruding items included in them, so people often place mining rigs in garages or places that only stick out a little. While you *can* hook a monitor up to a mining rig and use it as a regular computer at times, most people only use them to mine. Remember, mining can be full-time, and one can work 24 hours a day.

What are the types of mining rigs you can make? There are three vastly different choices when you are building your rig.

ASIC

First up is the ASIC rig. ASIC stands for Application-Specific Integrated Circuits. These are specially-made devices created with one sole purpose in mind. This is the most important, powerful choice when you want to start a career in crypto mining. They are more than just computers, which is essential to remember. An ASIC rig is a tool made for one thing and one thing only. In this case, that one thing is mining. This is a dedicated piece of machinery built to get the job done.

Creating or buying an ASIC is hard because they are so good at what they do. Their impressive performance skills mean that many people looking to get into mining want an ASIC. That means they are hard to come by. While eventually getting your hands on an ASIC is worth it and probably your best bet at a successful mining career, finding one will take much work. You will have to rely on third-party sellers or a very, very, *very* savvy tech friend who can make one for you. Remember, this won't resemble the personal computer you use at home to surf the web or play video games. This is an entirely different beast.

There is some controversy surrounding ASIC builds too. These compelling devices have been accused of toying and messing with other mining devices on the network, and that has caused them to be subject to a lot of disdain and finger-wagging. You need to remember that when you create or buy an ASIC, especially if you care about the well-being of other miners on the network. Still, this is the most powerful and impressive computer for mining.

GPU

The GPU approach to mining is a great way to go if you want to mine and, say, watch Netflix in your spare time or play games with your friends online. They can be more than just a mining rig, unlike an ASIC build. That makes them exceedingly popular and also relatively easy to create and maintain.

A GPU rig is a favorite for someone looking to build their computer. While it is still difficult and requires much computer knowledge, it isn't impossible and nearly as daunting as shopping for an ASIC.

There are two types of GPU rigs: simple and dedicated miners. You can guess what a dedicated miner is. That is a GPU computer that is made only of mine. This is the right path if you want to dive headfirst into crypto mining and want to devote much time to unlocking and encrypting the blockchain.

But what if you want to share your computer with the others in your house? What if you are an avid World of Warcraft player or use your computer for homework? Then you will want the simple miner, the second type of GPU computer. You can use this device to mine *and* do other typical things that a personal computer does. The ability to choose between these two options is an excellent incentive for people looking to try their hands at mining.

What about the downsides? There is a major one when buying or making a GPU computer. That is the price. Creating or buying one of these devices can be pretty expensive. Unlike the ASIC model, a GPU relies heavily on a graphics card. Graphic cards can get expensive, especially if you are looking for a high-end one that will get the job done.

It isn't just the graphic cards that end up impacting your wallet. Your GPU will need a lot of bells and whistles and a few add-ons to keep it running in top form. You will need cooling devices and a robust electricity system. And if your GPU hits a bump in the road and needs repairs, you will have to spend a lot of money to do that effectively.

Despite its setbacks and challenges, the GPU is a beautiful way to start your mining career and can serve multiple purposes. That makes the hefty price tag more worth it.

CPU

CPU mining is the third and, at a time, the most popular way to mine. Why is CPU mining so prevalent in the crypto community? Because it is a straightforward way to mine. It is also relatively inexpensive. But when we say it is cheap, we mean building the device itself doesn't cost as much as alternatives. Upkeep and other factors of CPU mining do cost a lot and can be a massive headache as you move further in your mining career.

When we speak of the simplicity of CPU mining, we are talking about the quick setup required. You can start crypto mining right now if you have a suitable computer. You can download an app on your CPU device using the CPU method and get to mining almost immediately. This is a very enticing and promising reason for many and why scores of people tend to start CPU mining over buying or creating a GPU or ASIC rig. CPU mining takes way less effort, and getting started doesn't take much time.

But CPU mining has its drawbacks, and they are related to pricing. While creating a CPU rig isn't very expensive (in fact, you might already have a CPU rig and not even know it), the upkeep prices are frustrating and high. For one, using a CPU rig will make your electric bills skyrocket. One of the biggest complaints about mining is the cost of electricity once you get started, and, sure enough, a CPU rig will hog up a lot of your power and strain your local grid. This isn't nearly as simple as a typical computer; you are not simply flipping a switch and turning on a monitor. The system and process a CPU rig goes through to mine are long; complicated, and lengthy. It will constantly be chugging along and sucking up much power. You will see the price on your monthly statement shoot up after some time. That alone is enough reason to scare many people away.

But the electricity bill isn't the only thing that will hurt your wallet. No, the price of cooling your system and maintaining it costs just as much as the power running your rig. These machines must be tended to often; a lot can go wrong. When something goes awry, you will step in and put down a pretty penny to fix it. Altogether, these rigs will suck a lot of money out of your bank account. It will all be worth it if you successfully mine a block and get its payout. If not, you will be spending much money with minimal reward.

These three types of rigs all have their benefits and their downsides too. The most common drawback for all three models is the price. Whether with maintenance, repairs, electricity, or something else, mining on one computer costs a lot of money. A lot can go wrong, and each mis-step-misstep will drain your funds. Maintaining one of these rigs is almost more expensive than having a small child.

Consider buying and running a mining rig like a business. It will cost much money, but so does successfully owning a company. You will need to invest significant sums and hope you are rewarded with something that pays you back at the end of the process. We have spoken of how much money you can make with mining; you could generate a fortune if you find luck in the field. If you think of mining as a hobby, it will be costly. But the hefty price tag will be more palatable if you approach mining like a career or business.

How Much Will a Mining Rig Cost?

We have spoken a lot about how expensive crypto mining is. We have made no secret that it will cost you a pretty penny and may only pay out for a short time, if ever.

But how much money are we talking about? Just how hefty is the price tag related to crypto mining? How much money will it set you back? Is it worth it?

The short answer is no; it probably isn't worth it for most people. The long answer, however, is that it could be worth it if you do it the right way and are comfortable spending a lot of cash. This isn't some hobby you pick up at your convenience; it is something you must dedicate a lot of time and energy to.

When building your computer, you will create a large chunk of change to create a rig that can do the job right. The graphic card needed for a CPU mining rig is at least $700. Some cost quite a bit more than that, too; it depends on what you are comfortable using. Remember, cutting corners and going cheap with any part of your rig will cost you in the long run and affect your computer's ability to mine successfully. It is hard to spend money like this, but it is even harder to do all this work for absolutely nothing while other computers race by you in terms of power.

The graphic card alone will hit your bank account hard. From there, the other components aren't much cheaper. There are examples of people building a crypto mining rig for around $3,000, but that is the bare minimum of what you can spend, and that sort of computer will not be very promising or deliver many chances for success.

On the other hand, some people have spent more than $10,000 on their rigs. That is more expensive than many cars. Even then, there is no guarantee of success. You can spend thousands of dollars on a rig and still walk away empty-handed. Are your chances improved based on how much money you spend? Yes, they are. But do not think spending $10,000 automatically means you will be racking in the Bitcoin.

The price of the computer isn't the only thing you will consider when getting into mining. Remember the electricity you will be using to mine. The total can add up fast and send some people straight into bankruptcy court.

We all have electricity bills and are familiar with their average price. You know that during the height of winter and summer, your power bill is going to skyrocket because of the consumption needed to keep you and your family warm or cool. But even the highest bill you've come across pales compared to what you will experience if you start crypto mining at home.

Research has shown that the cheapest electricity cost for mining a single Bitcoin is more than $3,000. That is an astronomically high number, and it's on the lower end of the spectrum. You will have to spend about $3,000 to mine a single coin in the cheapest states in the nation. If you live in a state with higher power prices, you could drop $6,000 to mine your Bitcoin. That quote, on top of the cost of creating and maintaining your rig, is tough to swallow. It is tough to accept if you aren't getting anything in return for all that cash spent. At that rate, it could take weeks or months to get a return on your investment, and that is only if your rig works perfectly and is lucky enough to mine a coin.

You can see the risk and rewards associated with crypto mining regarding how much you will spend. The cost of building and maintaining your rig is enough to scare many people away from attempting to make money this way. But when you remember the value of your rewarded Bitcoin, it sounds more promising. Just remember that, like everything related to cryptocurrency, your success isn't guaranteed, and it is doubtful that it will happen quickly.

Is Mining Legal?

Crypto mining, like cryptocurrency as a whole, isn't legal all over the globe. While most nations allow cryptos like Bitcoin and other altcoins, some countries do not allow them. Live in Egypt, Ecuador, Nepal, Pakistan, and Morocco. You will not be able to purchase or trade cryptocurrency and will not be able to mine.

However, in other countries, you can buy and mine freely. That doesn't mean it will always be that way, however. As cryptocurrency becomes more popular and disrupts the traditional monetary system, more and more people in power, like politicians, have come forward, pushing back against it and hoping to limit or outright restrict it. If that happens in the country you live in, your ability to mine and buy crypto will become a thing of the past and could put you in serious legal jeopardy.

This is one of the other risks of crypto mining. The crypto landscape is changing constantly, for better and worse. It is not only the value of coins that remains volatile. The opinion and future outlook for cryptocurrency also always feel in flux. In the months and years ahead, some nations will successfully ban crypto and the ability to buy, trade, and mine coins.

This unpredictability is a considerable drawback to mining. Imagine spending thousands upon thousands of dollars on mining. Imagine starting to make a profit off of it. Imagine it becomes banned in your region, and you are effectively breaking the law. All of that money, all of that time, all of that energy - down the drain. That is the risk you run by participating in an industry still seen as new and different and a bit suspicious by those in power.

It is important to note that if you live in a country that hasn't limited or banned cryptocurrency, you are doing nothing wrong by crypto mining. You are free to do so and should feel no shame. But you do need to consider the political and economic environment you live in. If there is a chance that cryptocurrency could be banned where you live, you should proceed with caution before you start to put time and money into becoming a crypto miner.

What About Mining Pools?

You may have read about mining pools as an intelligent and cheaper alternative to creating and running your mining rig. This is an easier route, especially if you want to save money. However, it has its drawbacks as well.

What is a mining pool? It is a group of miners all working together to unlock and encrypt a Bitcoin and earn a reward. As you can imagine, the resulting coin doesn't just go to one miner. Instead, all participants split the payout. That means the whole lump sum won't just go to you, even if your computer is the one that finally cracks the code. You are agreeing to split the earnings with those in your pool. That is terrible news if you want all the Bitcoin for yourself. But it also means you can reap a massive windfall of money even if your rig isn't the one to find success.

These mining pools are run by third parties who rely on the network of computers in each collection. This is indeed a more straightforward and far more profitable way to mine. The work's weight isn't on you and your rig; it is spread evenly across your pool. However, it is again important to note that there is no sure thing in mining, even when you are part of a pool.

Bottom Line: Should I Crypto Mine?

Like everything related to cryptocurrency, there needs to be more clarity around mining. Some people feel it is a sure thing, a great way to get rich quickly. Others, however, think the payout related to mining is impossible and that all it will ever be is a massive waste of time and money.

The reality is somewhere in the middle. No, it is not a get-rich-quick scheme and should never be considered one. And it is also not a complete and utter waste of time. Likely, you will never get rich by crypto mining, but you stand a chance at making some money. Will that amount of money make the price of computing and electricity worth it? That depends on your success and what you are comfortable with.

What is a Fork?

You have heard of a fork before but probably haven't heard of one about finance, have you? But forks are a significant part of financial institutions, especially cryptocurrency. And they can make or break an entire cryptocurrency.

A hard fork is when nodes of the newest version of a blockchain no longer accept the older version(s), which creates a permanent divergence from the previous version of the blockchain.

Adding a new rule to the code essentially creates a fork in the blockchain: one path follows the new, upgraded blockchain, and the other continues along the old path. Generally, after a short time, those on the old chain will realize their blockchain version is outdated or irrelevant and quickly upgrade to the latest version.

A fork in a blockchain can occur in any crypto-technology platform—not only Bitcoin. That is. because blockchains and cryptocurrencies work the same way no matter which crypto platform they're on. You may think of the blocks in blockchains as cryptographic keys that move memory. Because the miners in a blockchain set the rules that drive the memory in the network, these miners understand the new rules.

However, all miners must agree on the new rules and what comprises a valid block in the chain. So when you want to change those rules, you need to "fork it"—like a fork in a road—to indicate that there's been a change in or a diversion to the protocol. The developers can then update the software to reflect the new rules.

Through this forking process, various digital currencies with names similar to Bitcoin have come to be: bitcoin cash, bitcoin gold, and others. For the casual cryptocurrency investor, it can be difficult to tell the difference between these cryptocurrencies and to map the various forks onto a timeline. To help sort this out, we have composed a history of the essential Bitcoin hard forks of the past several years.

There are several reasons why developers may implement a hard fork, such as correcting essential security risks found in older versions of the software, adding new functionality, or reversing transactions—such as when the Ethereum blockchain created a hard fork to reverse the hack on the Decentralized Autonomous Organization.

After the hack, the Ethereum community almost unanimously voted in favor of a hard fork to roll back transactions that siphoned off tens of millions of dollars worth of digital currency by an anonymous hacker. The hard fork also helped DAO token holders get their ether funds returned.

The proposal for a hard fork did not exactly unwind the network's transaction history. Instead, it relocated the funds tied to the DAO to a newly created smart contract to let the original owners withdraw their funds.

DAO token holders could withdraw ETH at approximately 1 ETH to 100 DAO. The DAO curators withdrew and distributed the extra balance of tokens and any ether that remained due to the hard fork to provide "failsafe protection" for the organization.

CHAPTER 8

How To Stay Safe with Crypto

We have examined and talked about some of the many upsides of investing in Bitcoin and cryptocurrencies and the incredible power of blockchain. There are quick returns on investment, the accessibility of starting a new account, and the lack of restrictions from government bodies attempting to slow you down. Indeed, there is much to celebrate about crypto and the new and easy ways it allows to make money and become a part of such an exciting market.

There hasn't been anything like cryptocurrency, and its benefits are seemingly endless and truly impressive. It is a breath of fresh air to investors, bringing in newcomers who have never invested or traded before and want to get in on the ground floor of something special.

Unfortunately, it also brings out a fair number of scammers. As we have said before, there needs to be more clarity about cryptocurrency; a lot that people need to learn and a lot that is easy to inflate or muddle. A certain vagueness comes with cryptocurrency because the media needs to report and describe it accurately and because of its somewhat complicated nature. If you need to become more familiar with technology, cryptocurrency may make you scratch your head. However, there are still people looking to invest even though they need help understanding what they are doing. That is a recipe for disaster, and a scammer's dream come true.

Scamming has sadly become a substantial part of the cryptocurrency world because of the confusion around crypto and the lack of regulation and oversight from significant institutions. However, you are not destined to be taken advantage of by a scammer. There are ways to avoid these criminals looking to make a buck off of you. You need to be prepared and aware of what to look for because, sadly, navigating through scammers is becoming a regular part of cryptocurrency.

What Are Crypto Dangers?

The unfortunate thing about cryptocurrency scams is that there are many of them, and they seem to be only growing. Scammers have found many ways to capitalize on new investors and profit from their lack of knowledge and overall need for clarification about buying and trading crypto.

The truth is that crypto scamming has become a significant industry, and many people make far more money ripping off others than actually investing in crypto itself. In 2019, more than $4 billion was made by scammers. More than many companies make $4 billion is an astonishing amount of money. You can see why so many nefarious people worldwide want to get in on such a scandalous way of making money.

Scams are a scary thing. Not only are they scary because they can steal your money, your information, and, ultimately, your safety. They are also tricky because they hurt the overall health of Bitcoin and cryptocurrency. When a scam becomes prominent and well-known, it scares people away from investing in Bitcoin. As we have noted before, the strength of the crypto market relies on peoples' faith and trust in the system. If that waivers, the entire market will decline and trend downward. So while any scam is terrible for those affected, it can cause a ripple effect that will only harm the future of Bitcoin and the investments of those involved.

Many scams exist and are running rampant across the web. The most common scams would be fake Bitcoin exchanges online or Ponzi schemes. Let's start with the Ponzi scheme first since it is something you have seen in all sorts of industries and have for decades.

The Ponzi Scheme

A Ponzi scheme is when you pay into some business or investment with a promise of a significant return on your investment. It may be a small business that needs some starting cash but will pay you back your money with interest in less than a year. Maybe a brokerage investor is starting his firm and looking to put your money into some sure-thing stocks that will make you a massive profit in no time. Whatever the situation, a Ponzi scheme needs your money upfront with the guarantee that you will get it back - and then some - shortly after that.

The tricky thing about Ponzi schemes is that investors often see some money, which usually ensures that everything is above the board and properly working. In reality, though, the schemer is paying out profits to early investors using the latest batch of money. As long as more people are putting into the pot, the scammer can continue to distribute just a little bit of money to those who have invested and lure them into paying more. In reality, there isn't nearly as much money to go around as they promise, and eventually, the house of cards will collapse, and the significant sums promised will suddenly vanish.

The most unfortunate thing about Ponzi schemes is that it is tough for scammed investors to get their money back. They can never get back the total amount they put in because the scammer has often spent it all on him or herself. That is true for Bitcoin scams too.

How does a Bitcoin Ponzi scheme work? Usually, they promise to make the entire idea of Bitcoin trading and investing easy on you. They say they will remove the middleman by buying crypto and do all the hard work for you. All you need to do is provide payment, and they will invest for you but will still show you the progress your coins are making and will keep you up to date on how successful your investment is.

The problem is that they likely need to invest more. These scams hope they can trick you by showing you fake statements with falsified numbers. You will think you are doing great and will not ask to sell your coins. Or you may ask for just a sliver of your profits so far, which they can afford to part with. However, they are giving you other peoples' money while taking in even more to keep their scam alive. The moment the system is figured out, it will collapse, and no one will walk away with anything.

Another Ponzi approach to Bitcoin revolves around crypto mining. There have been several instances of up-and-coming businesses offering you to invest in mining. As we have discussed, crypto mining is a highly complicated process requiring much work and processing power to create, encrypt, and verify the ever-growing blockchain. However, if your system is one of the lucky ones to mine a block successfully, you will be rewarded with a Bitcoin, which can net you thousands of dollars.

Schemers across the globe know that mining is a very confusing thing that most people know little about. But they also know that many people know the great payout possible if you are successful in mining. So these schemers lure people in with the promise of a significant sum of cash at the end. They promise they have the computing power and the know-how; they only need the money to get things up and running.

In 2019, a band of scammers was busted after creating a business called BitClub Network. They ran the scam for years. They solicited more than $722 million from investors by promising them a part in a giant crypto mining pool. They swore up and down that significant profits were coming and that investors could make even more money if they recruited others to join in. In the end, the investors walked away empty-handed.

The Ponzi scheme is an easy trap to fall into. It plays upon your desire to make money quickly and without much effort. Scammers know precisely what to say and how to lure you in. They are smooth talkers who make themselves seem knowledgeable, friendly, and eager to help. In reality, they are preying upon those who do not know better. It is a horrible way to make money and one you should always look out for.

Make sure you see proof of your profits and do not invest in shady businesses that cannot prove how much you are making. Fact-check any potential scam, look into and do some research online. Ideally, avoiding any situation that could be a Ponzi scheme is best. Get-rich-quick plans seem too good to be true because they almost always are. You will make money slower and more efficiently than some say, so if someone tells you you can, you should be very weary.

Fake Bitcoin Exchanges

South Korea, 2017. Financial authorities made a significant bust in that country. The alleged criminals were running a scam called BitKRX. What did BitKRX do? They promised investors that they were the country's most powerful Bitcoin trading platform and took millions upon millions of dollars from people looking to turn a profit and make money off cryptocurrency.

These sorts of fake websites are becoming all too popular over the years. The bigger Bitcoin becomes, the more significant these scams become too. They prey upon folks who do not know much about investing and do not know the intricate details of buying and trading Bitcoin. They know they want to make money at the end of the day, and these fake exchange sites promise that. But they are also reasonable rates that are unheard of and frankly unreasonable. They promise you will invest for next to nothing, and the process will be painless and quick. In reality, they are taking advantage of you and simply stealing your money. None of it is buying Bitcoin or other altcoins; none of it is going into any market. They are merely pocketing your cash, and you are left with nothing.

Fake Bitcoin Exchanges are tough to combat because it is so easy for scammers to create authentic-looking sites that feel like the real thing. And for those who have yet to do the proper research, they are easy to fall for. Many people assume there are many real cryptocurrency exchange sites across the web. In reality, there are far less than you think. The moment you hear of a brand new exchange site promising too-good-to-be-true rates, you need to proceed with extreme caution because it is likely a scam and a way for you to lose it all and gain nothing.

The truth is that investing in Bitcoin should be done through one of the few genuinely reputable online exchanges. They are easy to find; a short Google search can find the most popular and reliable ones. Anything aside from those few is not worth your time. Refrain from trying to make extra money when finding an exchange, and be aware of finding the next best thing full of unheard-of rates and promises. You should take This part of Bitcoin trading seriously and avoid all risks. If you make much money off Bitcoin, it will not be because of the exchange site you buy into. Instead, you will make money by investing wisely and trading at the right time. Do not fall for a scammer who will tell you otherwise.

Scamming Emails and Fake Sites

Scamming emails have grown in popularity over the last few decades, and you cannot go a few days with some junk email promising you something rewarding and out of this world. These emails immediately go into your junk folder, and with good reason: they are trash. But that doesn't stop them from coming.

Why do spam emails still exist decades after the creation of modern email? Because someone is falling for it. It may be hard to believe, but these scammers make their money somehow. Even though nine out of ten people can recognize and ignore a scam email, one person may go for it. That is sometimes all a scammer needs to make their money.

The same is valid for spamming emails related to Bitcoin investing. Most people will not fall for it. Most people will recognize spam as spam, immediately ignore it, and keep it from wasting time. But there are people out there who need to become more experienced with Bitcoin and will be tricked into responding to a spam email, and then they will soon be losing their money.

They are creating an email address and official-looking correspondence that feels like the real thing isn't hard. There are many ways to impress potential investors and dupe them into giving away money. A spam email creates a letterhead and logo that looks real. These scam artists will state that they work for an effective and reputable service. They will use that company's artwork and logo in their emails. They will also create email addresses that look just like the real thing. But upon closer inspection, it would become evident that they are using old tricks that scammers have had for ages. They will replace the letter O with a zero or something along those lines, something that will trick the reader into thinking that things are valid and legitimate.

All the scams associated with Bitcoin and cryptocurrency exploit people looking to get rich quickly. That is an easy way for them to get their foot in the door and promise something that everyone wants: money, lots of it. The desire to get rich quickly is one you will need to disregard when you start investing in cryptocurrencies altogether. Do not expect to make millions overnight. Instead, you should be prepared to make your money slowly but steadily if you make the right choices and invest and trade smartly. You look in the wrong place if you attempt to make tons of money quickly.

There are other ways that scammers can take money from you. There are fake mobile apps that aren't legitimate and will only drain you of cash; malware is embodied on scammer sites that will hack into your account and take your banking or email information. There are even other scams related to Bitcoin like people claiming to be from the IRS and demanding you pay back taxes on sums you raised via cryptocurrencies. If you are not paying attention, there are plenty of ways for people to make money from you. What we listed are just some of the many approaches scammers will take. You must pay attention, stay informed and always keep yourself safe. Investing in Bitcoin offers you the chance to make money; that is true. But falling victim to a Bitcoin scam only promises heartbreak and financial ruin.

Will Crypto Be Banned? Why Do People Distrust It?

As you have heard repeatedly, there is a level of distrust aimed at Bitcoin and cryptocurrency that is unparalleled. Many people do not understand Bitcoin and believe in the most hyped and sensationalized conspiracies. Some people believe that Bitcoin is only used by hackers, scammers, and people who want to steal your hard-earned cash. Other people think that Bitcoin can easily *be* hacked and stolen, and there is no reason to invest because it will be taken from you by some criminal computer pro. Other people think that it cannot be used anywhere or that it has no value at all.

Many confused and unfounded thoughts about Bitcoin have led to rampant speculation and skewed biases and views. However, others know better. Some people know the particulars of Bitcoin and cryptocurrency and how it works. They are realists; they understand the benefits and the disadvantages of Bitcoin. Still, they choose to rail against Bitcoin and fight tooth and nail to ensure it doesn't find a solid footing in the modern world. Why do these people fight so vigorously against Bitcoin and its potential? What are they afraid of? Why do they hate it so much? Why is such anger directed at Bitcoin by the people who should know much better?

(Traditional) Money is Power

It is important to remember just how powerful and essential money is. There is no way to deny that, nothing to debate about that statement. People say that money is the root of all evil, and that may be true. But it is also the root of all power. And when someone has power, they want to hold onto it.

It is worth noting that someone isn't evil just because they want to control their power and keep things as they are. There is a solid argument to be made there. The world's entire course can collapse when things change too drastically or quickly. Some people legitimately want to hold onto their gained power because they genuinely believe the alternative could spell doom for economies and the people within them. Not everyone who wants to keep the status quo strong is a money-hungry monster. People have goals, expectations, biases, and desires. It isn't wrong to fight for what you genuinely believe is right.

Many people who have gained much power in governments and major corporations have done so with money. They have made much money and spent much money to get to where they are now. They have done this using fiat currencies. Fiat is a term used to describe conventional currencies, like the Dollar, Yen, etc.

The thing about fiat currencies is that they only really have value because the governments say they do. For example, the United States government has said that the dollar is the only valuable currency in the United States. If they came out one day and declared that seashells were the new, only accepted currency in America, seashells would now have value, and the dollar would be a flimsy piece of paper that meant nothing. Any tangible assets do not technically back fiat currencies. There is a term that you may see when reading about money. It says "backed by the full faith and credit" of the government. That means the government believes in that currency, which is why it is valuable. It has been chosen, deemed appropriate, and that is why you use it.

As technology has advanced, that means less and less to some people. But for those in power, the fiat currency that nations have used for generations must stay the only, unrivaled form of payment. That is the sort of currency they have amassed that is the sort of currency that makes the world go around, that is the sort of currency that keeps corporations thriving and the stock market booming. If fiat currencies didn't have as much value because they had legitimate competition, the power wouldn't be as strong. Money is power, and only one type of money can be recognized: the money that the powerful use. That is fiat currency.

Governments want to avoid new forms of currency because they need to learn how to handle it. They must learn how to monitor, tax, or control it properly. Current governments have great control over how much money is in circulation and how much it gets taxed. They can track money because they handle money. If fiat currencies lost their power and more people turned to cryptocurrency, the government would not be as in control, and that is something they desperately want to avoid.

Without control over currency, governments of the world would not be able to control fiscal policy, crime, and the world of business. Remember, the financial elite who control the puppet politicians have a lot invested in the current system and will do everything they can to keep it in place. They will even create their own Central Bank Digital Currency (CPDC) to continue to control the system. But that will only help Bitcoin to thrive and not shut it down.

Those in power think the concept behind Bitcoin or cryptocurrency is good. Some think the idea is revolutionary and essential; some genuinely believe in branching off and starting something new. However, many people know that things can get messy if the power is divided between those who currently have it and others. What will happen to the economy? What will happen to the business industry? So many things would be altered if cryptocurrency became more mainstream. Most notably, the balance of power would shift. They do not want that.

Unfortunately, that is why so many have turned to innuendo and downright conspiracies and lies about cryptocurrency. Some politicians and industrialists have come out and said that they do not want to see cryptocurrency thrive because it stands a chance of disrupting how things are currently run. That is an honest view of things. Others have spread misinformation about Bitcoin and all forms of cryptocurrency, saying it is easily hacked, has no value, and will drain your bank account and leave you in ruins.

The truth is that many of these people know the reality: that cryptocurrency isn't easily hackable but, in fact, very safe. Bitcoin does have value, just not based on the dollar or fiat currency. Lastly, it will not drain your bank account and will not leave you in ruins. It is less dangerous and more safe than the dollar and many other forms of traditional money.

But the problem doesn't just lie in the fact that some people do not like cryptocurrencies and Bitcoin. There is no crime there. Nothing can stop them from hating Bitcoin and spreading falsehoods about it. The problem arises when these same people hold government office, use their power to spread lies further, and push laws that limit people's ability to use and buy Bitcoin openly. That is when things cross over into the downright wrong.

While some genuinely want what is best for consumers and buyers, others do not wish for Bitcoin to become popular because that means they stand a chance of losing the vast amount of power they have gathered over the years. Often, you see these people spreading rumors or misinformation about Bitcoin in hopes that it will prevent the cryptocurrency from finding a new home with investors all over the globe.

These people, along with those who do not trust the power of Bitcoin and are coming from a place of genuine care and concern, sometimes come together to pressure lawmakers to pass legislation that will stop Bitcoin in its tracks. So far, no one has been able to stop the development of Bitcoin in the most significant countries, like the United States. In this country and others, Bitcoins remain free and unregulated. But that hasn't stopped attempts to limit or outright ban it.

States Fight For (And Against) Bitcoin

Bitcoin was initially seen as a stateless - and nationless - digital currency that could be accepted everywhere and would have no regulations no matter where you were spending it. One of the most exciting aspects of the premise behind Bitcoin was that you could use it anywhere and use it on anything. There should be no reason why Bitcoin shouldn't be universally legal and unchecked in all jurisdictions, not just in the United States but worldwide.

However, that has yet to be the case. As stated, many countries worldwide have enacted specific rules for and against Bitcoin and other cryptocurrencies. The same is valid for individual countries in the United States. Since the federal government has so far tried to stay out of the cryptocurrency battle, deciding not to regulate it and let the people run it themselves, some states have stepped up to either support or push back against the rise in popularity of Bitcoin.

Some states are better than others for Bitcoin. Because of state-level laws signed by numerous governors, Bitcoin is more efficiently used and traded, bought in some states, and more complex to come by and support in others.

For example, New York has long been a nemesis of Bitcoin. Considering how many people of power associated with Wall Street live in New York state, this isn't surprising. It would stand to reason that these influential people would use their connections with the governor to limit the power of Bitcoin. That is precisely what happened because New York has never supported Bitcoin. All online exchanges must disclose their global client base to state officials in New York. To some, that sounds like a massive invasion of privacy. This is just an example of the ways that New York State has tried to stymie the power of Bitcoin.

New York Governor Andrew Cuomo created a Bitcoin task force to study the use and intricacies of Bitcoin, so there may be changes in the future if the task force finds nothing to fear with Bitcoin. Supporters of cryptocurrency are hoping that's the case.

Another state that has come out swinging against cryptocurrency and Bitcoin is Rhode Island. Their senator, Sheldon Whitehouse, has long railed against Bitcoin and has said it is a way for foreign interference in America's business. He was a significant supporter of state-wide legislation that heavily taxed online exchanges and all cryptocurrency transactions. This shows that not only Sheldon Whitehouse thinks that Bitcoin and crypto can be a tool for foreign governments and adversaries.

Other states, such as Arizona, have created specific laws and taxes that oppose welcoming Bitcoin. This has hurt the base of supporters in those states and has made significant pushback from cryptocurrency fans. It flies in the face of the ideas and purpose behind Bitcoin, which has always been about a universal currency that governments would not hold back because it didn't need them. Bitcoin can thrive independently without any federal body of power's regulation, oversight, or help.

But it cannot exist without them. The fact is that Bitcoin would always go head-to-head with governments. There is no way around that. These strict laws being pushed by certain nations and states show that Bitcoin may exist outside the system but remains inside it significantly.

Thankfully, not all states are trying to limit the power and strength of Bitcoin. Other regions in America are supportive of cryptocurrency. For example, Colorado passed a law 2018 encouraging state agencies to use blockchain technology to keep their confidential records secret. That was seen as a massive sign of support for the crypto community. This was also matched by legislation allowing cryptocurrency donations in political campaigns and a bill that exempted cryptocurrencies from specific securities regulations. Colorado has proven that it isn't afraid of Bitcoin. It sees the value in the technology behind it.

Although it is usually known for its conservative politics that many would think could put them on the opposing side of Bitcoin and cryptocurrency, the state of Texas has shown itself to be an ally in advancing Bitcoin-related technology. That state has become a hub of crypto mining facilities; multiple central crypto mining locations exist throughout Lone Star State. This is partly due to the cheap cost of electricity and energy in Texas since using power is a significant part of crypto-mining, and the more expensive it is, the more complex the mining becomes. But Texas has welcomed many mining companies because of the business, income, and employment it brings.

California, unsurprisingly, is another state which has tried to embrace Bitcoin and cryptocurrency. Their governor signed a law 2014 that affirmed that "various forms of alternative currency such as digital currency" are legal payments when purchasing goods. Many major crypto companies in the world are located in California, such as Kraken, Ripple, Coinbase, and more.

The most crypto-friendly state in the union would be Wyoming. The least populated state is among the most engaging and positive regarding Bitcoin and cryptocurrencies. Wyoming has passed multiple laws to recognize and support cryptocurrencies. Their state legislature even created a bill that grants digital currencies the same legal status as other money. Because of their extended support for cryptocurrencies, including Bitcoin, Wyoming has become home to many crypto companies and has received its fair share of praise from the community that uses them. Wyoming might not be the first place you think of when you talk crypto, but it should be. It has shown time and again that it supports the future of cryptocurrency.

Some states favor Bitcoin and will do much to help advance it; others are against it and pushing legislation limiting it. The fight continues and will for some time. As long as the federal government stays out of the fray, it will be up to individual states to decide how Bitcoin and cryptocurrencies are regulated. Though that may mean it is sometimes a tough road, crypto fans support this approach because many need more confidence in federal officials. They fear that crypto proves too much of a risk and danger to the federal government, so they prefer they stay out of the arguments altogether. The more hands-off the government is, the better.

However, that doesn't mean the United States government has never dipped its toes in the fight and limited cryptocurrency. They have created an outright ban on at least one cryptocurrency. That decision spotlighted how politics and foreign affairs can mix and potentially make a massive mess for the future of cryptocurrency.

CHAPTER 9

What's Next For Crypto and Blockchain

What Could Happen With Crypto in the Future?

Cryptocurrency and blockchain have become incredible global phenomena in just a short time. No one can argue that it could become even more powerful and thriving in the years ahead. However, some people say about what a future for crypto looks like. Which direction will it go?

Many people see Bitcoin as the currency of the future, so speculation about what is next for it has run rampant since its inception.

So, what does Bitcoin's future hold? Many people think it is on the verge of a significant breakthrough that will take it further than ever. What would that breakthrough look like? Some speculate that a major retailer will begin accepting Bitcoin shortly. If a business such as Target, Walmart, or Amazon started to take Bitcoin as a currency, that would be a game changer. If that were to happen, you can expect to see the value of Bitcoin skyrocket by leaps and bounds in no time at all.

If a significant retailer welcomed Bitcoin, it would send a strong message to other businesses worldwide that cryptocurrency is here to stay and can be trusted and accepted safely. It would also send a massive message to average investors across the globe that significant business icons are now warming to the idea of cryptocurrency. That would drive people to online exchanges, looking to spend their money on crypto finally, and that would only make the industry boom even more.

If a retailer started accepting Bitcoin shortly, an immediate ripple effect would be felt and seen. It would increase the value of all cryptocurrencies, not just Bitcoin. People would be looking to make money off crypto and wouldn't want to focus solely on Bitcoin. However, Bitcoin itself would become even more significant and even more wanted. Headlines and news stories would splash across every newspaper and network on Earth. It would be one of the biggest business stories of the year.

This possible development is what many people have been waiting for. Fans of Bitcoin have been anticipating the day that a more significant retail business takes the first step and starts taking Bitcoin as payment at their locations. For years now, the holy grail has been Amazon since Bitcoin users know how convenient spending Bitcoin at Amazon could be. However, that online market hasn't embraced the idea yet, and Amazon has refused to budge on its resistance to Bitcoin.

Bitcoin proponents have been focusing on other retailers in hopes that they take the first step since Amazon has seemed hesitant over the years. They have their sights set on places like Best Buy and other businesses that provide many customers with the latest technology, gear, and devices. Some campaigns have convinced these businesses to accept Bitcoin and cryptocurrencies, but more headway has yet to be made. The possibility of this happening remains the biggest question for the future of cryptocurrencies. This is the most significant step for it to become mainstream, which many crypto fans see as necessary.

If a significant retailer remains outside the reach of Bitcoin shortly, that isn't the end of the road for crypto. No matter what, the future for crypto remains bright. Why? Because more people are flocking to crypto than ever before. Year after year, the currency attracts new investors looking to enter the market, and every time someone buys in, the value only goes up. That is why you have seen the price of various cryptocurrencies, most especially Bitcoin, skyrocket over the years.

However, if Bitcoin and other crypto fail to have some large name companies latch onto them and join in, you can expect to see their need to be clarified and met with trepidation from casual investors. You can also expect many successful business people and politicians to continue to rail against crypto and attempt to bring it down.

In the years ahead, a more significant fight will likely be waged against Bitcoin and its peers. We have already seen that beginning in India, Egypt, and the United States. Cryptocurrencies have made billions of dollars quickly, and money equals power in most countries. And new energy can be scary for those who have held old power for a long time. It is seen as a new threat that can unseat those in control and needs to be kept in check before it becomes too strong. Many Fortune 500 CEOs are looking to reel crypto in the years ahead, and they have mighty friends who can make that happen.

As for blockchain, the future potential is endless. As more and more major companies and industries discover the power of blockchain, it will only grow in popularity and continue to become more impactful worldwide. Blockchain started solely to facilitate the use of Bitcoin and cryptocurrencies. But it has become part of the healthcare industry, shipping and transportation, automobile companies, and even payroll technology.

Blockchain has never had such a promising future. It has become more than just a companion technology for Bitcoin and cryptocurrency. It has taken on a life of its own and still stands a chance to alter nearly every business in the world - if they are willing to accept it.

CHAPTER 10

How Blockchain Will Affect Your Life, Your Friend's Life & Your Families Lives!

What are the Real World Applications of Blockchain

Blockchain is already spreading worldwide and significantly affecting everything it touches in only the best of ways. What are some of the industries that are benefitting the most from blockchain and all it provides?

Healthcare

Take the pharmaceutical industry, for example. New rules to ensure drug integrity from manufacturing to consumption could save up to a million lives each year. Life sciences and healthcare companies create unique serial numbers for units of medication and pieces of equipment, which are scanned, captured, and verified at their point of origin.

Applied correctly, blockchain can take track-and-trace serialization to the next level, cutting costs, elevating security and trust, eliminating error-prone data movements, and enabling real-time supply chain transparency. Additional verified information is appended using blockchain as each item moves through the supply chain. These data blocks cannot be tampered with and are collectively validated by all stakeholders. The result is an end-to-end system that is simpler and more secure than anything we have seen before. It is more private, transparent, and efficient, with less risk, and meets and exceeds global serialization requirements.

The world of fashion is also embracing blockchain. CGS, an organization providing business applications, enterprise learning systems, and outsourcing services, is hearing from fashion, apparel, and consumer goods clients that they are looking at new ways to streamline the supply chain through blockchain.

Food Safety

From the supply chain perspective, blockchain can enable trust between trading partners and consumers. With blockchain technology, consumers can see the garment's entire lifecycle from the farm to the shelf. Consumers are going from blind trust to a complete understanding of the journey of that garment. With blockchain, an item's sustainability and compliance can be tracked on the raw materials and manufacturing processes."

Food safety is a significant industry that is incredibly important. Without it, all of society would suffer. And now, blockchain is arriving to make the entire system run better, smoother, and more efficiently.

IBM is partnering with food suppliers, including Dole, Nestlé, and Walmart, to regulate food safety better using blockchain. In the global food supply chain industry, all growers, suppliers, processors, distributors, retailers, regulators, and consumers can gain permission access to information about the origin and state of food in their transactions. All members of the ecosystem can use the blockchain network to trace contaminated foods to their source in a short amount of time to ensure they are quickly removed from store shelves.

The World Wildlife Fund is also using blockchain to better track seafood if you can believe it.

Consumers are calling for fully-traceable seafood that does not come from illegal fisheries or those that abuse human rights. Wholesale and retail seafood buyers are asking for improvements in transparency and traceability to reduce the risk of their brands being associated with dubious and illegal activities. Layered into the real-time information coming from other electronic technology platforms, blockchains can provide the unprecedented supply chain transparency and traceability that retailers and consumers want.

Oil & Gas

Oil and gas companies have taken to blockchain too, and they're already making millions more because of it. Blockchain in the energy sector allows users to monitor transactions, control output, and verify the origin of certificates.

There is a blockchain-based trading project with participants such as BP, Shell, Statoil, Gunvor, Koch Supply & Trading, and Mercuria commercial enterprises and, from banking, ABN Amro, ING, and Societe Generale. They developed a digital platform for managing transactions in the energy market. The project's authors aim to reduce the dependence on traditional paper contracts and the kilograms of paper documentation used in favor of a digital registry.

Blockchain will allow the energy sector to reduce operating costs, accelerate domestic trading operations for all its energy supply chains and increase the reliability of their operations. Most projects are currently under development, but industry representatives have long understood their relevance and importance. Undoubtedly, over time, the number of blockchain solutions in various sectors of the economy will increase significantly, and the benefits of their implementation will become quite apparent.

Automotive

Blockchain in the automotive industry is seen as a tool for storing and transmitting data by smart cars. In addition, the technology can be used to store data about specific cars in various registries. Blockchain will not allow for the falsification of data about a car. For example, after a vehicle is put on the market, all data about it, including information about service and repairs, will be stored using blockchain. As a result, the owner of a car will be able, at any time, to check the number of repairs it has undergone, accident data, and other information.

Auto industry players have been exploring the possibilities of blockchain for several years. Two years ago, Toyota announced a new program to introduce blockchain into its innovative car technology, where a distributed registry is used as the basis for exchanging data between intelligent vehicles. A similar project is being implemented by General Motors, which patented its technology in 2019. Volkswagen is developing blockchain technology that allows intelligent cars to exchange information about road conditions. According to its developers, the project could reduce the number of accidents caused by poor-quality road surfaces, challenging weather conditions, or other accidents.

Election Fraud

It's not only financial transactions that work with blockchain but any data transmission. This system infrastructure benefits voting because voting is a small piece of high-value data. Out of necessity, modern voting systems are primarily stuck in the last century, and those that want to vote must leave their homes and submit paper ballots to a local authority. Why not bring this process online? Some have tried, but it has proven difficult to put faith in the results due to significant security gaps.

Blockchain can solve the many problems discovered in these early attempts at online voting. A blockchain-based voting application does not concern itself with the security of its Internet connection because any hacker with access to the terminal cannot affect other nodes. Voters can effectively submit their votes without revealing their identity or political preferences to the public. Officials can count votes with absolute certainty, knowing that each ID can be attributed to one vote, no fakes can be created, and that tampering is impossible.

Voter apathy has seen the number of people showing up to cast their votes dwindle in recent years, even as it has become more critical. In America alone, the number of people who vote is far lower than those who *can*. Apathy in the voting booth hurts the country in many ways. With an involved populace, the government can go down the right path. People need to be engaged, and people need to care. Blockchain can help people believe in voting much more than now.

These miserable and sad numbers would rise by providing an irrefutable and easy way to vote from one's phone or PC. Blockchain is paving the way for a direct democracy, where people can decide the course of policy themselves rather than rely on representatives to do it for them. While the rules of a political election may have to be changed to make way for such a transparent system, blockchain is also ideal for informing business decisions, guiding general meetings, polling, censuses, and more.

The use cases for blockchain voting software are many and diverse. Its ability to engage and manage a constituency is crucial to the future of society, not just to produce a transparent outcome but to encourage all people to participate in their communities. The technology is still in its infancy but maturing alongside the young voters. It will one day help and be a crucial part of our collective future.

Conclusion

What Does the Future Have to Offer Crypto?

Many people are left wondering what is ahead for all forms of cryptocurrency. Over just over a decade, it has exploded in popularity and functionality and made so much money for many people. Still, cryptocurrency remains in its adolescent phase and still has much room to grow. It feels as though, despite its repeated appearances in so many headlines, many people are still in the dark about cryptocurrency, and it has yet to break through the mainstream. What is next for cryptocurrency? Will it rival the dollar? Will Bitcoin break through the $70,000 value mark? Will cryptocurrency find its way into some major retailers? And if it does, what happens then?

Let's discuss the chance of crypto being used in big, established businesses and stores because, if that happens, cryptocurrency's popularity - and value - will grow by a whole lot in a short time. Since you are now an investor in cryptocurrency, this will significantly affect you in some incredible ways. But is it even possible? Will it happen?

What about Amazon? Is crypto headed toward Amazon? That's unlikely, to put it gently. Amazon is a behemoth of a company, the world's largest retailer. You would think it would soon adopt cryptocurrency and Bitcoin and allow users to buy their products with cryptocurrency.

You would be wrong. Amazon has never accepted any crypto and doesn't have any plans to. In 2014, the shopping giant said it hadn't gotten into the crypto game because it didn't see a demand from customers to use it. Since then, speculation has reigned about Amazon using Bitcoin in the future. However, the assumption has been largely unfounded because Amazon has made few moves to suggest it would warm to the idea any time soon.

Why won't Amazon accept Bitcoin? There are multiple rumors. One of the largest ones is that Amazon founder Jeff Bezos doesn't like cryptocurrency. He is a mighty man, one of the richest on Earth, and there is a good chance he isn't fond of a new currency that isn't the one that made him so successful. He may prefer regular, cold, hard cash like many wealthy citizens. The newspaper he owns, The Washington Post, published a critical piece about Bitcoin in 2016. Its title was "R.I.P. Bitcoin. It's Time To Move On." Many people saw that as a sign that Bezos was actively working against the growth of all forms of crypto.

But there are other reasons why Amazon may be shying away from crypto. Some speculate that Amazon isn't fond of crypto because it is too volatile. That is a legitimate reason to be wary of it. The value of crypto fluctuates wildly, much more than the dollar does. How would Amazon and its third party online retailers price their products for Bitcoin when the worth of Bitcoin is all over the map? If the Bitcoin market settled down for a year or so, you might see Amazon begin using it.

Amazon has many behind-the-scenes deals with major credit card companies like Visa and Mastercard. Both major brands are not fond of Bitcoin and how it is shaking up the monetary business. To make the credit cards happy, Amazon may not accept Bitcoin until all parties can get along. However, it will be a long time before companies like American Express and others warm to Bitcoin because they are seen as a direct competition that is coming to change the status quo.

Perhaps another reason Amazon isn't using Bitcoin is that it is contemplating creating its cryptocurrency exclusive to the site. That would not be a surprising move at all. It wouldn't even be that original of an action. There are other eCommerce sites much more minor than Amazon that created their forms of crypto. These currencies are growing in popularity and can only be used in the areas they are designed for. If Amazon were to introduce its line of crypto, it would be a huge success and could even rival Bitcoin. That would be a significant reason why they are slow to accept it, because they may someday be doing direct competition against it.

It seems unlikely that Amazon will ever accept Bitcoin as a form of payment on their site. That is unfortunate and a massive blow to the crypto community. If a business as huge and ubiquitous decided to embrace crypto, it would be seen as a significant success story and make Bitcoin's popularity skyrocket seemingly overnight. Amazon holds the keys to making crypto and Bitcoin far more successful, but they aren't doing anything to promote its growth among average shoppers.

How Blockchain Will Revolutionize Everyone's Lives

Far too many people think of blockchain as the way to get Bitcoin or cryptocurrency. And far too many *more* people don't think about blockchain at all.

That's a shame because, in the years ahead, there is a perfect chance that blockchain truly will revolutionize the world and the lives of everyone you know. It might have changed your life already. You might not even know it yet.

What blockchain does is decentralize a system? It only focuses some data in one spot but sorts it and spreads it across a vast network. This network is always self-checking, updating, and tending to itself. It is always accurate and nearly impossible to infiltrate and disrupt or hack.

It is best to think of blockchain as a living and breathing creature, a creation that exists on its own and is self-sufficient and always stronger and safer than nearly any alternative.

Looking at it that way, you can see why blockchain can take the world by storm. From automobile creation to shipping and production of products to healthcare companies and even voting in local elections, blockchain can make everything run better, faster, safer, and more independently and efficiently.

Blockchain takes the pressure off the workers and puts it on a system and infrastructure that can withstand a lot. There are drawbacks to the blockchain, just like there are drawbacks to any approach, but it is safe, and it is almost always reliable.

More companies and businesses need to see the value and potential of blockchain. It has already founds its way into so many major players in the world, but there is so much more room to grow. If it does take hold even more, you can expect to see so much of your life perform better. There are many practical ways blockchain can be adapted to the everyday world, but many have yet to be discovered.

Blockchain is here to stay. It has allowed cryptocurrency to grow and blossom, and it will ultimately change so many other things. Blockchain *does* have the power to revolutionize your life and the world around you. It already has. And it's only just begun.

Thank You

You could have picked from hundreds of other books, but you bought mine, and I appreciate it. Thank you so much for purchasing my book.

Not that you enjoyed (I hope) my book, can I ask you for a tiny favor? Can you please post a review on the platform? You posting a review is the best way to support the work of independent authors like me.

Your feedback will help me keep writing the books that will help you get the desired results. It means a lot to me to hear from you.

I am happy for anyone to reach out to me for help, comments, collaboration ideas, or feedback at

brian@brianscottfitzgerald.com

Visit my author page with this link or Scan this QR code

https://www.amazon.com/author/brianscottfitzgerald.

www.ingramcontent.com/pod-product-compliance
Lightning Source LLC
LaVergne TN
LVHW100250210926
848480LV00003B/885